FV

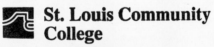

St. Louis Community College

Forest Park
Florissant Valley
Meramec

Instructional Resources
St. Louis, Missouri

GAYLORD

Filipino American Lives

In the series, *Asian American History and Culture,* edited by Sucheng Chan and David Palumbo-Liu

A list of books in the series appears at the back of this volume.

Filipino American Lives

Yen Le Espiritu

Temple University Press
Philadelphia

Temple University Press, Philadelphia 19122
Copyright © 1995 by Temple University
All rights reserved
Published 1995

⊗ The paper used in this publication meets the
requirements of the American National Standard for Information
Sciences—Permanence of Paper for Printed Library Materials,
ANSI Z39.48-1984

Printed in the United States of America

Text design by Anne O'Donnell

Library of Congress Cataloging-in-Publication Data

Espiritu, Yen Le, 1963–
    Filipino American lives / Yen Le Espiritu.
      p.   cm. — (Asian American history and culture)
    Includes bibliographical references (p.).
    ISBN 1-56639-316-7 (C). — ISBN 1-56639-317-5 (P)
    1. Filipino Americans—California—San Diego—Biography.
  2. Filipino Americans—California—San Diego—Interviews.   3. San
  Diego (Calif.)—Biography.   I. Title.   II. Series : Asian American
  history and culture series.
  F869.S22E9   1995
  305.89′921073′0922—dc20
      [B]   94-48081

To the
Filipino American Community
in San Diego

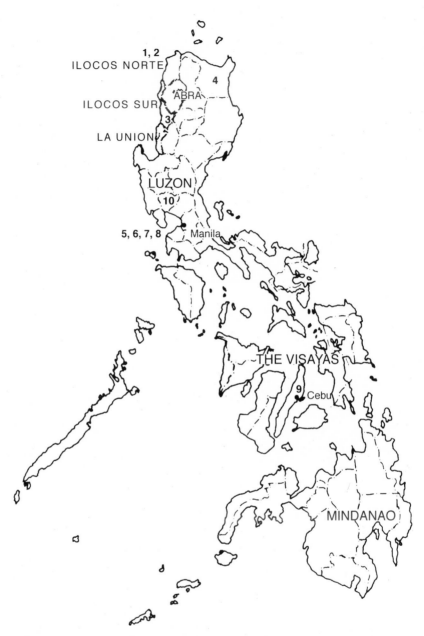

Birthplaces of Interviewees Born in the Philippines: 1, Saint Nicholas, Ilocos Norte—A. B. Santos; 2, Sarrat, Ilocos Norte—Juanita Santos; 3, Bulag Bantay, Ilocos Sur—Nemesia Cortez; 4, Piat, Cagayan—Ruth Abad; 5, Manila—Luz Latus; 6, Manila—Paz Jensen; 7, Manila— Dario Villa; 8, Manila—Daniel Gruta; 9, Cebu City, Cebu—Edgar Gamboa; 10, Santa Rita, Pampanga—Leo Sicat.

Contents

Preface

As an ethnic studies professor at the University of California, San Diego, I meet and befriend many Filipino American students. Either in my Asian American Studies courses or in our informal conversations, the students' questions and interests largely concern issues of identity. Frustrated by the lack of materials on Filipinos in the United States—particularly readings that deal with the second generation—some students have elected to conduct original research through independent studies with me, and I have encouraged them to pursue their research questions further in graduate school. Responding to the scarcity of materials and my students' hunger for information, and prompted by my own interest in the construction of identities, I began a study on Filipino Americans in San Diego in 1992.

I did not set out to produce a collection of first-person Filipino American narratives. Originally I intended to understand the multiple facets of Filipino American identities, paying particular attention to regional, generational, gender, and class differences. Using the life-history method as the main tool of research, I wanted to trace the connections between the life experiences of Filipino Americans and their changing sense of identities. As I collected these life histories, however, I came to realize the importance of presenting some of these accounts in full—not only because they are rich and compelling, but also because the narrators desire to see their life stories in print. In December 1992, Sucheng Chan, the co-editor of the Asian American History and Culture series published by Temple University Press, suggested that I produce two books: a study of Filipino American identities *and* a collection of life stories of Filipino Americans in San Diego. This book was born out of that suggestion.

A few words about my research methods are necessary. Using the "snowball" sampling technique, I started by interviewing Filipino Americans whom I knew and then asking them to refer me to others who might be willing to be interviewed. In other words, I chose participants not randomly but rather through a network of Filipino American contacts whom the first group of narrators trusted. To capture the diversity within the Filipino American community, I sought and selected narrators of different backgrounds and with diverse viewpoints. The interviews, tape-recorded in English, ranged from three to ten hours each and took place in offices, coffee shops, and homes.

My questions were open-ended and covered three general areas: family and immigration history, ethnic identity and practices, and community development among San Diego's Filipinos. While all the narratives began as responses to my questions, the interviewing process varied widely: some narrators needed to be prompted with specific questions, while others spoke at great length on their own. Some chose to cover the span of their lives; others focused on specific events or periods that were particularly important to them.

I believe that my own immigrant background—I came to the United States from Vietnam at the age of twelve—facilitated the interviews because these storytellers did not view me as a disinterested outsider but as a fellow Asian American who shared some of their life processes. Indeed, I did not wish to be detached and often shared with them my own struggles in becoming an Asian American in the United States. In addition to minimizing the inequalities inherent in a researcher-subject relationship, my self-revelations often triggered long-forgotten memories and thus prompted more storytelling. The fact that I am married to a Filipino American also opened doors, with many interviewees telling me that "you are practically one of us."

Thus far, I have interviewed some ninety men and women, fourteen of whom are profiled in this book. The narrators are men and women, old and young, middle class and working class, first and second generation, with diverse immigration histories ranging from those of the working students who came before World War II, to the *manongs* in the fields, to the stewards and officers in the U.S. Navy, to the "brain drain" professionals, and to the Filipinos who were born and/or raised in the United States. I chose their narratives for the diverse backgrounds they reveal, for their completeness, and for what they can tell us about Filipino American history in general and about Filipino American experiences in San Diego in particular. These accounts chronicle more than the pivotal events in the narrators' lives, for they also document their changing sense of identity and their evolving understanding of race and gender relations in this country.

Initially, I thought of dividing the book into sections by immigration categories: the first wave, 1903–35; the second wave, 1945–64; the U.S. Navy recruits, 1900–1992; the post-1965 immigrants; and the U.S.-born Filipinos. But I soon realized that this heuristic device, while useful, is not suited to the complexity of people's lives. For example, although six of the fourteen narrators are Navy-related, it would be too simplistic to categorize them only as "Navy people." Connie Tirona's narrative (Chapter 3), for example, is not only about life as a Navy wife but also about the history of the *manongs* and the experiences of American-born Filipinos who grew up in the 1930s and 1940s. Similarly, A. B. Santos's narrative (Chapter 1) focuses on the experiences of both nonsponsored Filipino students who arrived before World War II and Filipino draftees during the war. In the end, I opted for an organization based loosely on age rather than periods of immigration.

Although the book focuses on San Diego, it offers multifaceted and nuanced portraits of Filipino American life because most of the narrators have also lived in the Philippines, or Hawaii, the East Coast, the Midwest, and other parts of the United States. To place the San Diego community into the larger Filipino American historical context, I have written an introduction detailing Filipino settlements in other parts of the country, particularly in Hawaii and the Pacific Coast, but also in the Midwest, the South, and the East Coast. Beside providing much-needed information, this overview shows how the San Diego community both differs from and is similar to Filipino American communities elsewhere. Readers interested in further information on other communities can refer to my bibliography.

The life-story accounts in this collection are the result of a collaboration between the narrators and me. Unlike those oral historians who transcribe verbatim everything that is said, I have edited and rearranged the raw interview data into more coherent and concise texts. In all cases, I have taken great care to retain the flavor of the narrators' speech patterns. The participants had complete editorial discretion for their stories: they received copies of their edited narratives, made changes in them, and approved them for publication. Thus all had the opportunity to tell their life stories as they wanted them to be told. Although some revised and added to the content, the majority of the narrators were more interested in correcting grammatical and spelling errors so that their accounts read as smoothly as possible. Because they know that the book would have an audience wider than the Filipino American community, they made it clear that they wanted to present their stories in "proper" or "academic" English. As Sucheng Chan pointed out in *Hmong Means Free* (1994), Asian immigrants know too well the costs of speaking "improper" English and thus take great care to "clean up" their prose whenever possible. While some scholars may criticize these editorial changes, as a non-native English speaker I respect and understand the narrators' wish to express themselves eloquently.

I hope this collection adds to the literature on Filipino Americans, particularly to the knowledge about the San Diego community, the Navy experience, the post-1965 immigrants, and the younger generation—all gaps in the existing material. While this book has obvious relevance for students of Filipino and Asian American studies, ethnic studies, history, sociology, and biography, I want it to be accessible to any reader who wishes to understand the experiences of Filipinos in both the Philippines and the United States. Most of all, I want the book to be a source of information for the younger generations of Filipino Americans—for those like my husband, who were born in the Philippines but were raised primarily in the United States; and for those like my two children, who were born in this country, who are half-Filipino, and who probably will learn little about that part of their history in U.S. schools.

San Diego   Yen Le Espiritu
May 1994

Acknowledgments

I thank the Vice Chancellor of Academic Affairs at the University of California, San Diego, for an Affirmative Action Faculty Career Development Grant that provided me release time to collect many of the life stories, and to the UCSD Academic Senates for several small grants that enabled me to obtain the research assistance needed to complete this book. I am grateful to Enrique Bonus for providing invaluable assistance while completing his doctoral dissertation at UCSD, to Elaine Pablo for helping to compile the bibliography, to Ross Frank for preparing the map of the Philippines, and to Sucheng Chan for lending me important materials for the book. Most of all, I am indebted to the Filipino Americans I interviewed. Without their cooperation, hospitality, and support, this book would not have been possible.

Introduction

Filipino Settlements
in the United States

Although a majority of Filipinos have come to the United States only since the liberalization of immigration laws in 1965, the history of Filipinos in this country dates back to the middle of the 1700s. As early as 1765, Filipinos lived along the southeastern coast of Louisiana. Congregated in the marshlands of Louisiana's Barataria Bay (about thirty miles south of New Orleans), these Filipinos were believed to be descendants of Filipino seamen who had escaped Spanish galleons—ships that carried cargoes of luxury goods between the Philippines and Mexico from 1565 to 1815.[1] Today, with a total population of more than 1.4 million in 1990, Filipinos compose the second largest immigrant group as well as the second largest Asian American group in the United States.

Despite the long history of the immigration and settlement of Filipinos in the United States, very little sound research has been published about either their past or their contemporary life. As E. San Juan, Jr., maintains, the existing studies on the historical development of the Filipino community in the United States "have been sketchy, superficial, and flawed in their methodology and philosophical assumptions."[2] Lamenting the neglect of Filipino Americans in the literature on U.S. immigration, ethnicity, and communities, others have declared that Filipinos are the "forgotten Asian Americans"; that "not much is known about them"; and that on this group there is "no history. No published literature. No nothing."[3] However, most scholars and writers stop short of asking *why* this is the case. In a rare analysis, Oscar Campomanes argues that the institutional invisibility of the Philippines and Filipino Americans is connected to the historical amnesia and self-erasure regarding the U.S. colonization of the Philippines in particular and U.S. imperialism in general.[4] Employing a cultural perspective, Cecile Cruz asserts that the academic neglect of Filipinos stems from the erroneous assumption that the Philippines lacks an "authentic" indigenous culture. This perspective echoes Renato Rosaldo's contention that most anthropologists have ignored the Philippines because they perceived it as "too Westernized,"

1

with "no culture" of its own.[5] These observations suggest that recent Filipino American history can best be understood within the context of the colonial and postcolonial association between the Philippines and the United States.

The Impact of the U.S. Colonization of the Philippines

In 1898, following the Spanish American War, the United States assumed colonial rule of the Philippines, thereby extending its "Manifest Destiny" to the Pacific. After intense debate, Congress finally decided to retain the Philippines as a U.S. possession—ostensibly to prepare the archipelago for eventual independence. Battling to oust their new overlords, Filipino nationalists held off U.S. rule for several years.[6] From the very beginning, superior American fire power put Filipino troops at a dreadful disadvantage. In the opening battle in Manila, "dead Filipinos were piled so high that the Americans used the bodies for breastworks." After this initial rout, the Philippine Army quickly resorted to mobile warfare, whereby they took advantage of their superior knowledge of the terrain and the ardent support of many Filipinos. Harassed and attacked throughout the islands by determined peasants, the Americans slowly realized that the major foe of U.S. imperialism was not the Philippine Army but rather the Filipino people.

A series of bloody "pacification" campaigns ensued. Unable to penetrate the guerrillas, the Americans began to attack the population at large, burning barrios, destroying storehouses and crops, poisoning wells, slaughtering farm animals, and killing noncombatants. In the notorious Samar campaign in late September 1901, General "Howlin' Jake" Smith ordered his troops to ravage the province and to kill "everything over ten." Three months later, in another brutal campaign, Major General J. Franklin Bell set out to destroy Batangas. According to statistics compiled by U.S. government officials, by the time Bell was finished, at least one hundred thousand people had been killed or had died as a direct result of the scorched-earth policies. In 1902, through superior military force and the collaboration of the conservative and moneyed Filipinos, the Americans finally put an end to the armed nationalist resistance. Although it is difficult to determine how many Filipinos died resisting American aggression, estimates of the combined death toll from fighting, disease, and starvation ranged from several hundred thousand to one million. According to Sucheng Chan, many of the brutal facets of the Philippine American War remain largely hidden from the public.[7]

Although guerrilla warfare continued for several more years, on July 4, 1901, William Howard Taft had taken the oath of office as the first civil governor of the Philippines. The U.S. occupation affected all segments of Philippine society. Politically, the Philippine government was modeled after that of the United States.[8] To win over the existing leadership of the Philippines and to pacify many Filipino nationalists, the United States adopted the policy of Filipinization—the gradual substitution of Filipino personnel for American administrators and clerks in the colonial government. As early as 1900, Filipinos began assuming positions in the municipal, provincial, and later, in the national governments. However, Americans still controlled the strategic positions that allowed them to formulate and implement policies. Under U.S. colonial rule, the Philippine national economy changed significantly.[9] Foremost among the changes were the further development of the agricultural export economy (begun under Spanish rule), with sugar in the lead, and the growing dependence upon imports for such basic necessities as rice and textiles. By its tariff regulations and the subsequent free trade between the two countries, the United States fostered this export-import policy and kept the Philippines an unindustrialized export economy.

As a civilian government replaced military rule, the cultural Americanization of the Philippine population became an integral part of the process of colonization. Convinced that education was one of the best ways to pacify the Filipinos, U.S. colonizers introduced universal public education and revamped Philippine educational institutions and curriculum using the American system as its model and English as the language of instruction. Filipino historian Renato Constantino contends that through this policy the colonial educational system became an instrument of assimilation or Americanization. With the use of U.S. textbooks, "young Filipinos began learning not only a new language but a new culture. Education became miseducation because it began to de-Filipinize the youth, taught them to regard American culture as superior to any other, and American society as the model *par excellence* for Philippine society."[10] Infected with colonial culture and with grand illusions about the United States, Filipinos soon started to migrate to what they had been taught to think of as the land of opportunity and fair play.

The Beginning of Filipino Emigration to the United States

The first Filipinos to come to the U.S. mainland were students on government scholarships. As part of their effort to acculturate Filipinos and to augment their devotion to the United States, the territorial government sent several hundred individuals (predominantly males) to study in U.S. colleges and universities during the first decade of this century. Highly selected, these *pensionados* often were the children of prominent Filipino families whose loyalty the colonial regime hoped to win. Screened from twenty thousand applicants, the first group of one hundred government-sponsored students sailed from Manila to the United States in October of 1903. The *San Francisco Chronicle* reported their arrival, stating that the goal of their venture was their Americanization. By the early 1920s, almost all of the original *pension-*

ados had returned home to well-paying positions in agriculture, business, education, engineering, and government.[11]

The achievements of the *pensionados* inspired other young Filipinos to seek their fortunes through U.S. education. Between 1910 and 1938, about fourteen thousand Filipinos migrated to the United States as nonsponsored students. Although they came as laborers, these young men fully expected to earn enough money to attend U.S. schools. Regardless of their qualifications, racial discrimination relegated them to unskilled and menial occupations; some aspiring students took years to save enough money to go to school. A. B. Santos (Chapter 1) was one such student. Arriving in San Diego in 1922 at the age of fifteen, he worked as a dining-room helper at the Coronado Hotel while attending Coronado High School. Years later, as a student at San Diego State College (now University), Santos worked full-time one semester and then went to school full-time the next. Juggling work and classes, Santos took four years to finish two years of course work.

Nonetheless, before the Great Depression, the Filipinos' hopes for higher education had seemed possible. According to Chris Friday, between 1920 and 1925, an estimated two thousand (or 15 percent of the Filipinos in the continental United States) attended high school or college. By the end of the decade, the number had increased dramatically. In 1928 alone, approximately a thousand enrolled in classes. The depression years shattered the Filipinos' dream of success through education. In 1932 only eight hundred Filipinos attended school; in 1935 just five hundred; by 1939 the number had fallen to three hundred. Confronted by the economic devastation of the 1930s, many working Filipino students joined the American labor movement and fought to secure equal treatment for all races. Economic necessity and widespread discrimination forced many self-supporting students eventually to abandon their goals of completing their studies and returning to the Philippines. Stranded by the Great Depression and lost ambitions, most of these "unintentional immigrants" lived out their lives as laborers in the United States.[12]

According to Barbara M. Posadas and Roland L. Guyotte, the pre–World War II Filipinos in Chicago were among these "unintentional immigrants." Originating around 1905 with the arrival of the *pensionados* and expanded during the 1920s with the coming of self-supporting students, Chicago's Filipino community was composed principally of students. H. Brett Melendy reported that in 1907, the University of Illinois, with thirteen students, had the largest enrollment of Filipinos in the country.[13] In 1917, the U.S. Bureau of Insular Affairs counted forty-five Filipinos attending school in Chicago or Evanston out of a nationwide total of three hundred and thirty-seven. Like their counterparts elsewhere in the United States, Chicago's working students alternated quarters at school with periods of full-time employment, thus stretching their stay in the United States into unplanned-for years. The onset of the Great Depression further exacerbated their plight as they scrambled to find work to finance their education. At the University of Chicago, the number of full-time Filipino students dropped from forty-six in 1926–27 to ten in 1933–34. By the time of Pearl Harbor, the majority of Chicago's Filipino students had been forced to abandon their studies and became like the Filipino immigrant laborers who had immigrated to Hawaii and the West Coast.[14]

Filipino Workers in Hawaii

Filipino migration to Hawaii was tied to the fortunes of the islands' sugar companies. By the last decade of the nineteenth century, the sugar industry had become so massive that the prosperity of Hawaii depended largely upon its continued expansion and prosperity. Because sugar cane cultivation is so labor-intensive, plantation owners needed a constant flow of cheap and compliant labor to work their expanding properties. Filipinos were the last immigrant group to arrive on Hawaii's sugar plantations.[15]

In 1906, Hawaiian sugar planters sent Albert F. Judd to Manila to recruit three hundred Filipino workers. However, after six months of strenuous campaigning, Judd was able to enlist only fifteen laborers, who came not from Manila but from Luzon's northern province of Ilocos Sur in the coastal area of Candon. After the 1908 "Gentlemen's Agreement," which restricted the emigration of Japanese laborers and the 1909 strike by Japanese plantation workers, which threatened sugar production in the islands, the planters mounted an aggressive and well-organized program to import massive numbers of Filipino workers. Filipinos had become the favored source of labor because of their unusual legal status, for until the passage of the Tydings-McDuffie Act in 1934, Filipinos could migrate freely to the United States, protected by their colonial status as U.S. nationals. Moreover, because the Philippines was a "ward" of the United States from 1905 to 1935, the Hawaii Sugar Planters' Association (HSPA) could rely on the assistance of American colonial officials there. Although the territorial government supported the HSPA's recruitment efforts, the Philippine sugar interests and legislature, through physical force and steep taxes, strained to halt Hawaiian recruiting, as they needed labor for their own growing sugar industry.[16]

In the next two decades, HSPA labor recruiters concentrated on the Philippines as "the only available source of a permanent labor supply and the only hope of the future under existing laws."[17] So successful were their efforts that, for the first time, the Hawaiian planters could report an adequate supply of labor. Between 1907 and 1919, 28,500 Filipinos arrived in Hawaii; between 1920 and 1924, 29,200 did. The termination of Japanese immigration in 1924 resulted in a surge of Filipino arrivals in Hawaii—a total of 44,000 during the second half of the 1920s.[18] The Filipino migration was overwhelmingly composed of young men. In 1920, some four thousand Filipinas resided in the islands; by 1930, their number had increased to over ten thousand, but women still represented only 16.6 percent of the Filipino population.[19]

By the middle of the 1920s, it was no longer necessary for HSPA recruiters to offer free round trips as an incentive to Filipino migrants. As Filipinos became increasingly Americanized and as some successful individuals returned home from Hawaii triumphantly, so many Filipinos were eager to migrate to Hawaii that the HSPA ceased recruiting in 1926. Hopeful migrants not only were willing to pay their own passage, they even bribed the recruiters to assure being chosen. Some educated people tried to pass themselves off as illiterates in order to circumvent HSPA policy to recruit the physically strong and the less educated, who were thought to be more likely to remain on the plantations and perform the menial work they were hired to do.[20] A former Filipino plantation worker in Kauai recalled how he had by-passed the recruiters' inspection:

> I was told that if you have education, if you talk English that . . . you'll not be accepted. Besides that, if your look is like student, you cannot be accepted there, the same. But, in order that I could get in, I had to go and roughen my hand by having calluses on the back of the knuckles so that when the inspector will see, "Oh, you are hard working man, so you can go". . . . That's how I got in. And I had to avoid speaking any English. Otherwise, I cannot get to Hawaii.[21]

During the 1930s, however, the demands for Filipino exclusion and a labor surplus in Hawaii reduced the flow of migrants to a trickle.

Prior to 1915, attempts to recruit Filipinos were concentrated in the vicinity of Manila City in central Luzon and of Cebu City in central Visayas; accordingly, more Tagalogs and Visayans, natives of these areas, were among the earliest to emigrate. These efforts generally had poor results, however, since recruits from urban areas usually lacked agricultural experience and also had more economic opportunities than their rural counterparts.[22] HSPA agents thus shifted their recruiting efforts first to the Visayan Islands and then to the Ilocano region in northwestern Luzon. From 1919 to 1928, two-thirds of the Filipino laborers migrating to Hawaii were from the Ilocano-speaking provinces. Visayans, primarily from the hard-pressed eastern Visayan provinces, comprised the second largest group.[23]

The recruiters' shift to Ilocos Norte, Ilocos Sur, and their adjoining provinces was deliberate. A rural people who toiled in the least developed region in the Philippines, the Ilocanos filled the needs of the HSPA for unskilled laborers "who wouldn't be too unhappy to do manual work in the plantation, ten hours a day."[24] To understand the forces propelling emigration from the Ilocano region, one first needs to consider the changes in the Philippine economy brought about by both Spanish and U.S. colonial rules, the foremost being the shift to an agricultural export economy (led by sugar) in the last quarter of the nineteenth century and the growing dependence on imports for such necessities as rice and textiles. Instituted by the Spanish, these economic policies were continued by the United States through tariff regulations and subsequent free trade between the two countries. According to Miriam Sharma, these economic changes significantly dislocated the native economy. In the Ilocano area, the shift to an agricultural export trade destroyed the region's important textile industry, thus retarding its economic development. With no investment in other manufactured exports to replace textiles, "the main industry in the area then became the production, reproduction, and subsequent export of human resources."[25] By 1910, when HSPA agents were scouting the Philippines for laborers, the Ilocanos, having suffered severe economic displacements and dislocations, willingly emigrated.

The arrival of Filipinos in Hawaii changed the ethnic composition of the sugar plantations' work force. In 1915, Filipinos formed only 19 percent of the workers and the Japanese 54 percent; by 1932, Filipino workers predominated, constituting 70 percent, and the Japanese were 19 percent.[26] To defuse the organizing efforts of their ethnically diverse work force, planters stratified employment by race and paid different wages to different nationalities for the same work. Viewed primarily as instruments of production, Filipino workers were given the least desirable jobs and housing and earned the lowest wages. Laboring ten to twelve hours a day in the cane fields, they carried out the tedious and backbreaking tasks of hoeing, hauling, planting, and weeding during the cultivation, and cutting, hauling, loading, and fluming during the harvest. For this type of labor, from 1915 to 1933 Filipino men earned eighteen to twenty dollars a month, and women twelve to fourteen dollars. As late as 1932, the dwellings allotted to Filipinos were still of poorer quality than those furnished to other plantation workers. This segregation system was so entrenched that by the mid-1940s, many more Filipinos than Chinese and Japanese in Hawaii remained unskilled workers, dependent on the plantations.[27] In 1930, according to the U.S. Census, fewer than five thousand Filipinos lived in Honolulu. Composed mainly of ex-plantation laborers (and a small group of U.S. Navy and Army men), most of these urban dwellers worked in canneries, hotels, and private homes as domestic and day laborers.[28]

Like other plantation workers in Hawaii, Filipino laborers had little control over their time and activities. Roused by the screams of the plantation siren at dawn, they spent their days laboring under the watchful eyes and abusive treatment of the *lunas* (foremen). A retired Filipino worker described the control that plantation managers had over their laborers: "In the plantation, if you stay off work without permission, or go to the doctor, the camp police will go up into your house, and bring [sic] crowbar and open the door. If you are not in the house, he looks up the attic and everywhere."[29] In her narrative, Connie Tirona (Chapter 3) describes the hard life that her parents endured as laborers in Hawaii in the late 1920s: "It was sad, because my father said that they were so mistreated by the different crew bosses. . . . They would leave for work before the break of dawn and return long after dusk. The women like my mother would do the cooking, and some of them would go to work in the fields along with the men." As a noncitizen labor force, Filipinos had few protections from such exploitation. Whereas other nationalities theoretically could appeal to the representatives of their homelands for assistance, the Filipinos, as colonial subjects of the United States, had no representation either in the Philippines or in Hawaii.

But the Filipino plantation workers did not yield to their oppressive conditions, but rather engaged in labor militancy to improve their lives. As H. Brett Melendy reported: "The Filipinos proved that they would not be used, cheated, or forced into serfdom for long. They fought hard for equality in labor's struggle over wages, hours, and working conditions."[30] In 1920, in the first interethnic workers' strike in Hawaii, Filipino plantation workers, led by Pablo Manlapit, joined forces with Japanese laborers to demand greater control over their working conditions and a greater share of the profits they had produced. Because together they constituted more than 70 percent of the work force in Oahu, the 1920 Japanese-Filipino strike brought plantation operations to a sudden stop. Although the strikers were eventually defeated, the plantation owners agreed to improve housing, sanitation, and recreational facilities, raise wages, and distribute monthly bonuses.[31]

In April 1924, Pablo Manlapit called another Filipino strike, which lasted eight months and involved some two thousand workers on twenty-three plantations. The most violent incident in the strike—and in Asian American labor history—occurred in the Hanapepe plantation on Kauai. During a fight between two factions of Filipinos, a sheriff's posse invaded the strikers' camp and fired their rifles into the crowd, killing sixteen and wounding many others. Blamed for the Hanapepe incident, in which four policemen were also killed, strikers and their leaders were arrested, tried, and imprisoned. Many were later deported to the Philippines.[32]

Filipino laborers also resisted their oppressive conditions by leaving plantation work. From the mid-1920s through the 1930s, more than fifty thousand Filipinos headed for the U.S. mainland. One-third were reemigrants from Hawaii,[33] many having been blacklisted for their alleged participation in the 1924 strike.

Filipino Workers Along the Pacific Coast

Large-scale emigration of Filipino agricultural workers to the U.S. mainland coincided with their influx to Hawaii. The 1920s was a decade of dramatic increase in their numbers, with some forty-five thousand Filipinos migrating to the Pacific Coast. The 1921 and 1924 immigration acts, which barred Asian immigration and restricted European immigration, prompted West Coast farmers and canneries to turn to Filipinos to help fill the labor shortage created by the exclusion of the Chinese, Japanese, Koreans, and South Asians.[34]

Filipinos were scattered across the nation: in 1930, 3,480 were in Washington, 2,011 in Illinois, 1,982 in New York, 1,066 in Oregon, 787 in Michigan, and hundreds of others in states like Colorado, Kansas, Virginia, Maryland, Pennsylvania, Mississippi, Montana, Idaho, Texas, and Arizona. But the majority concentrated in California. From 1923 to 1929, Filipinos streamed into the state at the rate of over 4,100 a year. Between 1910 and 1930, the Filipino population in California had increased from only 5 to 30,470. The majority of these immigrants had little formal education and came primarily from the Ilocano region.[35] Almost all came as single young men without families. Out of every hundred Filipinos who migrated to California during the 1920s, 93 were males, 80 of whom were between sixteen and thirty years of age.[36]

In large metropolitan areas like Seattle, San Francisco, Los Angeles, Chicago, and New York, Filipinos worked in restaurants as dishwashers, busboys, or kitchen helpers; in hotels as bellboys, bed makers, or elevator attendants; and in private homes and apartments as servants, janitors, or maintenance men.[37] But most of the Filipinos—about 60 percent—flocked to agriculture. Although they were the largest group of Asian laborers along the Pacific Coast in the 1920s, few became tenant farmers or independent farm owner-operators. By the time large numbers of Filipinos immigrated to the American West, various anti-alien land regulations had been passed, legally forbidding them to lease or buy agricultural land. As a result, Filipinos, unlike Japanese immigrants, never managed to climb the agricultural ladder; the majority toiled in the fields as unskilled migrant laborers.[38]

Unlike plantation workers in Hawaii, who remained in one place, Filipino farm laborers on the mainland moved with the crops. Given the great variety of crops grown along the Pacific Coast, something needs to be harvested virtually every month, but each harvest lasts only two to six weeks. This specialty agriculture created a migratory labor force that moved with the harvests.[39] From the 1920s to the 1970s, Filipinos (and Mexicans) on the Pacific Coast formed the backbone of this harvest labor supply. Under the leadership of labor contractors, Filipinos moved in crews of five to fifty from job to job and pooled funds to help meet car payments, fuel, food, and lodging.[40] In the 1930s, a Filipino agricultural laborer in California earned an average wage of twenty to twenty-five cents per hour. Out of this meager sum, from sixty to seventy-five cents a day would be deducted for room and board.[41]

Viewed by racist growers as ideally suited for "stoop labor," Filipino farm workers remained in high demand until the Great Depression, following the ripening fruit and vegetables as they developed specialized roles in western agriculture. In Washington, Oregon, Montana, and Idaho, they picked apples, hoed hops, topped beets, and dug potatoes. In California, moving from the San Joaquin Valley to the Salinas Valley to the Imperial Valley, Filipinos dominated the agricultural labor force, pulling carrots, picking strawberries, cutting celery, and harvesting grapes. They were also the predominant workers in the cultivation of asparagus—a multimillion dollar industry. In 1925, Filipinos constituted over 80 percent of the asparagus labor force, numbering approximately seven thousand.[42] Because of the long hours of stooping, extreme heat, and dust involved, cutting asparagus is the most difficult job a farm worker can do, with even experienced, able-bodied laborers passing out from heat prostration and exhaustion.[43]

Filipino laborers also lived and worked within a gender-skewed context. Legally prohibited from marrying white women, most Filipino laborers were lonely bachelors, destined for a harsh life without families. Missing the company of small children, these single men adopted and pampered the few Filipino children that were around. Born in 1929, Connie Tirona's (Chapter 3) childhood days were surrounded by bachelor friends of her parents. In her narrative, she describes the joy that her family's visits brought to the lonely *manongs*[44] who labored in the Sacramento–San Joaquin area:

> [Our family] went to see them almost every week or every other week. . . . It was so beautiful there when we visited them. . . . The *manongs* would fix up their rooms immaculately. . . . After eating they would play guitars and mandolins, and we, as little children of the families, would sing and dance. . . . They were so happy. I especially remember when we sang the Visayan songs. You could see the tears on the faces of those grown men. . . . As I was drifting off to sleep, I could hear them laughing as they started to sing nostalgic songs from the Philippines. . . . After such weekends, the *manongs* prepared for another grueling week of hard work.

Because they were predominantly single men, Filipino workers could be housed inexpensively. A Japanese grower told an interviewer in 1930 that he preferred to hire Filipinos because "these Mexicans and Spaniards bring their families with them and I have to fix up houses; but I can put a hundred

Filipinos in that barn" (pointing to a large firetrap).[45] Housed in dilapidated, crowded shacks or in tents, Filipino laborers endured harsh climate, unsanitary living conditions, and the lack of privacy. Philip Vera Cruz, a pioneering Filipino laborer, recalled: "The first camp I lived in had a kitchen that was so full of holes, flies were just coming in and out at their leisure, along with mosquitoes, roaches, and everything else. . . . The toilet was an outhouse with the pit so filled-up it was impossible to use."[46]

Familial and friendship networks helped Filipino workers to cope with the daily punishment of agricultural labor. In virtually every area of the American West where Filipinos labored in large numbers (California, Oregon, Washington, Idaho, Colorado, and Alaska), they established strong and lasting cultural, religious, and community organizations. Among the most important were fraternal associations with elaborate rites of initiation. Some of these groups, such as the Dimas Alang and the Legionarios del Trabajo, spanned great geographic distances. Equally important were regionally and provincially based organizations of immigrants who came from the same area in the Philippines. In Seattle, for example, Ilocanos, Tagalogs, Pangasinans, and Visayans formed their own associations to perpetuate the traditions and folkways of their home regions and to provide mutual aid to their members. Regardless of size, these community organizations provided the earliest immigrants with a substitute for the extended families left behind in the Philippines.[47]

As in Hawaii, Filipinos on the mainland fought oppressive working conditions through labor activism. In the Salinas Valley, where they comprised 40 percent of the agricultural work force, Filipino field workers were especially militant. Harsh words from a boss or sudden wage cuts would prompt them to evacuate the fields. In 1933, after the American Federation of Labor (AFL) refused to organize a union on their behalf, the valley's lettuce pickers formed the Filipino Labor Union (FLU). The following year, the FLU led Filipino workers in a strike, demanding union recognition, improved working conditions, and higher wages. This violent strike ended when local vigilantes burned the camp to the ground and forced the determined strikers to flee for their lives.

Filipino labor activism eventually jolted U.S. organized labor into accepting them. In 1936, the AFL granted a charter to the Field Workers' Union Local No. 30326, composed of Mexican and Filipino laborers, and in 1940, it chartered the Federal Agricultural Laborers Association, a Filipino union.[48] Filipinos in the San Joaquin valley were also the ones to launch the historic Delano grape strike in 1965, which catapulted the United Farm Workers Union and its leader Ceasar Chavez into the limelight of the nation's farm labor struggles.[49]

Filipinos also toiled in the canneries of the Pacific Northwest and Alaska. Deemed a good source of income, cannery jobs were particularly attractive to Filipino students who needed a quick way to make money during the summer. Manuel Buaken reported that in 1930, 500 of the 4,210 Filipinos contracted during the cannery season were college and university students; 800 others attended various trade schools.[50]

As the Northwest's major metropolitan area, Seattle became the hub for "Alaskeros"—Filipino cannery hands who toiled in the Alaskan fisheries. There, in the city's International District, they doubled up in their hotel and boardinghouse beds, waiting out the winter months before sailing north to work from late spring to late summer. According to Bruno Lasker, in 1931 Seattle's Filipino summer population consisted of only a few hundred, while its winter population rose to some thirty-five hundred.[51] Filipino students at the University of Washington provided an important source of labor for the canneries—so much so that contractors were obliged to cultivate a relationship with them by helping to fund their Filipino Club. The presence of the Alaskeros significantly increased the number of Filipino residents in Washington State, which grew between 1910 and 1930 from seventeen to approximately thirty-five hundred.[52]

Recruited by Chinese and Japanese contractors on the West Coast, nearly a thousand Filipinos joined the Alaskan fishery work force in 1921 and by the mid-1930s had become the backbone of the cannery crews. In 1928, Filipino cannery hands in Alaska numbered 3,916, compared to 1,445 Japanese, 1,269 Mexicans, and 1,065 Chinese. Yet despite their numerical dominance, very few Filipinos became contractors because of the Chinese and Japanese oligarchy. Having entered the cannery labor market later than these two other Asian groups, Filipinos predominantly worked as unskilled laborers in mechanized plants. Those permitted to advance at all were halted at the rank of foreman. In charge of recruiting and managing their countrymen, these foremen received relatively high renumeration and special treatment.

Given the narrow access to cannery jobs, Filipino workers were forced to rely on those who might take advantage of them—the Chinese and Japanese contractors and Filipino foremen. Dependent on advances doled out by Chinese and Japanese contractors, Filipino workers often accumulated considerable debt—as much as a month's wages—before the canning season had even begun, as unscrupulous contractors forced them to buy lodging, food, clothes, and bedding at inflated prices from their stores. In some instances, contractors disappeared with the seasonal wages of a whole Filipino crew. Filipinos in positions of power also often took advantage of their countrymen, sometimes demanding half a month's pay or more just for the promise of a cannery job. If a Filipino complained too loudly, he found himself without a cannery job in subsequent years. The victimization of fellow ethnics is a common phenomenon in immigrant labor as the more seasoned migrants take advantage of the new arrivals who usually don't speak English and cannot fend for themselves.

With the onset of the Great Depression, the upward mobility Filipinos had hoped might come to them through cannery work disappeared. Between 1929 and 1933, wages for unskilled cannery positions dropped by 40 percent. More than other Filipinos, students felt the sting of the Depression through the elimination of cannery jobs and severe wage cuts, which forced them to find other seasonal jobs that left little or no time for school. Faced with the dismal realities of the 1930s, Filipinos tried to open the canning industry in new ways, particularly through unionization. On June 19, 1933, Filipino laborers entered the AFL as the Cannery Workers and Farm Laborers Union (CWFLU), Local 18257. Because of Seattle's proximity to Alaska, the city became the union's headquarters.

Uniting the Filipino community behind a unionization drive proved no easy task. Before the Depression, the myriad of small-group affiliations—the family, friendship, and ethnic networks—had helped Filipinos to brave exploitative employers, contractors, and foremen. During the Depression, however, members of these same associations competed for jobs and disagreed on the solutions to their deteriorating conditions in the cannery industry. In spite of its best effort to unite the community, the CWFLU made little headway. Not until the 1936 murders of two top Filipino union leaders and their elevation to martyrdom did Filipinos rally behind the CWFLU. Negotiating for higher wages, better hours, and improved working conditions for its members, the CWFLU empowered Filipino cannery workers to unite against some of the worst abuses of employers and contractors. In 1938, Filipinos finally eliminated the contract system; from then on, cannery workers were hired through the union hall.

During the late 1920s and 1930s, as the Filipino population grew and as the Great Depression engulfed the nation, white resentment against Filipino laborers intensified. Anti-Filipino spokespersons also portrayed the largely single Filipino men as sexual threats who sought the company of white and Mexican women at taxi-dance halls. Between 1928 and 1930, competition for jobs as well as concern over "hybridization" culminated in a series of race riots in Washington and California meant to drive Filipinos out of various communities. The most explosive and most publicized incident took place in 1930 near Watsonville, California, where four hundred white vigilantes attacked a Filipino dance club, beating dozens of Filipinos and killing one. In 1933, the California state legislature amended antimiscegenation laws to include Filipino-white marriages. Twelve other states had similar restrictions.

In the midst of the Depression, exclusionists also sought—unsuccessfully—to repatriate Filipinos. Although the 1935 Welch Bill appropriated $300,000 to pay for the fare of Filipinos who would voluntarily return to the Philippines, only 5 percent of those in the United States (2,190 out of

45,000) took advantage of this offer.[53] To enable the government to restrict the number of Filipino immigrants, their legal status as U.S. nationals had to be changed. In 1934, yielding to anti-Filipino forces, the U.S. Congress passed the Tydings-McDuffie Independence Act, granting the Philippines eventual independence, declaring Filipinos to be aliens, and cutting Filipino immigration to a trickle of fifty persons a year.[54] Filipinos who served in the U.S. armed forces, especially in the U.S. Navy, were among the few who were exempted from this immigration restriction.

Filipinos in the U.S. Navy

Filipino nationals are the only Asians who have served in the U.S. armed forces in sizable numbers without holding U.S. citizenship. This arrangement emerged out of the colonial process, specifically the extensive U.S. military presence in the Philippines. It was during the Philippine American War at the turn of the century that the United States established its first three military bases in the Philippines.[55] Since then, the Philippines has housed—at times unwillingly—some of the United States' largest overseas air force and naval bases. Even after the Philippines' formal independence in 1946 the U.S. military installations remained, and the Military Bases Agreement of the following year allowed the United States to lease five major bases and at least twenty minor military installations for ninety-nine years at no cost. Although the agreement was signed in 1947, its preliminary terms had been arranged prior to World War II, in effect making it an agreement between the United States and its colony, not between two sovereign states.

Despite the official pretext that the bases served the security interests of both the United States and the Philippines, they primarily protected U.S. economic and political investments in the region. In the post–World War II era, these bases served as springboards as well as training and supply stations for U.S. military interventions in China, Indonesia, Korea, and Vietnam. With the "fall" of China to Mao Zedong's forces in 1949 and the outbreak of war in Korea in 1950, the bases in the Philippines became critical to the U.S. security in terms of "containing" Communism. After the end of the Vietnam War, they represented U.S. commitment to remain a power in the Asian-Pacific region.

For Filipino nationalists, the bases symbolized the colonial legacy and U.S. dominance over the Philippines. For many others, however, they represented economic opportunities. In 1987, the U.S. bases were the second largest employer after the Philippine government, providing jobs and an annual salary totaling more than $96 million to over sixty-eight thousand Filipinos. They also fueled local economies, sustaining businesses that catered primarily to the base personnel. For these reasons, local, provincial, and some national officials and business leaders lobbied to keep the bases in the Philippines. However, after a 1991 vote for national sovereignty by the Philippine Senate, the last U.S.-controlled base (Subic Bay Naval Station) was turned over to the Philippine government in 1992, some ninety-four years after the first U.S. troops landed in the Philippines.[56]

During the ninety-four years of U.S. military presence in the Philippines, U.S. bases served as recruiting stations for the U.S. armed forces, particularly the Navy. Soon after the United States acquired the Philippines from Spain in 1898, its Navy began actively recruiting Filipinos as stewards and mess boys. From a total of nine persons in 1903, the number of Filipinos in the U.S. Navy grew to six thousand by World War I and hovered around four thousand (or 5 percent of the total Navy manpower) during the 1920s and 1930s. After the Philippines achieved full independence in 1946, the United States no longer could unilaterally authorize recruitment of Filipino nationals, since they had become citizens of their own country. To sidestep this obstacle, U.S. officials inserted a provision in the 1947 Military Bases Agreement (Article 27) granting its Navy the right to continue to recruit Filipino citizens. With the onset of the Korean War in the early 1950s, the U.S. Navy allowed for the enrollment of up to two thousand Filipinos per calendar year for terms of four or six years.[57]

For many young Filipino men, a career in the U.S. Navy had been a life-long dream. In some towns (and in many families), particularly those surrounding U.S. bases, joining the Navy had become a tradition. Beside serving as recruiting stations, these bases—centers of wealth amidst local poverty—exposed the native populace to U.S. money, culture, and standards of living, generating a strong incentive for enlistment. The economic incentive to join the U.S. Navy was high: the salary of a Filipino enlistee often placed him among the top quarter of his country's wage earners. Filipino recruits also used their service in the Navy to gain U.S. citizenship—the springboard for escaping from poverty.[58] During the 1960s, some one hundred thousand Filipinos applied to the U.S. Navy each year, but few were admitted due to a high reenlistment rate of 94 to 99 percent among Filipinos.[59] By 1970, in large part due to the grave economic, political, and social problems besetting the Philippines, there were more Filipinos in the U.S. Navy (fourteen thousand) than in the entire Philippine Navy.[60] In 1973, when the U.S. Navy reduced the number of Filipino recruits from two thousand to four hundred per year, approximately two hundred thousand applied for the few coveted slots. According to the U.S. Navy Chief of Legislative Affairs, in the 1970s about forty thousand potential Filipino enlistees were available at any given time.[61]

Prior to and during World War I, the U.S. Navy allowed Filipino enlistees to serve in a range of occupational ratings such as petty officers, band masters, musicians, coxswains' mates, seamen, machinists, firemen, water tenders, commissary stewards, officers' stewards, and mess attendants. However, after the war the Navy issued a new ruling restricting Filipinos, even those with a college education, to the ratings of officers' stewards and mess attendants.[62] Leo Sicat (Chapter 6), a graduate of the University of the Philippines, described the indignity he felt in steward school: "At the school, we were taught how to cook and bake, how to set the table, and how to position the silverware, and the glass and the cup. They basically taught us the job of a waitress. Personally, I was so insulted. I was almost a chemical engineer, and I came to the United States just to become a steward."

Barred from admission to other ratings, Filipino enlistees performed the work of domestics, preparing and serving the officers' meals, and caring for the officers' galley, wardroom, and living spaces. Ashore, their duties ranged from ordinary housework to food services at the U.S. Naval Academy mess hall. Unofficially, Filipino stewards also have been ordered to perform menial chores such as walking the officers' dogs and acting as personal servants for the officers' wives. Even when they passed the relevant qualifying examinations, few Filipinos were allowed to transfer to other ratings—unless they were the personal favorites of high-ranking officials who agreed to intervene on their behalf. In 1970, of the 16,669 Filipinos in the U.S. Navy, 80 percent were in the steward rating.[63]

In the early 1970s, responding to the demands of the civil rights movement and to a senatorial investigation on the use of stewards in the military, the U.S. Navy amended its policies to grant Filipino enlistees the right to enter any occupational rating. In 1973, the first year of the new Navy policy, Filipino nationals served in fifty-six of the eighty-seven ratings available for enlistees. But they were not distributed evenly among these ratings. According to Navy statistics for that year, over 40 percent of Filipinos remained stewards. Of the balance, the majority congregated in clerical jobs such as personnel man, disbursing clerk, storekeeper, and commissary man.[64] This rating concentration—the result of both job availability and ethnic clustering—suggests that Filipinos in the U.S. Navy continue to share common experiences.

These Navy-related immigrants form a distinct segment of the Filipino American community. Because of their similar background in the U.S. Navy, these Filipino men and their families cultivate informal but lasting social networks. In fact, many Filipino Navy retirees prefer living near their "old Navy comrades with whom they spent a great deal of time while in the service."[65] Consequently, U.S. cities with large naval facilities, such as San Diego, have sizable Filipino communities made up largely of Navy families. Following in their fathers' footsteps, some Filipino Americans have also joined the U.S. Navy—but now as officers. For example, Daniel Gruta (Chapter 10), whose father and three uncles were Navy enlistees, became a naval officer after graduating from the U.S. Naval Academy in 1986.

Filipinos During World War II and the Postwar Years

World War II marked an important turning point in the history of Filipinos as well as other Asians in the United States. The military exploits of Filipino soldiers—both in the Philippines and in the United States—did a great deal to reduce white prejudice against Filipino Americans. Their wartime services also earned many U.S. citizenship and helped to rescind exclusion laws, thus making renewed immigration from the Philippines possible. According to H. Brett Melendy, from 1946 to 1965, thirty-three thousand Filipinos immigrated to the United States and contributed to a 44 percent increase in the Filipino American population during the 1950–60 census period.[66] Leaving a war-torn country, the postwar Filipino immigrants, who included war veterans, war brides, students, and skilled and unskilled workers, scattered throughout the United States. During the 1950s, Filipinos in California congregated primarily in the San Francisco Bay area and Los Angeles. Other mainland cities in which sizable Filipino populations developed were, in order of rank, Seattle, Chicago, New York, and Washington, D.C.[67]

When the United States declared war against Japan in December 1941, President Franklin D. Roosevelt incorporated the Philippine armed forces into the United States Armed Forces in the Far East (USAFFE). University student reserve officers and nurses in the Philippines were also inducted for military service.[68] Fighting alongside American soldiers in defending Baatan and Corregidor during the spring of 1942, the heroism and courage of Filipino troops were widely publicized in newsreels and newspaper headlines across the United States. The wartime performance of Filipinos forced whites to view and treat Filipinos in the United States more favorably.[69] Although Roosevelt had pledged citizenship to Filipino nationals who took up arms against the Japanese, a federal act rescinded that pledge in 1946. Only four thousand Filipino World War II veterans were able to gain U.S. citizenship before the rescission.[70]

Meanwhile, large numbers of Filipinos in the United States were inducted into the armed forces.[71] Their status as U.S. nationals forgotten, many became citizens through mass naturalization ceremonies held before induction. According to A.B. Santos (Chapter 1) who was drafted into the U.S. Army in 1943, "[When] I reported to Los Angeles, . . . they swore me in as a U.S. citizen. I did not even have to file an application." Because most Filipinos were males of draft age, some sixteen thousand were called up under the first draft in 1942. Over seven thousand recruits served in the segregated First Filipino Infantry Regiment and the Second Filipino Infantry Regiment of the U.S. Army. Although the U.S. Navy tried to enlist Filipinos as mess attendants, nearly one-third of the draft-age Filipino males in the continental United States volunteered for the Army. In 1944 over one thousand Filipino Americans infiltrated the Philippines via submarine to gather intelligence for General Douglas MacArthur's headquarters in Australia. Engaged in sabotage to destroy Japanese communications, Filipino soldiers accelerated the recapture of the Philippines by U.S. forces in 1945.[72]

World War II also changed the economic fortunes of Filipinos by opening employment in labor-starved war industries. In agriculture, California's attorney general reinterpreted the land laws to allow Filipinos to lease and buy land. The war also forced the United States to reopen its gates to Filipino and other Asian immigrants. In 1946, seeking to demonstrate U.S. commitment to democracy, Congress passed the Luce-Celler Bill, permitting the entry of one hundred Filipino immigrants annually and granting Filipinos the right of naturalization. As citizens, qualified Filipinos were able to secure professional licenses and upgrade their occupational status. As the country's industrial base expanded, many found jobs in factories, in trades, and in wholesale and retail sales. Nevertheless, in California in 1960, agriculture remained the largest employer of Filipinos, with 3 percent classified as farmers and farm managers and another 28 percent as farm laborers and foremen.[73] Filipino veterans also made use of the G.I. Bill to attend college and to purchase property. Sociologist R. T. Feria has noted that shortly after the war, many Filipinos in Los Angeles bought homes and small farms that had been vacated by the Japanese who had been incarcerated in "relocation camps."[74]

It was during the postwar years that Filipino women first came to the United States in significant numbers. The majority immigrated as U.S. dependents: some, such as Juanita Santos (Chapter 1), had met and married U.S. servicemen in the Philippines—including a sizable number of Filipino Americans serving in the U.S. Navy; others came to join their Filipino husbands already in the United States; still others, such as Ruth Abad (Chapter 2), entered as "repatriates"—dependents of U.S. citizens who had lived in the Philippines before World War II. According to David Reimers, nearly half of the Filipino immigrants (16,000) between 1946 and 1965 came as wives of U.S. servicemen.[75] Single Filipinas came to the United States primarily as students. As in the case of Luz Latus (Chapter 4), an unknown number married U.S. citizens and stayed in the United States after their schooling was completed.[76]

The postwar immigrants also included the last batch of Filipino plantation workers. Facing a postwar shortage of cheap laborers, the Hawaiian Sugar Planters Association requested the U.S. Department of Interior, by provision of the Tydings-McDuffie Act (section 8), to permit unlimited Filipino immigration to the islands. Exempted from the immigration quota of 50 persons a year, that is applied to Filipino immigration to the mainland, in 1946 some 7,361 Filipinos migrated to Hawaii to work on its sugar plantations. Many arrived to beat the quota of 100 persons a year that would go into effect following Philippine independence.[77] In sharp contrast to the restrictions imposed on the immigrant plantation laborers of the 1920s, women and children were allowed in the 1946 group. Most of these families, which included 710 women and 1,425 children, settled on the island of Kauai.[78]

Post–1965 Filipino Immigrants

Contemporary Filipino immigration has been shaped by changes in U.S. immigration legislation and by political, economic, and social conditions in the Philippines. The 1965 Immigration Act, which abolished the national-origins quotas and permitted entry based primarily on family reunification or occupational characteristics, dramatically increased the number of Asian immigrants. In the twenty years following passage of the 1965 act, about 40 percent of the legal immigration to the United States has come from Asia.[79] The Philippines has been the largest source, with Filipinos comprising nearly one-quarter of the total Asian immigration. In 1961–65, fewer than 16,000 Filipinos immigrated to the United States, compared to more than 221,000 in 1981–85. Since 1979, over 40,000 Filipinos have been admitted annually, making the Philippines the second largest source of all immigration, surpassed only by Mexico.[80] The 1990 U.S. Census counted close to 1.5 million Filipinos in the United States, 50 percent of whom reside in California. Hawaii and Illinois ranked next, with close to 170,000 and 65,000 respectively.

The 1965 Immigration Act alone, however, does not explain why so many Filipinos have come to the United States in the last quarter-century. The ties forged between the Philippines and the United States during the ninety-plus years of colonial and postcolonial rule have also contributed to this influx. Beside creating strong military and business connections between the two countries, this colonial heritage has produced a pervasive cultural Americanization of the population, exhorting Filipinos to regard the American culture, political system, and way of life as superior to their own.[81] Infused with images of U.S. abundance peddled by the educational system, the media, and relatives and friends already in the United States, Filipinos quickly took advantage of the 1965 changes in the immigration law to emigrate.

The grave economic conditions in the Philippines have also pushed frustrated Filipinos to leave for the United States. During the 1960s, the Philippine economy registered high growth when President Ferdinand Marcos implemented an economic plan that depended solely upon U.S. war efforts in Vietnam. When U.S. forces withdrew from Vietnam, the Philippines was left with an economic infrastructure ill-suited to local needs.[82] By the end of the Marcos era in 1986, the Philippines was bankrupt and inflation was rampant. Weighed down by the cost of servicing a gigantic foreign debt and heavily dependent on agricultural exports, the Philippine economy suffers from massive unemployment and inequality in the distribution of income and wealth.

Driven off the land, many peasants migrate to Manila in search of livelihood, but the city does not have enough industries to support its burgeoning population.[83] Also, since the 1960s, the Philippines has had an oversupply of educated people. With U.S. aid, the Philippines underwent an "educational boom" after World War II. In 1970, one-quarter of the college-age population in the Philippines was enrolled in colleges and universities, a ratio second only to that of the United States. But this growing army of college-educated Filipinos faced extremely limited employment prospects. Heather Low Ruth estimated that in the late 1960s, jobs were available for only half the college graduates in the Philippines.[84] Under such grave economic conditions, many Filipinos seized the opportunity to work abroad as permanent immigrants in the United States or as short-term contract workers all over the world.

But the push to leave the Philippines was also political. Declaring martial law in 1972, President Marcos prorogued the legislatures, controlled the media, suspended the writ of habeas corpus, and arrested many of his alleged political opponents. According to a U.S. congressional report, there were between five hundred and one thousand political prisoners in the Philippines at the end of 1978.[85] During the Marcos era (1965–1986), an estimated three hundred thousand Filipinos emigrated to the United States.[86] In 1983, the U.S. Immigration and Naturalization Service (INS) reported that 208 Filipinos had filed for political asylum that year. However, only eighteen were granted asylum.[87]

As soon as martial law was declared in the Philippines, the Filipino American community organized against Marcos's dictatorship. The first U.S.-based opposition group was the National Committee for the Restoration of Civil Liberties in the Philippines (NCRCLP). Shortly thereafter, exiled former Philippine senator Raul Manglapus organized the Movement for a Free Philippines (MFP). Edgar Gamboa (Chapter 8), an anti-Marcos student activist, was among those who left for the United States to escape "the tentacles of Marcos's repressive government." Once in the United States, he joined the MFP to protest the Marcos dictatorship. Critical of Marcos's corruption and alarmed by his political repression and violation of human rights, these opposition groups alerted the American public to the plight of political prisoners and to the regime's use of torture and execution of alleged opponents. Convinced that U.S. economic assistance enabled the Marcos regime to maintain its totalitarian rule, the main goal of these groups was to stop such aid.[88]

Since the 1960s, the Philippines has been the source of the largest number of white-collar professionals to immigrate to the United States.[89] Because of the shortage of medical personnel in this country, particularly in the inner cities and in rural areas, doctors, nurses, and other health-related practitioners are overrepresented among the recent Filipino immigrants. Just as the early Filipino immigrants were recruited for farm labor, by the 1970s recent medical graduates in the Philippines were recruited to work in U.S. hospitals, nursing homes, and health organizations.[90] However, as indicated in the narratives of Luz Latus and Edgar Gamboa (Chapters 4 and 8, respectively), strict licensing procedures and the racial discrimination in the United States have forced many Filipino medical professionals to work in jobs for which they are overqualified or that are totally unrelated to their knowledge and expertise.[91]

Since 1960, women have dominated the Filipino immigrant population,[92] a phenomenon that can be accounted for in part by the need for health professionals in the United States. In the Philippines, according to Antonio Pido, women are the majority in all health-related professions (including nursing, pharmacy, medical technology, and institutional food services) except for medicine, where the numbers of male and female physicians are nearly equal. Because their occupations are high on the list of preferred professions for U.S. immigrants, Filipino women, married or unmarried, can apply as the principal immigrants under the 1965 Immigration Act.[93] For example, when Joey Laguda's mother (Chapter 12), a medical technologist, entered the country, she carried the primary immigrant status, with her husband and children entering as her dependents.

Since the 1970s, the Philippines has been the major source of foreign-trained nurses in the United States, with at least twenty-five thousand Filipino nurses arriving between 1966 and 1985. In fact, many women in the Philippines still study nursing in the hope of securing employment abroad, and many of the nursing programs in the Philippines are accordingly oriented toward supplying the U.S. market.[94]

Not all of the contemporary immigrants from the Philippines are professionals, however. Instead, the dual goals of the 1965 Immigration Act—to facilitate family reunification and to admit workers needed by the U.S. economy—have resulted in two distinct chains of emigration: one of the relatives of Filipinos who had left for the United States prior to 1965 and another chain of highly trained immigrants who entered during the late 1960s and early 1970s. During the period 1966–75, the two groups entered in about the same proportion. However, in 1976–88, the proportion of occupational preference immigrants dropped to 19–20 percent of the Filipino total, while the proportion of family preference immigrants rose to about 80 percent. This shift was the result of tightened entry requirements for professionals in the mid-1970s and their subsequent reliance on family reunification categories.[95]

Because new immigrants tend to have socioeconomic backgrounds similar to those of their sponsors, family reunification immigrants such as Nemesia Cortez (Chapter 7) represent a continuation of the unskilled and semiskilled Filipino labor that had emigrated before 1965. In contrast, professionals who immigrate, such as Paz Jensen and Edgar Gamboa (Chapters 5 and 8, respectively), originate from the middle to upper social, economic, and educational sectors of Philippine society, and they in turn sponsor relatives with the same backgrounds.[96] As a result of these two distinct groups of immigrants, the contemporary Filipino American community exhibits more class diversity than it did in the past.

By allowing resident Filipino Americans to bring their relatives into the United States, the family unification provisions of the 1965 law rejuvenated the established Filipino communities in Hawaii, California, and Washington, and supported a proliferation of regional, hometown, and even village associations.[97] But such organizations do not bridge class differences, because immigrants with professional backgrounds tend to settle in suburban neighborhoods, beyond the reach of their compatriots, and form their own communities and organizations. Having minimal ties to the pre-1965 Filipinos, these professionals join voluntary associations that cater primarily to their particular class interests and needs. Because employer sponsorship, rather than family sponsorship, influences the destination of occupational immigrants, large numbers of post-1965 immigrants have by-passed the Pacific Coast and settled in the Northeast and Midwest.[98] This is particularly true for health-care workers who have been recruited to fill the shortage of medical personnel in older metropolitan areas in the Northeast. For example, in 1984 nearly half (46 percent) of the Filipino nurses who had received their licenses within the preceding four years resided in the New York–New Jersey region. The Filipino community of Washington, D.C., provides a similar example. Characterized by high levels of education and middle to upper-middle levels of income, many if not most of these D.C. Filipino Americans are post-1965 immigrants. The new communities in which they predominate add to the complexity of the contemporary Filipino experience.

While class differences both divide established Filipino communities geographically and organizationally and create essentially new communities (each dominated by class), the common confrontation with U.S. racism may eventually lead to greater unity, at least for political purposes.

The Filipino American Community in San Diego

All of the narrators in this book reside in San Diego County, the third largest U.S. destination of contemporary Filipino immigrants.[99] Numbering close to ninety-six thousand in 1990, Filipinos were the county's largest Asian American group, representing approximately 50 percent of this population. Despite the long history of the San Diego community (dating back to 1903), it receives little mention in the literature. For this reason, I have selected narratives that illumine not only the Filipino American experience in general but also the Filipino American experience in San Diego in particular.

As in other parts of the U.S. mainland, the first Filipinos in San Diego were students. According to Adelaida Castillo, school records indicate that in 1903 a group of Filipinos between the ages of sixteen and twenty-five enrolled at the State Normal School (now San Diego State University). Lawrence Lawcock reported that nineteen Filipinos organized a Filipino Students' Club in San Diego that same year. Presumably arriving on government scholarships, these *pensionados* stayed only for one year, during which they studied algebra, drawing, botany, English, and music.[100] As illustrated in A. B. Santos's narrative (Chapter 1), the nonsponsored students who followed the *pensionados* scrambled to maintain themselves by combining work and study.

The prewar San Diego Filipinos also included laborers. While the farm workers concentrated in the agricultural communities of El Centro and Escondido, California, the urban laborers lived and worked in downtown hotels and restaurants. For example, according to A. B. Santos, in the early 1920s about eighteen to twenty Filipinos worked at the Coronado Hotel as busboys, janitors, and dining room helpers. Although numerically small (see Table 1), the prewar Filipino community was vibrant. Barred from renting or purchasing homes outside of the business district, most Filipinos lived in the downtown section of the city. There, around Market Street, Filipinos ran small restaurants and pool and gambling tables, and sponsored dances and other cultural events. Rizal Day—a yearly observance in honor of Philippine national hero Dr. José Rizal—was the most celebrated festivity, drawing several hundred Filipinos from all over the county.[101]

The virulent racism against Filipinos in San Diego—and in other parts of the country—declined after World War II. According to Ruth Abad (Chapter 2), before the war, Filipinos who were not U.S. citizens* could not own property "unless they married an American. And even then, the white people used to stone their homes. Also, some hotels . . . did not allow Filipinos to hold their dances in their ballrooms. . . . But after the war, the white people learned that Filipinos are good, so the prejudice faded." In the 1950s, non-Filipino women's clubs and churches began to invite Filipino folk dancers and speakers to teach them about Filipino culture.[102] Recalling her immigration to the United States in 1952 as a war bride, Juanita Santos (Chapter 1) mentions receiving "so many invitations" to the women's clubs of Coronado, Pacific Beach, Chula Vista, and La Jolla to speak about Filipino women.

---

*Like other Asian immigrants, Filipino immigrants were denied the right of naturalization. They became eligible for naturalized citizenship in 1946 with the passage of the Luce-Celler bill.

Because San Diego is the site of the largest U.S. naval base and the Navy's primary West Coast training facility, Navy men and their families have comprised a large proportion of the county's Filipinos since the early 1900s. According to Juanita Santos and Ruth Abad (Chapters 1 and 2 respectively), the majority of the Filipino families in San Diego during the 1940s and 1950s were Navy-connected. This association is reflected in the founding of pioneer Filipino organizations in San Diego—the Fleet Reserve Association and the Filipino American Veterans Hall (the first community center). Recalling her school days in the early 1960s, Anamaria Labao Cabato (Chapter 9) states that "there were a lot of Filipinos where I went to school [in National City]. We were all Navy children. I don't think any of my classmates were the children of professionals. Maybe their mothers were nurses, but it was the Navy that got them here." Even into the 1970s, the Navy presence was still prominent. According to Daniel Gruta (Chapter 10), Mira Mesa's proximity to the nearby Miramar Naval Air Station in northern San Diego made it predominantly a Navy town. The biggest store in town was not Alpha Beta [a Southern California supermarket chain] but the Navy Commissary store and the Navy Exchange at the Naval Air Station." Rubén Rumbaut reported that during 1978–85, more than 51 percent of the 12,500 Filipino babies born in the San Diego metropolitan area were delivered at the U.S. Naval Hospital.[103]

As in other Filipino communities along the Pacific Coast, the San Diego community grew dramatically in the twenty-five years following passage of the 1965 Immigration Act. New immigration contributed greatly to the tripling of the county's Filipino American population in 1970–80 and its doubling in 1980–90 (see Table 1). The arrival of the new immigrants has made it more difficult to maintain the closeness once shared by the smaller group. Reminiscing about the pre-1965 community, Juanita Santos (Chapter 1) states that "we used to be very, very close. We were one big family. When we had a picnic, Oh, my Lord, everybody would come. Now we don't know everybody like we used to."

The increasing geographical dispersion of the community is an obstacle to its cohesion. Once concentrated in South Bay communities such as National City, Chula Vista, and Imperial Beach, San Diego Filipinos now also live in the relatively newer and more affluent North County communities of Mira Mesa, Rancho Penasquitos, and Oceanside, which means that most Filipinos who live at opposite ends of the county know very little about each other. This north-south separation also reflects differences in class and immigration history, with most newly arrived professionals residing in the North County and most retired Navy people living in the South Bay. Consider the two boards of directors of the PASACAT dance troupe.[104] According to Anamaria Labao Cabato (Chapter 9), executive director of PASACAT, in the North County "we've got a financial adviser on the board, a senior

Table 1
Filipino Population in the United States, California, and San Diego, 1910–90

Year[1]	United States	California	San Diego[2]
1910	2,767	5	—
1920	26,634	2,674	48
1930	108,260	30,470	394
1940	98,535	31,408	799
1950	122,707	40,424	NA
1960	181,614	67,134	5,123
1970	336,731	135,248	15,069
1980	774,652	358,378	48,658
1990	1,406,770	733,941	95,945

[1]Up to 1950, the data are from H. Brett Melendy, *Asians in America: Filipinos, Koreans, and East Indians* (Boston: Twayne Publishers, 1977), whose sources include the annual reports of the U.S. Immigration and Naturalization Service and the U.S. Bureau of the Census. The figures for 1960 to 1990 were collated from the U.S. Census of Population and Housing for each area.
[2]Melendy's records for San Diego through 1950 were for the city itself; the numbers from 1960 to 1990 are those for San Diego County.
NA, not available.

financial analyst, an accountant who has his own business, a mechanical engineer, an auditor working for the Department of Defense. . . . Here in the South Bay, the board members are Navy retirees, civil servants, a couple of nurses, maybe one or two teachers. They do not have the business skills that the North County people have."

As the number of Filipinos in San Diego grew, so did the number of community organizations. According to my own estimate and that of the narrators in this book, there are currently 150 to 175 Filipino American associations in San Diego County—an exponential increase from the handful that existed prior to 1970.[105] The majority are town- or region-based associations, some of which have been started anew, while others have been revived by previously inactive groups. Bringing together individuals who originally came from the same town, province, or region in the Philippines, these social groups mainly sponsor annual banquets, picnics, dances, and town fiestas. In contrast, the primary goal of the professional and alumni organizations is to promote their particular class interests and needs. As Luz Latus (Chapter 4) stated, the principal aim of the San Diego Chapter of the Philippine Nurses Association of America is "to protect our profession and our nurses." The relative class homogeneity of these associations suggests that these professionals limit their contact largely to Filipinos of the same socioeconomic background.

Most of the narrators regard the proliferation of such organizations as divisive and detrimental to Filipino American political effectiveness. The following comment by Leo Sicat (Chapter 6) is typical: "If we are not unified, nobody is going to talk to us. We Filipinos don't get the respect that we deserve. We are not being heard." However, given its increasing diversity along class, regional, linguistic, and generational lines, the Filipino American community in San Diego—and elsewhere—needs a flexible organizational structure that will allow them to coalesce as well as to fragment, and to shift identity and reference groups to meet situational needs. A single organizational structure would leave them only two choices: to join or to withdraw. But if a more accommodating structure is allowed to develop, the proliferation of organizations, instead of being a detriment, may provide the strongest social and political support for Filipino Americans, linking them simultaneously to multiple levels of solidarity.

The Construction of Filipino American Identities

In the last quarter-century, the vast majority of immigrants to the United States have been people of color. However, despite their Third World origins, today's immigrants—unlike their European counterparts of the nineteenth century—have long been exposed to Western life styles, cultural practices, and consumption patterns, because the contemporary world, although still organized as separate nation-states, is in fact bound by a global capitalist system.[106] Owing to the accessibility of international travel, the increasing economic and political connections between developing and developed nations, and the worldwide diffusion of postindustrial, bourgeois mass culture, today's immigrants arrive with a working, if not intimate, knowledge of U.S. capitalist culture.[107]

The development of a global economy means that most recent immigrants are, in a sense, the offspring of American globalism.[108] This global context opens new perspectives on international migration, perspectives that place the study of migrants' identities within the *worldwide* historical context of differential power and inequality. Extending the issue of power beyond the context of the countries of settlement, this global view posits that the identity and experience of contemporary immigrants of color have been shaped not only by the social location of their racial group within the United States but also by the position of their country within the global racial order.

In the case of Filipino immigrants, the cultural, economic, and political relationships between the Philippines and the United States—imposed and maintained during the ninety-plus years of colonial and postcolonial rule—have provided and continue to provide the context within which they construct their identities. The position of the Philippines within the global racial order and the social location of Filipinos in the United States means that Filipino immigrants—regardless of their class status and familiarity with U.S.

culture—are defined as "nonwhite" and face the consequences of being so labeled.

As discussed, prior to World War II Filipinos were barred from becoming U.S. citizens, owning real property, and marrying whites. While such blatant legal discrimination against Filipino Americans (and other Asian Americans) is largely a matter of the past, Filipinos continue to encounter many barriers that prevent them from full participation in the economic, social, and political institutions of the United States. Most importantly, the economic mobility and cultural assimilation that enables white ethnics to become "unhyphenated whites"[109] does not lead to complete acceptance of Filipinos and other people of color as "Americans." As Connie Tirona (Chapter 3) declared, "Sometimes, I am not sure what it means to be an American. I am not equal to anyone. My color is different and that seems to be mattering all my lifetime."

Like Filipinos elsewhere, the narrators in this book actively resist the cultural racism and nativism of U.S. society. Juanita Santos (Chapter 1) counters arrogance with the "truth" about the Philippines: "I just wanted to 'educate' the other races that the Filipinos are as knowledgeable and cultured as they are. I wanted respect for my people. I wanted to project a positive image of the Filipinos and my native country." When a tall, blue-eyed doctor at Mercy Hospital asked Santos if there were schools in the Philippines, she shook her finger at him and said, "You know what, Doctor, you are ignorant. Our University of Santo Tomas is twenty-five years older than your Harvard University." Similarly, Ruth Abad (Chapter 2) founded the Filipino American Women's Club in part to "show off our culture, like our cooking, our costumes, and our folk dances." Other narrators responded to racism by resolving to outshine the offenders. For example, faced with racial tauntings by his classmates, Daniel Gruta (Chapter 10) "got even by outdoing them in school." Still others, like Luz Latus, Paz Jensen, Edgar Gamboa, and Dario Villa (Chapters 4, 5, 8, and 11 respectively), challenged institutional racism through their positions at work and/or their involvement in professional organizations.

To resist racial categorization, Filipino immigrants in the United States also have refused to sever their ties to the Philippines. They have assumed instead the role of *transmigrants,* generating and sustaining multistranded relations between the Philippines and the United States.[110] While some narrators in this book identify more with one society than the other, most have kept ties with family, friends, and colleagues in the Philippines through occasional visits, telephone calls, remittances, and medical and other humanitarian missions. In so doing, they have created and maintained fluid and multiple identities that link them simultaneously to both countries. As an example, while Luz Latus identifies herself as "an American citizen" who is "very much interested in and informed on what goes on in this country," her dream is to return to the Philippines to help "*my* country and *my* people" (emphasis added). According to Nina Glick Schiller and her colleagues, "through these seemingly contradictory experiences, transmigrants actively manipulate their identities and thus both accommodate to and resist their subordination within a global capitalist system."[111]

As transmigrants, Filipinos also engage in the process of transculturation, creating something new from the cultural resources of their countries of origin and of settlement.[112] This is particularly true among the "one-and-a-half generation"—those who came to the United States in their late childhood or teen years. In the following statement, Dario Villa (Chapter 11), who came to the United States in 1976 at the age of seventeen, describes his Filipino American world as a union of cultures:

> In my case, what I have is an amalgamation of values. I have been able to find a comfort zone between both cultures, taking the values that I learned as a kid and adopting the American values that I think will make me a much wholler, more knowledgeable individual. For example, I use both the Filipino value of family interdependence *and* the American value of independence to the best interests of myself and my family.

This active cultural construction challenges both the assimilationist and pluralist perspectives, which conceptualize identity as bipolar and linear, and thus overlook the emergence of distinct, new cultures that are qualitatively different from those of the immigrant homelands as well as from traditional American society.

In contrast, because U.S.-born Filipinos are not as able as their parents and the "one-and-a-half generations" to draw on the knowledge of an alternative way of life or on the social ties "back home," their identities are shaped largely by the dialogue of racial domination in the United States.[113] Connie Tirona, Anamaria Labao Cabato, Joey Laguda, and Lisa Graham (Chapters 3, 9, 12, and 13, respectively) detailed the social costs of being Filipinos in the United States. Beside witnessing the economic discrimination faced by their immigrant parents, all recalled being teased and harassed by their peers for their perceived racial differences. Connie Tirona described the world of prejudice of the 1930s: "I can remember walking to elementary school and being taunted at times. . . . I used to bring rice and fish to school for lunch because I love to eat both. It was a great meal for me. [But] the little girls would not sit by me." Joey Laguda similarly felt ostracized when his parents moved to North San Diego in the late 1970s: "Back then . . . the majority white population was not tolerant of any minorities. This I got to experience from watching racial fights my brothers were involved in and seeing the words 'Flips go home' spraypainted on the house of one of my best friends." These accounts reveal that Filipinos in both the Philippines and the United States live within, and in tension with, a racist system that defines white middle-class culture as the norm.

The racism of the larger society strongly influences the ethnic identification of second-generation Filipino Americans. Some respond by "assimilating": speaking only English, dating and associating primarily with Anglos, and slighting Filipino culture. Dario Villa (Chapter 11) recalled being shunned by the U.S.-born Filipinos because he was an "FOB" ("Fresh Off the Boat"): "I was ridiculed because my accent reminded them of their parents. It was their shame coming out at my expense. A number of times in my classes, there were Filipinas who giggled and displayed bodily discomfort when I spoke." Others, like Joey Laguda (Chapter 12), reacted to racism by developing "a real hatred for white people. . . . Filipinos were being slurred and slandered, and therefore it was right for us to retaliate. I was involved in many fights because of this. When I got angry about anyone thinking that I was less than human, I made sure they knew that I was someone to be reckoned with."

U.S. racism also reconfigures gender roles for some of the women narrators in this book. In contrast to the patriarchal, patrilineal, and patrilocal nature of Chinese, Japanese, and Korean societies, the gender structure in the Philippines is more egalitarian, and kinship is bilateral. In employment as well as in participation in economic, political, and social activities, women in the Philippines had and continue to have more or less equal status with men.[114] According to Paz Jensen (Chapter 5), "When I was growing up in the Philippines, women were already represented in almost all high positions. . . . There were so many role models of women involved in politics, in philanthropy, and in society." As of the mid-1970s, the Philippines was one of the few countries in the world where the number of women in postsecondary education equaled or exceeded that of men.[115] Luz Latus (Chapter 4) recalled the high aspirations that her father had for her: "He would have liked to see me become a teacher, a doctor, or a lawyer."

Given the relatively favorable status of women in the Philippines, many immigrant Filipinas like Luz Latus, Paz Jensen, and Lucie Gamboa (Edgar Gamboa's wife [Chapter 8]) have excelled in their professions, particularly when their skills match the needs of the U.S. labor market. But other Filipinas, like Ruth Abad (Chapter 2), encountered more restrictive female roles in the United States. Coming from a prominent family in the Philippines, there Abad did not have to do any household chores: "When I came home, the food was cooked, and the clothes were washed [by the helpers]." But in the United States, "I had to do everything, cleaning, cooking, and taking care of the children. It was endless. I used to cry. My maids in the Philippines had more days off than me." Although Abad was not the "housekeeping type," her class position in the United States, which is in part a consequence of the racism that restricts the economic opportunities of many Filipinos, forced her into a more restrictive female role. Abad's narrative reminds us that class, race, and gender are interlocking categories that affect all aspects of human life.

Most importantly, in almost all of the life stories that I collected in San Diego County, Filipinos (particularly the second generation) contend that their ethnicity has changed in both importance and content over time. For example, Anamaria Labao Cabato (Chapter 9) "felt inferior" in high school because she was a Filipina; however, in college, through her involvement with the PASACAT dance troupe, she became proud of her heritage because she "knew more about our culture than other Filipinos." Lisa Graham (Chapter 13), the daughter of a white American and a Filipina American, recalls being pressured to choose between the two groups: "In school, when we had to fill out those cards for nationality, I was always confused because I never knew what to put. . . . I wish they would have something like 'half-and-half,' because if you are not one full race, you don't know what to put down." Although the larger society insists that races are mutually exclusive, Graham eventually resists being shoved into one of the existing monoracial categories. In the following statement, she described the progression of the change in her ethnic identity:

> When I was younger, I used to say, "I am American, I am American. I am white." It was just because everybody seemed to be either white or black, a full race. . . . Starting in junior high, it became important for me to say that I was Filipino because of my mom. . . . But now my whole attitude is changing. Now I say that I am half-Filipino and half-white.

Stressing flux rather than continuity and multilinearity rather than unilinearity, the narratives in this book show that a Filipino American culture is not formed in isolation but in dialogue with and in opposition to the racist ideologies and practices of the United States. Each of the narratives reveals ways in which Filipino American identity has been and continues to be shaped by a colonial history and a white-dominated culture. It is through recognizing how profoundly race has affected their lives that Filipino Americans force their ethnic identities—identities that challenge stereotypes and undermine practices of cultural domination. It is in this sense that the ethnic experiences of Filipino Americans resemble those of other communities of color and diverge from those of European ethnics.

Endnotes

1. Larry Arden Lawcock, "Filipino Students in the United States and the Philippine Independence Movement: 1900–1935" (Ph.D. diss., University of California, Berkeley, 1975), 33–34; Maria E. Espina, *Filipinos in Louisiana* (New Orleans: A. F. Laborde & Sons, 1988), 1–7.

2. E. San Juan, Jr., "Mapping the Boundaries: The Filipino Writer in the U.S.A.," *The Journal of Ethnic Studies* 19 (1991): 117–31.

3. Fred Cordova, *Filipinos: Forgotten Asian Americans* (Dubuque, Iowa: Kendall/ Hunt, 1983); Amado Cabezas, Larry H. Shinagawa, and Gary Kawaguchi, "New Inquiries into the Socioeconomic Status of Pilipino Americans in California," *Amerasia Journal* 13:1 (1986–87): 1–21; Oscar Penaranda, Serafin Syquia, and Sam Tagatac, "An Introduction to Filipino American Literature," in *Aiiieeeee! An Anthology of Asian American Writers,* ed. Frank Chin et al. (Washington, D.C.: Howard University Press, 1974).

4. Oscar Campomanes, "The Institutional Invisibility of American Imperialism, the Philippines, and Filipino Americans," paper presented at the Annual Meeting of the Association for Asian Studies, Los Angeles, March 25, 1993.

5. Cecile Cruz, "Relocating Myths: An Analysis of Two Filipina Transmigrants," unpublished paper, University of California, San Diego, 1993; Renato Rosaldo, "Ideology, Place, and People Without Culture," *Cultural Anthropology* 3 (1988): 77–87.

6. Luzviminda Francisco, "The First Vietnam—The Philippine-American War 1899–1902," in *Letters in Exile,* ed. Jesse Quinsaat et al. (Los Angeles: UCLA Asian American Studies Center, 1976), 1–22.

7. Sucheng Chan, *Asian Americans: An Interpretive History* (Boston: Twayne, 1991), 16–17; see also Antonio J. A. Pido, *The Pilipinos in America: Macro/Micro Dimensions of Immigration and Integration* (Staten Island, N.Y.: Center for Migration Studies, 1986), 48.

8. Teodoro A. Agoncillo and Milagros C. Guerrero, *History of the Filipino People* (Quezon City: R. P. Garcia Publishing Co., 1970), 303–42.

9. Miriam Sharma, "The Philippines: A Case of Migration to Hawaii, 1906 to 1946," in *Labor Immigration Under Capitalism: Asian Workers in the United States Before World War II,* ed. Lucie Cheng and Edna Bonacich (Berkeley: University of California Press), 337–58.

10. To underscore the importance U.S. colonizers gave to education, the head of the Department of Education in the Philippines until 1935 was an American. Renato Constantino, "Identity and Consciousness: The Philippine Experience." Paper presented in symposium 3 of the VIII World Sociology Congress, Toronto, Canada, 1994, 39.

11. Lawcock, "Filipino Students," 92; Constantino, *The Philippines, A Past Revisited* (Quezon City: Tala Publishing Services, 1975), 310; William J. Pomeroy, "The Philippines: A Case History of Neocolonialism," in *Remaking Asia: Essays on the American Uses of Power,* ed. Mark Selden (New York: Pantheon Books, 1974), 171; Barbara M. Posadas and Ronald L. Guyotte, "Unintentional Immigrants: Chicago's Filipino Foreign Students Become Settlers, 1900–1941," *Journal of American Ethnic History* 9 (Spring 1990): 26–48.

12. Chris Friday, *Organizing Asian American Labor: The Pacific Coast Canned-Salmon Industry, 1870–1942* (Philadelphia: Temple University Press, 1994), 135; Generoso Pacificar Provido, *Oriental Immigration from an American Dependency* (San Francisco: R & E Research Associates, 1974); Lawcock, "Filipino Students." The discussion of "unintentional immigrants" is based on Posadas and Guyotte, "Unintentional Immigrants."

13. H. Brett Melendy, *Asians in America: Filipinos, Koreans, and East Indians* (Boston: Twayne, 1977), 32.

14. According to Barbara Posadas, "At a Crossroad: Filipino American History and the Old Timers' Generation," *Amerasia Journal* 13:1 (1986–87), 85–97, not all Chicago Filipinos were laborers. Several hundred fortunate Filipinos secured jobs with the Chicago Post Office and the Pullman Company. These workers became the "elite" of the old-timers in Chicago.

15. Lawcock, "Filipino Students," 665; Mary Dorita, *Filipino Immigration to Hawaii* (San Francisco: R & E Research Associates, 1975). See also Ronald Takaki, *Pau Hana: Plantation Life and Labor in Hawaii: 1835–1920* (Honolulu: University of Hawaii Press, 1983).

16. Dorita, *Filipino Immigration,* 3–11, 16–17. See also Miriam Sharma, "Pinoy in Paradise: Environment and Adaptation of Pilipinos in Hawaii, 1906–1946," *Amerasia Journal* 7:2 (1980): 91–117.

17. This statement was made by Hawaii's Territorial Board of Immigration in 1909, as cited in Dorita, *Filipino Immigration,* 11.

18. Figures computed by Sucheng Chan from Bruno Lasker, *Filipino Immigration to Continental United States and to Hawaii* (1931; reprint, New York: Arno Press, 1969), 347–53.

19. Chan, *Asian Americans,* 109.

20. Pido, *The Pilipinos in America,* 61; Dorita, *Filipino Immigration,* 40.

21. Ethnic Studies Oral History Project, *The 1924 Filipino Strike in Kauai* (Honolulu: University of Hawaii at Manoa, Ethnic Studies Program, 1979), 4.

22. Robert N. Anderson, *Filipinos in Rural Hawaii* (Honolulu: University of Hawaii Press, 1984), 3–4.

23. Figures are computed from Lasker, *Filipino Immigration,* 167. Most Visayans came to Hawaii in the first wave of immigration; few arrived after the mid-1920s.

24. Cordova, *Filipinos,* 28.

25. Sharma, "The Philippines," 337–58.

26. Sharma, "Pinoy in Paradise," 97.

27. Miriam Sharma, "Labor Migration and Class Formation Among the Filipinos in Hawaii, 1906–1946," in *Labor Immigration Under Capitalism,* ed. Cheng and Bonacich, 579–615. See also Ronald Takaki, *Strangers from a Different Shore: A History of Asian Americans* (Boston: Little, Brown, 1989), 140–42.

28. Roman R. Cariaga, *The Filipinos in Hawaii: A Survey of Their Economic and Social Conditions* (San Francisco: R & E Research Associates, 1974), 39–41.

29. Ethnic Studies Oral History Project, *The 1924 Filipino Strike,* 9.

30. Melendy, *Asians in America,* 94.

31. Takaki, *Strangers from a Different Shore,* 142–55; Chan, *Asian Americans,* 84–88.

32. The most detailed account of the 1924 Kauai strike is Ethnic Studies Oral History Project, *The 1924 Filipino Strike.*

33. Chan, *Asian Americans,* 18.

34. Melendy, *Asians in America,* 41–42.

35. California State Department of Industrial Relations, *Facts About Filipino Immigration* (San Francisco: 1930), 47; Takaki, *Strangers from a Different Shore,* 315.

36. Sonia Emily Wallovitts, *The Filipinos in California* (San Francisco: R & E Research Associates, 1972), 21.

37. In 1930, 25 percent of the Filipinos (11,400 out of 45,200) on the mainland worked in hotels, restaurants, and homes as janitors, valets, kitchen helpers, dishwashers, bed makers, busboys, and domestic servants; see Takaki, *Strangers from a Different Shore,* 316–17.

38. Chan, *Asian Americans,* 37–39.

39. Chan, *Asian Americans,* 37.

40. Melendy, *Asians in America,* 75–76.

41. Provido, *Oriental Immigration,* 27.

42. Lawcock, "Filipino Students," 484–85, 665; Provido, *Oriental Immigration,* 28; Melendy, *Asians in America,* 74.

43. Roberto V. Vallangca, *Pinoy: The First Wave: 1898–1941* (San Francisco: Strawberry Hill Press, 1977), 23.

44. *Manong* literally means "uncles," a term of respect used for the old-timers.

45. Interview cited in Takaki, *Strangers from a Different Shore,* 321.

46. Craig Scharlin and Lilia V. Villanueva, *Philip Vera Cruz: A Personal History of Filipino Immigrants and the Farmworkers Movement* (Los Angeles: UCLA Labor Center, Institute of Industrial Relations, and UCLA Asian American Studies Center, 1992), 5.

47. Chan, *Asian Americans,* 75–78. According to Chan, compared with the information available on Chinese, Japanese, and Korean community institutions, much less is known about the social organizations of the Filipino immigrant community. For information on the Filipino American community organizations in Washington, see Jon D. Cruz, "Filipino-American Community Organizations in Washington, 1900s–1930s," in *People of Color in the American West,* ed. Sucheng Chan, Douglas Henry Daniels, Mario T. Garcia, and Terry P. Wilson (Lexington, Mass.: D. C. Heath and Company, 1994), 235–45.

48. Chan, *Asian Americans,* 88–89; Takaki, *Strangers from a Different Shore,* 321–23.

49. Scharlin and Villanueva, *Philip Vera Cruz.*

50. Manuel Buaken, *I Have Lived with the American People* (Caldwell, Idaho: Caxton Printers, 1948), 201.

51. Lasker, *Filipino Immigration,* 21.

52. Provido, *Oriental Immigration,* 30. The next 4 paragraphs are culled from Friday, *Organizing Asian American Labor,* 125–48; and Cruz, "Filipino-American Community Organizations."

53. Emory S. Bogardus, "Anti-Filipino Race Riots" (1930), in *Letters in Exile,* ed. Quinsaat et al., 51–62; Howard A. De Witt, *Anti-Filipino Movements in California: A History, Bibliography, and Study Guide* (San Francisco: R & E Research Associates, 1976), 46–66; Takaki, *Strangers from a Different Shore,* 327–330.

54. Melendy, *Asians in America,* 27–28, 40–44.

55. This and the next 2 paragraphs are based on William E. Berry, Jr., *U.S. Bases in the Philippines: The Evolution of a Special Relationship* (Boulder, Colo.: Westview Press, 1989); and Roland Simbulan, *A Guide to Nuclear Philippines: A Primer on U.S. Military Bases, Nuclear Weapons, and What the Filipino People Are Doing About These* (Philippines: IBON Data Bank, 1989).

56. Bob Drogin, "Americans Bid Farewell to Last Philippine Base," *Los Angeles Times,* November 25, 1992.

57. Lasker, *Filipino Immigration,* 62; Jesse Quinsaat, "An Exercise on How to Join the Navy and Still Not See the World," in *Letters in Exile,* ed. Quinsaat et al., 96–111; U.S. Congress, House, Committee on the Judiciary House of Representatives, Special Study Subcommittee of the Committee on the Judiciary to Review Certain Immigration, Refugee, and Nationality Problems, *Report of Special Study Subcommittee of the Committee on the Judiciary to Review Immigration, Refugee, and Nationality Problems,* 93rd Cong., 1st sess., December 1973 (hereafter cited as Special Study Subcommittee).

58. The Nationality Act of 1940 and its amendments give aliens who have served 3 or more years in the U.S. armed forces the opportunity to become U.S. citizens without having to meet the usual requirements such as residence.

59. Special Study Subcommittee, 3.

60. Melendy, *Asians in America,* 96.

61. Special Study Subcommittee, 15.

62. Lawcock, "Filipino Students," 473.

63. Quinsaat, "How to Join the Navy"; Timothy Ingram, "The Floating Plantation," *Washington Monthly* (October 1970): 17–20.

64. Special Study Subcommittee, 16.

65. Quinsaat, "How to Join the Navy," 101.

66. Melendy, *Asians in America,* 249.

67. H. Brett Melendy, "Filipinos in the United States," *Pacific Historical Review* 43 (1974): 524–25.

68. Vallangca, Caridad Concepcion, *The Second Wave: Pinoy & Pinay, 1945–1965* (San Francisco: Strawberry Hill Press, 1987), 11.

69. Takaki, *Strangers from a Different Shore,* 358–59.

70. Citing their wartime contributions and their loyalty to the United States, many Filipino veterans have come to the United States to petition for naturalization. In 1990, nearly 50 years after the end of World War II, the United States finally restored citizenship rights to veterans who were stymied when Roosevelt's pledge was rescinded in 1946. See Paul Feldman, "A Battle for Rights," *Los Angeles Times,* February 19, 1994: B3.

71. Because of their status as aliens, Filipinos in the United States were exempt from military service. On January 2, 1942, President Roosevelt signed a law revising the Selective Service Act to permit these Filipinos to join the U.S. armed forces.

72. Cordova, *Filipinos,* 217–14; Melendy, *Asians in America,* 50; Lawcock, "Filipino Students," 576.

73. Melendy, "Filipinos in the United States," 531.

74. R. T. Feria, "War and the Status of Filipino Immigrants," *Sociology and Social Research* 31 (1946–47): 50–53; see also Takaki, *Strangers from a Different Shore,* 358–63.

75. David Reimers, *Still the Golden Door: The Third World Comes to America* (New York: Columbia University Press, 1985), 24–25.

76. Vallangca, *The Second Wave,* 53–54.

77. Melendy, "Filipinos in the United States," 522.

78. Vallangca, *The Second Wave*, 26.

79. Leon Bouvier and Robert Gardner, "Immigration to the U.S.: The Unfinished Story," *Population Bulletin* 41 (1986): 1–50.

80. Benjamin V. Cariño, James T. Fawcett, Robert W. Gardner, and Fred Arnold, *The New Filipino Immigrants to the United States: Increasing Diversity and Change*, (Honolulu: East-West Center, 1990), 2.

81. Pomeroy, "The Philippines," 171; Benjamin V. Cariño, "The Philippines and Southeast Asia: Historical Roots and Contemporary Linkages," in *Pacific Bridges: The New Immigration from Asia and the Pacific Islands*, ed. James T. Fawcett and Benjamin V. Cariño (Staten Island, N.Y.: Center for Migration Studies, 1987).

82. John M. Liu and Lucie Cheng, "Pacific Rim Development and the Duality of Post-1965 Immigration to the United States," in *The New Asian Immigration in Los Angeles and Global Restructuring*, ed. Paul Ong, Edna Bonacich, and Lucie Cheng (Philadelphia: Temple University Press, 1994).

83. Chan, *Asian Americans*, 149–50; David Joel Steinberg, *The Philippines: A Singular and a Plural Place* (Boulder, Colo.: Westview Press, 1990), 129–30.

84. Heathow Low Ruth, "Philippines," in *The International Migration of High-Level Manpower: Its Impact on the Development Process*, ed. The Committee on the International Migration of Talent (New York: Praeger 1970); Pido, *The Pilipinos in America*, 62; Takaki, *Strangers from a Different Shore*, 433.

85. Berry, *U.S. Bases*, 168.

86. Steinberg, *The Philippines*, 129–30.

87. Madge Bello and Vince Reyes, "Filipino Americans and the Marcos Overthrow: The Transformation of Political Consciousness," *Amerasia Journal* 13 (1986–87): 73–83.

88. Bello and Reyes, "Filipino Americans and the Marcos Overthrow," 76–78.

89. Rubén Rumbaut, "Passages to America: Perspectives on the New Immigration," in *America at Century's End*, ed. Alan Wolfe (Berkeley and Los Angeles: University of California Press, 1991), 208–44.

90. Pido, *The Pilipinos in America*, 85.

91. Takaki, *Strangers from a Different Shore*, 434–36.

92. Cariño et al., *The New Filipino Immigrants*, 13–14; Pido, *The Pilipinos in America*, 77–82.

93. Pido, *The Pilipinos in America*, 78–82. The third preference of the 1965 Immigration Act allows for the immigration of professionals and other highly talented persons whose skills were scarce within the U.S. labor market.

94. Paul Ong and Tania Azores, "The Migration and Incorporation of Filipino Nurses," in *The New Asian Immigration*, ed. Ong et al., 164–95.

95. Cariño et al., *The New Filipino Immigrants*, 11–12.

96. John M. Liu, Paul M. Ong, and Carolyn Rosenstein, "Dual Chain Migration: Post-1965 Filipino Immigration to the United States," *International Migration Review* 25:3 (Fall 1991): 487–513.

97. Liu, Ong, and Rosenstein, "Dual Chain Migration."

98. Joseph McCallus, "The Rhetoric of Journalism: The Filipino-American Press

and Its Washington, D.C., Audience" (Ph.D. diss., The Catholic University of America, 1987), 19–20; Alvar Carlson, "The Settling of Recent Filipino Immigrants in Midwestern Metropolitan Areas," *Crossroads* 1 (1983): 13–19; Peter C. Smith, "The Social Demography of Filipino Migrations Abroad," *International Migration Review* 10 (1976), 307–53; and Liu et al., "Dual Chain Migration."

99. Rumbaut, "Passages to America," 220.

100. Adelaida Castillo, "Filipino Migrants in San Diego, 1900–1946," *The Journal of San Diego History* 12 (1976): 27–35; see also Lawcock, "Filipino Students," 97.

101. Castillo, "Filipino Migrants in San Diego"; Adelaida Castillo-Tsuchida, *Filipino Migrants in San Diego, 1900–1946* (San Diego: San Diego Society, Title Insurance and Trust Collection, 1979).

102. Wallovitts, *The Filipinos in California,* 79.

103. Rumbaut, "Passages to America," 220.

104. PASACAT, the name of a Philippine folk dance, is the acronym for the Philippine-American Society and Cultural Arts Troupe in San Diego, whose objectives are to preserve the cultural heritages of the Philippines through music, song, dance, and drama.

105. My estimate of the number of Filipino American organizations is derived from the official membership list of the Council of Pilipino American Organizations (COPAO) and from the announcements of community organizations in the local Filipino American newspapers.

106. Immanuel Wallerstein, *The Modern World System* (New York: Academic Press, 1974); Saskia Sassen, *The Mobility of Labor and Capital: A Study in International Investment and Labor Flow* (New York: Cambridge University Press, 1988).

107. James T. Fawcett and Fred Arnold, "Explaining Diversity: Asian and Pacific Immigration Systems," in *Pacific Bridges: The New Immigration from Asia and the Pacific Islands,* ed. James T. Fawcett and Benjamin V. Cariño (New York: Center for Migration Studies in association with the East-West Population Institute, East-West Center), 453–74.

108. For a transnational perspective on migration, see *Annals of the New York Academy of Sciences* 645 (1992): entire volume.

109. Stanley Lieberson, "Unhyphenated Whites in the United States," *Ethnic and Racial Studies* 8 (1985): 159–80.

110. Nina Glick Schiller, Linda Basch, and Cristina Blanc-Szanton, "Transnationalism: A New Analytic Framework for Understanding Migration," *Annals of the New York Academy of Sciences* 645 (1992): 1–24.

111. Glick Schiller et al., "Transnationalism," 12.

112. The concept of transculturation was introduced by Cuban sociologist Fernado Ortiz, as discussed in Lambros Comitas, "Preface," *Annals of the New York Academy of Sciences* 645 (1992): vii–viii.

113. For a discussion of the construction of identities of second-generation Filipinos, see Yen Le Espiritu, "The Intersection of Race, Ethnicity, and Class: The Multiple Identities of Second-Generation Filipinos," *Identities: Global Studies in Culture and Power* 1:2 (1994):1–25.

114. Pido, *The Pilipinos in America,* 23.

115. Pido, *The Pilipinos in America,* 82.

Chapter 1

"We Have to Show
the Americans
that We Can Be
as Good as Anybody"

A. B. Santos and Juanita Santos

A. B. Santos⋆

Running away from Home

I hate to tell you how old I am because I am a very old man. I was born December 26, 1907, in Saint Nicholas in the province of Ilocos Norte. My mother was a housekeeper. My father was a traveling merchant. He was killed during World War II by the Japanese.

My grandfather was a really devoted Catholic. To show you how really devoted he was, he had five children, and when he harvested barley, rice, and other things, instead of dividing it into five portions, he made it six because he included the church. We all lived in the same block, the five families [of his children].

My grandfather's word was law in our family. When I was about fifteen years old, I overheard that my grandfather wanted to send me to the seminary. When I heard that, I ran away from home to Manila because I didn't want to go to the seminary. My grandfather asked why. I told him that it was because a priest cannot get married and I wanted to get married. Because his word was law, my parents had to obey him. But I outsmarted him by leaving.

So I went to Manila. I only spoke Ilocano at that time. I learned Tagalog

---

⋆Mr. and Mrs. Santos were interviewed together. He spoke first; she picked up the narrative at the point after they met in the Philippines.

37

in Manila. I had some relatives there, but I stayed only one night. Then I met some town mates who were much older than I was; I could have been their son. They were coming to the United States to look for jobs, so I decided to go with them.

Leaving for the United States

I did not know much about the United States, but I had heard from the Americans and the other Filipinos that there were many opportunities there. I had an American teacher who used to tell our class that in the United States, as long as you are willing to work and you are not weak, you can survive very well. So I was impressed with this. It was this kind of information that gave me all the courage. My town mates took care of me until we arrived in San Francisco.

At the time, it cost only 200 pesos to leave the Philippines, and I had that much money. To leave, I only had to buy a resident certificate and to have a resident certificate, you must be eighteen to show that you can go without consulting your parents. But I was only fifteen. So, instead of getting the resident certificate from my hometown, where they could check my birth date, I got it in Manila. That was all you needed. You didn't need any passport.

We arrived in San Francisco in 1922. At that time, I spoke a little English. People could understand me, but I had to repeat. I was good, especially in writing, because from kindergarten to my first year in high school the instruction was all in English, and the Americans were our teachers. In San Francisco, I stayed with some relatives, but I was uncomfortable about it because I didn't like imposing.

With the little money that I had, I went to an agency to look for work. A relative of my town mates was a contractor for a Salinas [California] farm, and he was looking for men to work picking sweet peas. I volunteered to go. About thirty of us young people went with him to Salinas to work. So my first job in the United States was picking sweet peas. I only worked there for two weeks. It was hard work for me. I ached all over, my back, my legs, because I was not used to it. The workers were a mixture: there were some Mexicans, Asians, Japanese. There were also some American high school students.

Working and Going to School in San Diego

My grandfather's godson was in San Diego working at the Coronado Hotel. When I wrote to him, he told me to come to San Diego. So I came. I stayed at a motel, and he came to meet me there. He was with a blonde American girl, and he had his arms around her. I was so surprised when I saw that,

A. B. and Juanita Santos with Congressman Bob Filner at a
community dinner-dance, San Diego, 1992

because in his letters to my grandfather, he seemed so religious. I went with him to the Coronado that night, to the dormitory. It was about two blocks from the hotel. I slept on the floor. My cousin had to hide me in the dormitory until I got a job at the hotel and was assigned my own room.

I got at job at the Coronado Hotel precisely because Ms. Adair wanted to help me. She was the head of the executive dining room, an Englishwoman, a very nice woman. It was around wintertime, and my job was to turn on the lights of the executive dining room in the morning, set it up, turn on the heater, and make sure that everything was in order. I had to learn where to put the spoons and so on. I used to get mixed up, because for me a spoon and a fork is enough. But for them, there is this and that, and the coffee cup you cannot put it on the left, and things like that.

I got up at three o'clock every day to make sure that the heater was already warm when the people got there. Then after that, I just fooled around, waiting for the guests to arrive. They usually came at six o'clock. And then at seven o'clock, I went downstairs to eat. Then after that, I went to school. So that was my job, and I was paid twenty dollars a month with board. In the housekeeping department, there were about six Filipinos. Busboys, there must have been about eight to twelve. And then in the dining room downstairs, there were two helpers. The head of the dormitory was a Filipino.

On Saturdays, the dining room was always busy because so many tourists came to visit. So after my job in the morning, I went back to the dormitory to study. That was the only time I could study, because everybody else was at work. Usually, it was very noisy; they played the guitars, yelling, singing, everything else, after their work. I was the youngest one, and I was the only one going to school.

I just went to school and enrolled myself. At first, because I had no credentials, they thought they should put me in junior high. But I told them that I had already started my first year in high school. I was the first and only Asian in Coronado High School. I was kind of apprehensive at times. Some of the students made fun of me and my accent. But one time, this girl Betty told them, "Don't make fun of him. He is much smarter than you are." Betty's family was staying at the hotel. They were on vacation from Oklahoma for the winter. I used to ride to school on my bicycle, while Betty rode in a limousine. Her family was very good to me.

I was determined to go to school. In the first place, I wanted to prove to my parents and my grandfather that I could survive without being a priest. With my very first pay check, I bought a very expensive hat for my grandfather. It cost me thirty dollars. And that made him change his attitude toward me. I was no longer the boy who was not going to amount to anything. I stayed there until I graduated from Coronado High.

I played the clarinet in the school band. That was my only school activity. We had rehearsals on Tuesday evenings. When we had rehearsals, Mrs. Pendleton (the wife of General Joseph H. Pendleton) would come to listen. General Pendleton was a retired major general from the Marine Corps. By the way, the Marine Corps Camp Pendleton in Oceanside was named after him. He was chairman of the board of trustees in the Coronado School

District then. One time during rehearsal, I had a solo, about four verses. It just so happened that when my solo came, my clarinet squeaked. It was very embarrassing for me, because it had never done that before. The band director asked me what was wrong. I told him that my clarinet reed was not good but that I could not afford to buy a new one. Five dollars was big money in those days.

Mrs. Pendleton overheard my conversation with the band director. When we had an intermission, she stood up and motioned for me to come to her. So I went. She put her arm around me and asked Mr. Green, the band director, who owned the students' instruments. When Mr. Green told her that the students owned their own instruments, she said, "I overheard this young man say that his clarinet was no good. Why can't the school buy the accessories for them?"

Apparently, Mrs. Pendleton talked to her husband about me, because he came to the school and I met him. He told me that he had enjoyed his tour in the Philippines. "Your people are nice," he said. He invited me to come to his house. So whenever I was not busy, I would go visit him. One time, I saw him on the ground weeding, so I said, "General, I can do that for you." We became friends. He told me to use one of the rooms in his house to study in. When I graduated, he was the one handing us the diplomas. I was the only Asian in the whole ceremony. When he gave me my diploma, he held my hand for some time.

College Years

When I graduated from Coronado High, I went to Berkeley. But when I arrived there, the tuition fee had increased three times for foreign students [at UC Berkeley]. I could not afford that, so I came back to San Diego. I went to see General Pendleton, because he was the only friend I knew. He advised me to go to San Diego State college [now University], because it was not that expensive. He also told me that I could stay in one of his rooms, since the college was too far for me to ride my bicycle. I welcomed his invitation, because there were no buses.

My first two years at San Diego State, I took preparatory courses. But I could not go to school the whole time. I had to work for my tuition. Then I took my license as a real estate and insurance salesman. I was selling life insurance, but my clientele was limited to Filipinos and Orientals in the Navy. I could not sell to the Americans. At that time, the Americans believed that Filipinos and other Orientals were just dishwashers and cooks because these were the only jobs of Filipinos in the Navy and these were the only Filipinos they knew. On Saturdays, I worked at the Coronado Hotel for extra money.

But even then, books were expensive and the tuition was high, so I would work one semester full-time and then go to school full-time the next semester. It took me four years to finish two years of course work. But thank God I was not kicked out, because there were some foreign students who were expelled. There was a Filipino who was a student there, but he could not make it. He made a C —. Then another one came, but the same thing happened to him. If you got a C — in any subject, out you went.

There were times when I ate only twice a day. I used to save money by not eating in the cafeteria on campus, because the food was more expensive there. So I had to walk from the campus to the corner and eat a hamburger there. They called me "the hamburger boy."

Back then, in the 1940s, Filipinos were not allowed to be taxicab drivers. So I went to the city council and lambasted them, "You only want us, the Filipinos, to fight for you in the battleground, but you don't even let us drive a taxicab in this city, which is supposed to be the finest city in America." I was in the newspaper. I was not afraid to tell them off, because I was as educated as they were. I was educated here, and I have lived in the United States longer than in the Philippines. I knew that I was smarter than so many of them.

Army Service During World War II

When World War II came, I got drafted into the U.S. Army. They drafted me in 1943 even though I was a foreigner, a noncitizen. It was during the week of my finals when I received a special-delivery letter to report to Los Angeles. So I went to the Selective Service and asked them to postpone my induction until Friday, so I could take my finals. On Saturday morning, I reported to Los Angeles. When I got there, they swore me in as a U.S. citizen. I did not even have to file an application. So that was how I became a U.S. citizen.

After my basic training at Camp Cooke, California, I was assigned to an American troop [unit] where I was the only Filipino. But I did not stay with that troop for very long. When I learned about the First Filipino Infantry Regiment, which was formed in 1942, I requested to be transferred there because I knew they were going to be assigned to the Pacific. I did not want to go to Europe.

The Filipino Infantry was sent to Oro Bay, New Guinea. From there, we were ordered to go liberate New Zealand. The liberation did not take long, because the enemy troops were not large. When I returned to Oro Bay, for some reason I was picked to go to General MacArthur's headquarters in Ollandia to receive my basic training in counterintelligence work. Ollandia is in the middle of New Guinea, about halfway between Australia and the Philippines. This was in 1944, and the United States was preparing to invade the Philippines. As you know, General MacArthur landed in Leyte on October 20, 1944. About half a month later, on November 6, I began my counterintelligence work in the Philippines.

The day that the Japanese surrendered, I ran back to my office and requested a discharge. I wanted to go back to the United States to complete my education. But they told me that they still needed me because I spoke several Filipino dialects, Spanish, and English. They assigned me to work for the U.S. Veterans Administration as a contact representative. That was when I met my wife, Juanita, in 1946.

~~~~~~~~~~~~~~~~~~~~~~~~~~~~~~~~~~~~~

Juanita Santos

Early Years in the Philippines

I was born in Sarrat, Ilocos Norte. According to my mother and my aunt, my birth date was March 30, 1918. But in 1952, when I applied for my passport to come to the United States, I discovered that on my birth certificate, my birth date was April 8!

My father and mother were both grade-school teachers. My father died when I was three years old. When I was in the third grade, we moved to Laoag, where Mama and Auntie taught in the elementary school across the street from where we lived. We always lived together in the same house— Auntie, Mama, my sister, my brother, and me.

I remember that one afternoon, our third-grade teacher opened a silver box sent by the U.S. Red Cross, and in it were trinkets—and I received a pearl necklace, *faux* of course, but to me then, it was the most beautiful treasure I'd ever had.

When I was in grade five, Auntie got married, and when she went to Baguio to join her husband, she asked Mama to let me go with her to be their eldest daughter. So I went with her, away from my own family. Uncle (my aunt's husband) was an accountant at the Trinidad Agricultural High School, and Auntie taught at the elementary school. Baguio is temperate like here [San Diego]; they grow flowers and vegetables like they do here. Because the school had teachers from different provinces who spoke different dialects, English was the way we could communicate. At that time, there were no children my age except the son of the school principal, an American, and the son of the division superintendent of schools, also an American. Both became my playmates.

After high school graduation, I went to Manila and lived in the YWCA dormitory, and took up pharmacy at the Philippine Women's University. At that time, it was an exclusive women's university. I wanted to take journalism but that profession was not considered "feminine" then. When the war came, I had to go home to my mother in Ilocos Norte. Because the guerrilla activities against the Japanese were becoming intense, my mother brought me back to my aunt and uncle, who had evacuated from Baguio to Caloocan, a suburb of Manila, where it was still relatively safe.

Marriage

After the war, I met A. B.—who became my husband—through a friend of mine, Gregoria. During the bombing of Manila, Gregoria walked for approximately two weeks to reach Caloocan, somehow escaping injuries and death. She stayed with our family in Caloocan until after the liberation of the Philippines. Gregoria's husband, Manuel, had gone to the United States at an early age and come back as one of the GIs. That's what they called the boys who were in the U.S. armed forces who liberated the Philippines.

Manuel had gotten out of the U.S. Army and was a driver for the U.S. Veterans Administration [USVA]. A. B. also was working at the USVA as a contact representative, a counselor. Gregoria brought Manuel to meet the family. When he met me, Manuel couldn't keep still. He kept moving and looking at me. Gregoria told me afterward that after seeing me that night, Manuel decided that I was to marry A. B. This was before I had even met A. B. So one night, Manuel and Gregoria brought A. B. to Caloocan. They picked me up the following day for a double date.

That June [in 1946], I had to return to college. I was taking pharmacy, and I was in my senior year. I wanted to finish. But that September, A. B. and I got married secretly. Well, not really secretly, since all his friends at the USVA, about twenty to twenty-five of them, and his cousin, were there. But my family did not know anything about it. That was because Mama did not want me to get married yet. She wanted me to finish my college first so as to be "complete." She wanted my diploma to be in my maiden name. So we got married "secretly."

A. B. surprised me with the marriage proposal. We were walking down a boulevard along Manila Bay when A. B. asked me to show him my church. So I took him there. After my prayers, I looked around but I did not see anybody. When I went downstairs to look for A. B., I saw him with a priest. The priest asked me to sit down and said, "My child, this man said that the two of you would like to get married." I looked from A. B. to the priest. I knew in my head that I was going to marry A. B., so I said "yes" to Father. I never actually said "yes" to A. B.

A. B. even lied to the priest, saying that he needed to get married soon. When Father asked him why, A. B. said it was because he might be reassigned to Japan very soon. I was twenty-eight and A. B. was thirty-eight years old when we got married. That November, Mama got sick. So when A. B. and I went to visit her at the hospital, A. B. confessed that we were already married. I received my B.S. in pharmacy in 1947.

After that, the Veterans Administration sent A. B. to the Cagayan Valley to be the manager of the USVA branch office there. I went with him. His friend, the division superintendent of schools, Mr. Miguel Gaffud, asked me to teach general science and U.S. history at the high school. The principal, Mr. Juan Manuel (who was the brother-in-law of former President Ferdinand Marcos), also selected me to teach folk dancing, and so I taught two hundred first-year and second-year high school students to dance two folk dances. When A. B. was transferred to Ilocos, Mr. Gaffud asked if I could stay behind with his family. He was happy to have me at the school. He later became the Philippine secretary of education.

I am most proud of having organized the *first* two Girl Scout troops in that high school. My troops and I won a place in the National Honor Roll of the Girl Scouts of the Philippines [GSP] that year! Miss Mariquit Castelo, the GSP executive director, flew to Cagayan to convince me to fly back with her to Manila to become the GSP national supervisor. A. B. was furious. He did not want me to go to Manila. So he told me to choose between that career and him. Well, Miss Castelo flew back to Manila without me. I was not free to do as I please. I was married!

In 1952, A. B. quit the USVA and returned to the United States. He came by himself in January. I was taking my master's degree in social work at that time, but I did not finish it because I wanted to join my husband. So in May, I left the Philippines for San Francisco.

When we went out on the day I arrived, the first person whom I saw was a very beautiful American lady with a hat that had flowers all around it, and she smiled at me. In the Philippines, you don't just smile at anybody. But here, she smiled. I thought to myself, "Well, this America must be as beautiful as this lady." When you leave your country, you leave everyone that you love, everything that is familiar. I was feeling so lost. But that beautiful lady, to me, she was America.

Working and Dealing with Racism in San Diego

In June 1952, we came to San Diego because A. B.'s brothers lived here. I did not know what to do with myself, but I knew I wanted to work. So I went to take up typing and bookkeeping. Then A. B. brought me to see the sisters at Mercy Hospital [a Catholic hospital in downtown San Diego]. He used to work there as a vegetable buyer. He also formed the Filipino American Catholic Society at Mercy Hospital. A. B. was a favorite of the sisters because he was a hard worker and an activist. He would rebel and tell the sisters off. That's what Sister Augustine and Sister Dorothy used to tell me. With the other Filipino boys, it was always "Amen," but A. B. was different.

As soon as we arrived at Mercy Hospital, Sister Augustine brought me to meet Sister Anna Marie, the supervisor of the pharmacy, because A. B. had told them that I had a pharmacy degree from the Philippines. So the sister hired me right away! I was very lucky. Sister Anna Marie was very supportive, very kind to me, but she was a terror to nurses who did not know their medicines.

When our son Michael was born in 1959, we decided that I should stay home and take care of him. It was only when he was in high school that I started working again, but only part-time so that I could be home when Michael was home.

In the 1950s, most Americans thought that Filipinos just worked in the kitchen. My first week at Mercy Hospital, I was typing the label for one of the prescriptions. And here came a doctor. He asked me, "Hey, do you know what you are doing?" When I gave him the label, he turned to Sister Anna Marie, my sister supervisor, and said, "Hey, Sister, she knows what she is doing." The sister told him, "Of course, she is just as educated as you are." The next thing he said was, "Are there schools in the Philippines?" I was shocked. I shook my finger at him—he was tall, very handsome, blue eyes—and I said, "You know what, Doctor, you are ignorant. Our University of Santo Tomas is twenty-five years older than your Harvard University." And you know what? Since then, my inferiority complex—being short, and very brown, and very Filipino—fell away, because if this educated man is ignorant, what more with the "ordinary" green, yellow, blue man on the street?

Once when I was reading the bulletin board [at Mercy Hospital], a woman came up to me and asked me if I knew how to read. I told her that I did. When she asked where I worked, I pointed to the pharmacy. She apparently did not believe me, because she went to talk to the sister, and when she came out of there, she just looked at me, up and down. But I didn't know that those were prejudices; to me, these people were just ignorant.

Another time, one of the sisters told me, "My child, are you lost? The kitchen is that way." I said, "No, Sister, I work at the pharmacy." At Mercy Hospital, there were some twenty or so Filipino workers in the kitchen. All of them were very nice, devoted family people.

Because of this ignorance, every time there is a Filipino program and I am the master of ceremony, if we have any professional on stage, I will always mention that she is a pharmacist, he is a doctor. . . . The other Filipinos in town used to say that I was prejudiced and that I only recognized professionals. But that was not true. I just wanted to "educate" the other races that the Filipinos are as knowledgeable and cultured as they are. I wanted respect for my people. I wanted to project a positive image of the Filipinos and my native country.

The Filipino Community in San Diego

When I first came to San Diego, there were very few Filipinos—maybe about one hundred families. We knew everybody. There were a few farmers. There was one Filipino family who owned a big farm in Chula Vista. At that time, their property was worth $250,000. That's a quarter of a million! And these people were not educated; they could hardly speak English. But they got divorced, and they had to sell.

Most of the Filipina women in San Diego in the 1950s were wives of Navy men. There was only one schoolteacher from the Philippines. She was also a GI bride. I was a minority. I was the first one to work at a pharmacy. And you know what, they [the other Filipinos] used to look down on me because I was one of the "educated" ones.

The first time that I attended a Rizal Day celebration sponsored by the Filipino community, I wanted to crawl under a chair. I was not looking down on them, but the people who were on the program did not speak very well, and the program was not the way it should have been. The following years, I waded in, and I helped them because they had to be taught. I shouldn't say they had to be taught, but I wanted to share what I knew, because at the Philippine Women's University, they taught us many things. It was not just books; it included social and civic training and everything.

In 1955, even though I was recuperating from surgery, in my bed I wrote a three-act play about Dr. José Rizal: Part I was the farewell party for Dr. Rizal; Part II was the three Filipino artists in Madrid; and Part III was Rizal writing his last farewell.* That year, the San Diego mayor attended the Rizal celebration, and that started the relationship between the Filipino community and the city of San Diego. And we, the Filipinos, became recognized and were respected.

In the 1950s, because the Filipino community was so small, it was very close-knit. Everyone loved getting together. We came from different regions in the Philippines, but it did not matter. We all spoke Tagalog. I didn't speak Tagalog very well, so I had to learn it fast. The Filipinos lived downtown, and around us. They were not spread out yet. There was one family in

---

*A Filipino national hero, José Rizal was accused of inspiring the Philippine Revolution to oust the Spanish colonial regime with his writings and was executed by a firing squad in 1896. Part I of the play refers to the farewell party in Rizal's honor as he left for Spain at the age of 21 to continue his studies; Part II re-enacts a discussion that Rizal had with two of his Filipino friends in Madrid concerning their roles in the impending Philippine Revolution; Part III features Rizal writing his farewell poems while being imprisoned in Fort Santiago.

Pacific Beach, three or four in Chula Vista, and later on, maybe after ten years, another family in Linda Vista.

At that time, we only had one main organization, the Filipino American Community of San Diego County. It was first founded by my husband in 1941, but when the boys had to go to war, they drifted apart. When A. B. came back, they wanted him to reactive it, but he was going to school and working at the time. He attended Cal Western University [now the United States International University], where he eventually earned his B.S. and master's degree in business administration. So it was never reorganized. In 1959, a Filipino businessman from Los Angeles, a Mr. Lopez, and A. B. organized the Filipino American Community Association. Because of his business interests, Mr. Lopez wanted to reactivate the association so that he could get to know the Filipinos in San Diego better.

Around 1970, the newly arrived professionals and the retired Navy men wanted to take over the association. When a new person got elected and it was somebody they did not like, they would leave and form another organization. Independence Day, Rizal Day, and the Miss Philippines Pageant—they wanted to take these over too. I have been trying to figure out why there is such a division and why we cannot get together.

The Filipinos should get together and work as a team because there are so many of us. We could be politically strong. You know, Bob Fillner (the California assemblyman of the 50th District and a former San Diego city councilman) recognized that he got elected because of the Filipinos in the South Bay. He told us at a victory event that if it were not for the Filipinos, he would not have won. So, you see, if we had an intelligent, educated, and motivated Filipino, we could put him in political office. But unfortunately, we are so divided. We are each to his own province or profession or whatever. I don't know if the community will ever be united. It is so splintered right now. We have so many organizations, over 140.

We used to be very, very close. We were one big family. When we had a picnic, Oh, my Lord, everybody would come. Now we don't know everybody like we used to. The Filipino community is so dispersed today—Poway, Mira Mesa, Oceanside, San Ysidro, National City, Imperial Beach. . . .

Community Involvement

I have always been very active in organizations, even when I was working full-time, because I wanted to share my expertise. I was a member of the Women's Club and the American Legion Auxiliary, and I was president of a few other community organizations. The American Legion has a Filipino Auxiliary unit, Leyte Unit 625, which is 99 percent Filipinos. There is only one American lady who is a member.

A. B. was a commander of the Legion for many years. He belongs to the elite organization, the 40 and 8, a group of distinguished leaders in the American Legion. They were not taking Filipinos or minorities before, but they invited A. B. to be a member. We were very proud of that. I think we have to show the Americans that we can be as good as anybody. I am not racist, but I want to push my race forward and upward. It makes you feel good when a Filipino shines.

I enjoy giving speeches on Filipino culture. I am the only Filipino to ever make a speech at the Crown Room of the Coronado Hotel. This was at a convention of the National Business and Professional Women's Club with representatives from all over California, Nevada, and Arizona. There were about seven hundred of them. They invited me to talk about the "Filipino Woman, Yesterday and Today." I was a hit. I got so many invitations after that—the Women's Club of Coronado, of Pacific Beach, Chula Vista, La Jolla—I cannot remember some. I must say that whenever I go before non-Filipino audiences, they tell me *never* to lose my accent because it is cute.

When we were having the antipoverty programs in the 1960s, I got involved in them, and I wished the Filipino organizations could have gotten involved as well. When we broached the subject to them, some said, "We are not poor. We don't need public assistance. We take care of our own." Nobody would volunteer to find out which social services were available or to learn how to write grant proposals. It is true that we take care of our own, but we also needed programs.

In the 1970s, the Filipino community finally had a social service program sponsored by COPAO [Council of Pilipino American Organizations] but we lost it after some ten years. We still have a Samahan Senior Center where our seniors go to get hot noon meals, learn English, play bingo—but of course, it is the dancing that they enjoy most.

When we first moved to San Diego, we used to live close to A. B.'s two brothers in southeast San Diego. We owned a house there. Then, we sold it and bought this one here in downtown San Diego. We bought this house not only because of the price but also because it is close to the buses. You see, I still do not drive.

Our son, Michael, thinks that this is not a very good location because it is downtown. He said to me, "You know, Mom, let's go to Carlsbad. It's beautiful there. We can have a house that overlooks the ocean. You deserve a better place than this." But I said, "I'll die there. How can I go downtown?" Here, the church is only two blocks away, and there is a market that I can run to if I don't have anybody to drive me. Then there are the buses. I can take the buses, and I can go anywhere any time without bothering A. B. or Michael. And the people around here, they know us. Also, it is not where the house is, it is the quality of the people who come into the house that matters.

Teaching Michael About Filipino Culture

When our son Michael was growing up, we were very active in the church, and the sisters told me that if he did not speak English, he would be put in the retarded classes. Gee, I didn't want him to be put in the retarded classes, so we only spoke English to him. So now he does not know how to speak our language. He graduated from kindergarten and elementary [school] as a valedictorian. He was an honor student in junior high and high school.

When Michael was a little boy, I overheard him and his classmates imitate their parents who spoke the English language with an accent. When the guests were gone, I took him aside and said to him, "Michael, do you know that by imitating the way these people speak, you are insulting Daddy and me, you are insulting the Filipinos." He never imitated any one again.

When Michael was six years old, we all went to the Philippines. We brought him to our hometown in Ilocos. I showed him churches built by the Augustine friars and said, "Michael, look at this plaque. It was built in the 1500s. So, you see, we were Christians even before the United States was discovered." We attended town fiestas featuring processions, competitions, folk dances, and feasts. But Michael is not too fond of Filipino cuisine—especially mine.

He got to meet his relatives, who were mostly teachers, so he knew that education is highly prized in the Philippines. When he visited the University of the Philippines and the University of Santo Tomas in Manila, I said to him, "Everybody in this country is interested in going to school and finishing college because it's the only way by which someone can rise from where they are in the social ladder."

Then we showed him an open market in Manila. When he asked me why I had brought him to "this stinking market," I told him it was because this was a part of my culture. After that, we went to a big supermarket, and I told him, "You see, it's the same kind of supermarket that we have in the United States. We have both here." He also visited Corregidor, where he learned of Filipino soldiers fighting side by side with American soldiers and saw the war memorials for the American and the Filipino war heroes.

So he knows part of the cultures of the Filipinos. He knew when he was six years old what a Filipino is and to be proud of it because Daddy, Mommy, and he are Filipino. So he never had the feeling of any conflict. He knew he is a Filipino. Of course, when he goes out the door, he is very American. It doesn't matter to us if he marries a Filipina or another race. It is his decision. I told him to have fun but to date only somebody whom he thinks will be worthy to be the mother of his children.

"I Am Still Very Active"

I am still very active in the community. Right now, I am a member of the board of directors of the Philippine American Community of San Diego County, which sponsors the annual Miss Philippines Pageant. The pageant is to show one and all that Filipinas are beautiful, intelligent, and talented! I am also president of the American Legion Auxiliary of Leyte 625. Because my husband is a World War II veteran, I like to help with their programs. They work so hard to help the veterans and the communities. These involvements keep me from being completely retired.

After more than forty years in the United States, I have gotten acclimatized to the mores of the United States. I see, and I accept. I don't look down; I don't look up. I just accept. But I am Filipino first. When I go out, I don't care what kind of person that I meet, professionals, European, American, or whatever, I have no inferiority complex—or whatever complex.

Chapter 2

"I Was Used
to the American
Way of Life"

Ruth Abad

"My Father Was an American"

I was born in Piat, Cagayan, on September 23, 1911. My father was an American born in Lexington, Kentucky. He was a captain in the Cavalry during the Spanish American War. This was in the 1900s [*sic*] when the Americans sent the Spaniards away and occupied the Philippines. When we were born, my father registered all of his children as American citizens.

My father met my mother in Cagayan. My mother couldn't speak English; all she knew was Spanish and our dialects—Itawas and Ibanag. My father could not speak the dialects, so he learned Spanish. After my father got out of the Cavalry, he practiced law. That was another reason why he had to learn Spanish. The court cases were all in Spanish, and most of the judges were Spanish-speaking. So at home we spoke English with my father and Spanish with my mother. But then, we spoke with the townspeople in our own dialects. I never learned Tagalog. I find it a hard language to speak.

My grandparents were landowners. My grandfather on my mother's side was a *gobernadorcillo,* like a mayor. They were prominent people in our town. At first, none of my mother's family wanted my father to marry my mother because he was an American. During the Spanish time, the Spaniards took Filipina women as concubines. They seldom married them. So my grandparents thought the Americans would do the same thing, taking Filipinas as their mistresses.

But my father was serious about marrying my mother. Because my mother was the only child still alive, my grandmother made my father promise not to take her away from the family. He lived with that promise. He never went back to the States. So we never met his side of the family. My parents got married in 1903. It was the first civil marriage in our town, because my father was a Methodist and my mother was a Catholic, and the church did not allow mixed marriages in those days.

They were eight children in our family, four boys and four girls. Because my father was an American, we were raised partly the American way. My father never learned to eat Filipino food. So we had two kinds of food. My father ate potatoes and bread and my mother wanted her rice and *pinakbet* [a vegetable dish] or *adobo* [a stew-like dish].

My father sent my oldest brother here [to the United States] to study. He came back home after he finished eighth grade. My father also wanted to send two other boys, Clifford and Henry, but my grandmother said to my mother, "Your husband is taking your children from you little by little." They still didn't trust him. So the rest of us didn't go to the United States to study. All of us graduated from high school in Cagayan.

My brothers went to college in Manila, which is about three hundred miles from Cagayan. They went to Santo Tomas, the University of the Philippines, and Mapua Engineering School. One took law. Another brother, Clifford, took dentistry, but he joined the army afterward. Henry took business administration. He was the one managing the estate of my mother. The youngest was Sam, who studied engineering.

And the girls became teachers. That was the only job that women could have then. Before the Americans came, women were expected to just get married and raise a family. During the Spanish time, only the rich could go to school, because you had to pay to go to school. The Spanish purpose was to spread Christianity, but the Americans wanted to establish democratic government. So the Americans introduced free education, and everybody wanted to go to school. The women became ambitious and wanted to become teachers.

Coming to the United States as a Repatriate

I came to the United States after World War II in 1945. I was already thirty-three years old. The U.S. government was repatriating all the dependents of U.S. citizens who had lived in the Philippines prior to the war. Because my father was an American, I was considered a repatriate. So I said, "This is my chance to go to the United States." The government paid for our passage through the Red Cross. My parents never made use of that trip. They never even came to the United States for a visit. My mother was not the type who liked to travel, but I was.

We lived in a small town, maybe twelve thousand people, where everybody was my mother's relatives, and everybody minded everybody's business. My father was the only American in town. I wanted a change. Also, I'd read about the United States in the many American magazines that Papa

*Ruth Abad (third from left) with three other past presidents of the
Filipino American Women's Club, San Diego, 1965*

subscribed to, and it sounded so exciting. I wanted to find out what kind of
life America had to offer. So when I had the chance to come to this country,
I took it. I also wanted to come to the United States to finish my education,
to study library science. And then maybe even join the U.S. Navy. I admired
men and women in uniforms, maybe because of my father and brother, who
were in the services. And I liked traveling, because I am the adventurous
type.

When I first came to the United States, I traveled with the chief executive
of the Red Cross to Denver, Colorado. Her husband was a pharmacist in
the Navy. So when he was transferred to San Diego, I came with them.
From San Diego, I was supposed to go to San Francisco to meet my brother
Clifford, who had been sent there by the Philippine Army. But on that same
day he was called to go back to the Philippines because of the Philippine
independence. So I did not even have a chance to get out of San Diego.
Before that, I didn't even know that San Diego existed.

Because I was used to the American way of life, I didn't have a difficult
time adjusting to life in this country. The United States was not a strange
place for me.

Marriage and Work

I met my husband in San Diego. I was working as a babysitter for a captain in the Navy, and my husband's cousin was working as a civilian employee in the Naval Training Center where I worked. He invited me to a dance to meet other Filipinos. My husband had a car, so he was the one driving us. That's how I met him. It was a blind date.

It didn't occur to me at that time to get married. What I wanted was to go to school or to travel. I was very independent. Papa trained us to take care of ourselves. It was not my ambition to get married, because I did not want to be stuck at home with the babies. I saw that when my sisters got married, they stayed home and took care of the children. They could not go anywhere because of the babies. That was not for me. I wanted to go out. But then when fate comes, you cannot counter it. My husband and I got married in 1946 in San Diego; I was thirty-four years old. I just wrote to my family about it. I didn't go back to the Philippines until 1964, when my mother died.

My husband came from the Ilocos region. Since so many Ilocanos lived in Cagayan, I knew the Ilocano dialect. But my husband never learned my dialect. Ilocanos are different; they will never give up their dialect. If they marry a person from Cagayan, she has to learn Ilocano. And the Cagayanos give in, so they all become Ilocanos.

My husband came to the United States in 1928 to join his father, who was working as a farm laborer. During those days, so many Filipinos came as farm laborers; some were schooled, and some were not. My husband graduated from high school in the Philippines, and he came to the States hoping that his father would help him to continue his schooling. But because of the Depression, his father could not help him. So he had to find his own way. He had to look for jobs, just odds and ends. Anything to support himself.

After we got married, I didn't work because I was having one child after another. I had four children, but I lost two. After that, I tried to look for work, because my husband was not making much. I looked for any kind of work. I tried waitressing. But my husband said, "I want you to be home when the girls come home from school. I don't want them wandering around." So I started babysitting the children in the neighborhood for seventy-five cents an hour.

I didn't really like staying home. I was not the housekeeper type. I told my husband, "Let's go back to the Philippines. Life is terrible for me here." But he said, "No, all these people in the Philippines would pay a fortune to bring their family here. Now you're here, and you want to go back there?"

I hated doing the housework. In the Philippines, even if you were an average family, you could afford to get helpers. We had helpers left and right.

I didn't have to do anything. When I came home, the food was cooked, and the clothes were washed. But here, I had to do everything, cleaning, cooking, and taking care of the children. It was endless. I used to cry. My maids in the Philippines had more days off than me.

I didn't regret coming to the United States, but I wanted to have at least a helper. My mother wanted to send me a helper, but my brother told her not to. He said that once the helpers are here for two or three years, they will leave me and go on to their own. Many times, I wanted to go back home, but I had no money to go home. My husband did not want to go, because he was working morning, noon, and night. So I had to bear it. It was hard.

At that time, my husband was working at Bishop's School, a private girls' school in La Jolla, as a dining room man. He served the girls in the cafeteria. He was receiving only sixty dollars a month, and we had to pay forty dollars a month for the house. After that, he took a civil service examination in North Island [a naval air station in San Diego], and he passed the exam. First he worked as a store clerk, and when they had an opening for a photography equipment specialist, he applied and got that job. Photography was his hobby. While he was working at Bishop's School, he used to work extra in a photography shop, helping the men there take and develop pictures. He worked there at North Island for twenty-one years until he retired.

In 1970, when the girls started going to high school, I started working again. I worked as a teacher's aide in Balboa School. After four years, I became the librarian aide. I did that for twelve years until I retired. I enjoyed my work very much.

When I started working, life got better, and I started to relax. I wrote to my brothers and sisters asking them to come here for a visit. I told them not to sell their property; just come and try it out for a year. After a year, if they didn't like it here, then they could go back. Eventually all of them came, and they never went back—in spite of all the property that we had there. But they got good jobs here, and they were able to buy their own homes.

San Diego in the 1940s and 1950s

After we got married in 1946, my husband and I lived in downtown San Diego. A lot of Filipinos used to live there, on Forty-fifth and Forty-sixth streets. Almost all of our neighbors were Filipinos. That was where the cheapest houses were. But then, in 1950 or 1951, they built Highway 5 right through our neighborhood. That sent the people away. We moved here to Paradise Hills. We liked the neighborhood because it was quiet.

San Diego was very different in the 1940s and 1950s. There was not much traffic. There was no Bonita yet. Bonita was a mountain then. We only had one small shopping center in National City. Then, after World War

II, the city expanded because so many people decided to live in San Diego. They came by leaps and bounds. The real estate people started building houses everywhere.

There were only a handful of Filipinos in San Diego then, about five hundred. Most of them were in the Navy. There were others who were farm laborers and domestic workers. And some were students; they worked in the farms, but they also went to school. There were very few Asians around. The Filipinos were the largest Asian group. There were no Vietnamese until after the Vietnam War. The Chinese were already here because there was a Chinatown.

After the war, Filipinos finally were able to own property.* Before, they could not own unless they married an American. And even then, the white people used to stone their homes. Also, some hotels like the U.S. Grant Hotel, the Coronado Hotel, and the El Cortez did not allow Filipinos to hold their dances in their ballrooms. There was a lot of prejudice against Filipinos. But after the war, the white people learned that Filipinos are good, so the prejudice faded. My father used to tell us about the discrimination against Filipinos in America. He said, "If you want to go to America, get an education first. Use your brains, then you can challenge anybody."

I personally did not experience any prejudice. It used to be that some restaurants would refuse to serve Filipinos. But we seldom went out to eat anyway. We ate at home to save money. My children sometimes complained that some of their classmates at school called them "Flip." But they fought back by calling those kids "white trash." I think discrimination still exists today, but to me, you should not go to a place where you think you are not wanted. Why go and look for trouble?

But there is also prejudice among Filipinos. There are some professionals who have better means than us, and they do not care to mingle with us. They keep themselves aloof. Maybe they do not have enough time to meet with other people. They are busy day and night. But if they don't like me, I cannot be bothered.

Organizing the Filipino American Women's Club

In the 1940s, the Filipino community had only one civilian organization, the Filipino American League, and two military organizations, the Fleet Reserve for the Navy and the American Legion for all the armed forces. They had a building here on Market Street, the Filipino American Veterans Hall.

Because there was no organization for the women, I decided to form the

---

*Before the war only citizens could own property. Filipino immigrants could not own property because they were denied the right of naturalization. They became eligible for naturalized citizenship in 1946 with the passage of the Luce-Celler bill.

Filipino American Women's Club. I used to read in the newspapers about the Mexican Women's Club, the Czechoslovakian, the French, so many. I said, "Then why not a Filipino Women's organization?" So I called Mr. Canta; he was the one who organized the Fleet Reserve and the American Legion. I asked him if there were any laws against forming a social organization. He said no and promised to support my efforts. I was inspired. I called some of the Filipina women I knew and told them about my idea. And that was how we, thirteen of us, formed the Filipino American Women's Club in 1949.

The founding members all came from different places in the Philippines. We had different dialects, so we spoke English to each other. We all knew English because it was taught in schools all over the Philippines. As soon as the Americans occupied the Philippines, English became the medium of instruction. The women also came from different backgrounds. Some were high school graduates like myself. Some worked as domestic helpers. Some came as students.

There were American and Mexican wives of Filipino men who wanted to join the organization. But when we wrote the bylaws and constitution, most of the women wanted to concentrate just on Filipina women. There were only three of us who were in favor of accepting the American women. Because I am half-American, I voted for it. But the majority of the Filipina women wanted to show that they can build this organization without the American women's help. So membership was restricted to anyone with Filipino blood in them. Of course, I was hated by the American women for that, because they thought it was my idea.

We also didn't want any men, because we didn't want any challenges from them. We felt that we were more outspoken when we were among ourselves. I liked the women's movement in this country because it gives women a chance to express their opinions, because we cannot always say "yes, yes," to a man. In our home, I always stand up for what I want. When it came to finances, my husband was the head. But when it came to social things or the education of our daughters, then he listened to me.

It was discouraging at first, because the men didn't trust that we could start the Women's Club. They said, "Oh, it will not last. These women will pull each other's hair out." They thought we wouldn't be able to do much. But we started sponsoring many activities. We celebrated Mother's Day and Father's Day. Then we had the anniversary and installation dinners. Then we had the Miss Sampaguita beauty contest for the teenagers. (Sampaguita is the national flower of the Philippines.) We also used to feed Filipino sailors who had no place to go; they really appreciated that. And when Filipinos take their citizenship oath, we hold a reception for them.

We also got involved in the larger community. We got in touch with all the leaders in town, with the human relations people. We invited them to our programs, and we asked them to include us in their programs. We wanted to show off our culture, like our cooking, our costumes, and our folk dances. For example, we were invited by the people in Del Mar to present a Philippine night. So we presented all the Philippine dances, and we explained to the audience how those dances originated. My sister-in-law was the dance teacher. She was a schoolteacher in the Philippines, and she taught folk dancing there. We even tried to have a Filipino group teaching Tagalog to our children.

Regionalism and Unity Among Filipinos in San Diego

The Filipino American Women's Club is the oldest organization in the [San Diego] community. Now there are so many Filipino organizations. If you come from Leyte, you have your own group. If you come from Cebu, you have your own group. And these clubs have coronation almost every Saturday. There's the coronation of Miss Pangasinan, Miss Cavite, Miss Leyte, Miss Cebu, Miss Asian—Oh, so many! And then you have the professional organizations—the Filipino lawyers' group, the doctors' association, the nurses' association.

We cannot unite the Filipinos. This has always been a problem, because everybody wants to be president. That's the trouble with us Filipinos. No one wants to give in. They love power. It's in their blood. In the mid-1960s, the Council of Pilipino American Organizations [COPAO] was organized as an umbrella group in order to unite the Filipino community. The Women's Club used to be a member of COPAO. But then some members were disappointed because when we had activities, COPAO didn't help us. They didn't attend, they didn't help us sell tickets, and they didn't advertise our events. That's why I said, "What's the use of joining COPAO when they don't even help us?"

The Women's Club is steady. We raise money, and when help is needed and we can afford it, we give. We are trying to encourage the young ones to join, because the old people are dying. In fact there are only three of us alive now from the original thirteen members; the rest are gone. I don't want the organization to die.

We have many new members who are very enthusiastic and are good leaders. One of our aims is to develop leadership skills. If the women had talents, they could be a candidate for president. That way, they can develop their leadership skills by learning how to preside at a meeting and how to interpret the bylaws and constitution. In fact, most of the women presidents of the different organizations in San Diego were former presidents of the Filipino American Women's Club. Some of the Filipino women are very shy. They are [self-]conscious about their ability to communicate in English. They are afraid that they will not be understood. But we tell them that as long as they are speaking English, they will be understood. So just speak out and say what they want.

Raising Daughters in the United States

I raised my daughters the American way because we lived here, and I didn't want them to be ignorant of the American ways. My husband and I spoke automatically in English, so the children never learned the dialects. But we fought in Ilocano when we didn't want the children to understand. When our daughters were grown, they met Filipino children who spoke the dialects and asked us why we never taught them the Filipino language. I told them, "Well, because I thought that it was not necessary. To survive here, you have to learn their ways and their language."

But we always taught the children about the Philippines. When we formed the Women's Club, we used to sponsor Philippine folk dances. So we made them participate in the dances, wear the costumes, and learn the culture of the Filipinos. We tried to keep them eating Filipino food, although they prefer sandwiches and hot dogs. It was easier for us to prepare the American food, because with the Filipino food, there is so much work.

The women of our generation were more conservative. But our children were born here, and sometimes we have a hard time with their ways. We have that old-fashioned way of telling the children, "Don't talk when your mother is talking." But the children here are very outspoken. We cannot discipline them the way we were disciplined by our parents.

In the Philippines, we always have chaperons when we go out. When we go to dances, we have our uncle, our grandfather, and auntie all behind us to make sure that we behave in the dance hall. Nobody goes necking outside. You don't even let a man put his hand on your shoulders. When you were brought up in a conservative country, it is hard to come here and see that it is all freedom of speech and freedom of action. Sex was never mentioned in our generation. I was thirty already when I learned about sex. But to the young generation in America, sex is nothing!

I do not tell my children whom to date. As long as we know whom they go with and where they go, it is okay. We just give them advice, but they can take it or leave it. We tell them not to do anything that they'd regret. At first, we tried to match the children up with our friends' sons, but that didn't work. Both of my daughters are married to Americans. I told them, "I married the man I love, so do the same. I'm not the one that promises to sleep with him or live with him for the rest of my life. So it is up to you."

My children are more lenient with their own children than we were with them. My daughter allows her eighteen-year-old to go camping with her friends and their boyfriends. That's the way she sees it, but I don't see it that way. So that's why when my children asked me to come and live with them after my husband passed away, I said no. I told them, "Go ahead with your life style, and I'll go ahead with mine. I might not like the way you bring up your children, and I'll butt in, and we might fight." So I live by myself now.

My grandchildren consider themselves American. There is not much we can do to change that. But I want them to know where they came from. I tell them about the Philippine culture and history, such as the fact that there is a lot of Spanish influence in our clothes, like the puff sleeves on the dresses and the skirts. We were ruled by the Spaniards for three hundred years, so the Spanish influence was strong. Then the Americans came and ruled us for fifty years. So the only *real* Filipinos are those in the non-Christian tribes. They live in the mountain provinces, especially in the Moro land in Mindanao. They were driven there when they refused to convert to Christianity.

I consider myself to be more American now that I am here. Some Filipinos buy beautiful homes, but they only use their house to show off. They don't eat in their good dining room; they eat in the kitchen. And even though they live here now, some of them still eat with their hands. I have seen a couple of families like that. My children said, "Mama, they don't use forks and knives in that house. They eat with their hands!" That's the way they were brought up. But we will never do that, because we were never brought up that way.

Politics

Although I am active in the Filipino community, I am not really involved in politics. I don't believe the politicians. In the Philippines, I used to fight with all the candidates. So I cannot be a good politician, because to be a politician, you have to tell lies, you have to bluff people. And I don't like that. To me, politics is not really honest. You have to be pretentious to be a good liar, to be a bluffer.

I haven't voted since they killed Kennedy. I am so disgusted with politics. They always kill the good man who tries to do good for all. Last year [1992], in National City, there were three Filipinos running for city council. All three lost. What they should have done was to decide among themselves which one should run, so they wouldn't end up dividing the Filipino vote three ways. The Women's Club does not endorse any candidate or any political party. We are not involved in politics.

We are in a country where whites are in power. To fight back, I think we need to organize as Asian Americans. Then they cannot ignore us. If there is only one group, they will not listen. But it is very challenging to try to unite the Asians, because the Vietnamese think they are better, the Filipinos think they are better, and so on. The Asians are fond of challenging each other. There is no unity. Everybody wants to be a leader. Instead of pushing a leader, we drag him down. I think that's the Asian custom. They don't want to give in.

Chapter 3

"Sometimes, I Am Not Sure What It Means to Be an American"

Connie Tirona

Farm Laborers in Hawaii

My parents were recruited to Hawaii as laborers sometime between 1920 and 1926. My father was from Aklan province in western Visayas. He stopped attending school after the seventh grade. I remember him telling me that he had to give up his education because he had to work to send his brothers and sisters through school. He joined the Philippine Scouts. For him, it was an adventure because of the chance to meet the American officers. He wanted to learn more about the United States.

My mother lived a very sheltered life. At that time, women were taught to stay home and learn homemaking skills to prepare for marriage. She only had a third-grade education. Her parents felt that was sufficient for a female. Her father owned a ferryboat in the Visayan Islands, so people could travel from one island to another. So they must have been middle class or upper middle class.

It was a hard decision for my mother to go to Hawaii, coming from a very sheltered life. There were four or five other Filipinas who came at the same time that my mother did. Later on, when we were in California, they would meet often and tell the old stories about Hawaii, and I would just sit there and listen. There were nostalgic stories as well as sad ones, like the time my mother had a miscarriage coming over [in] steerage. They came over in steerage class on one of the American President liners, and their fare was paid by the recruiters.

My parents were sent to the Wailua Sugar and Pineapple Plantation. They lived in labor camps. I learned all this from my father, so this is oral history. It was sad, because my father said that they were so mistreated by the different crew bosses.

At that time, only Ilocanos and Visayans were recruited to Hawaii. It was my understanding that this was because they were the farmers. The Tagalogs were more the intellectuals. What I heard from my parents was that at first, Filipinos in those labor camps saw themselves as either Ilocanos or Visayans. My parents were Visayans. But they became "Filipinos" because of what was happening to them: the violence against them; they were mistreated. They united against the Portuguese foremen and the "*haoles*" [whites]. My father learned to speak Ilocano fluently because Ilocanos and Visayans were always put to work together, and the Ilocanos also learned to speak Visayan. Some of my children's godparents are Ilocanos. So regionalism didn't matter to either group because they had suffered the same indignities.

The Filipinos also got along with the Japanese [in the labor camps.] Because of the different ethnic groups in these camps, "pidgin English" became their common language bond. My mother learned to cook many Japanese dishes. I think that was because they were all together in the work camps. They all had to work hard, and this is why they became so close-knit with each other.

Theirs was a hard life. They would work from very early in the morning until late at night. They would leave for work before the break of dawn and return long after dusk. The women like my mother would do the cooking, and some of them would go to work in the fields along with the men. But again, they said there were some fun times when they would get together and have their famous cockfights. Among other things, they would make this fermented drink from coconuts. So, despite an oppressive work atmosphere, there was some joy.

My parents stayed in Hawaii for about five years. My father was able to leave the plantations and work in the shipyard. Some of their Filipino friends in Hawaii who had gone to the mainland asked them to come and join them there because there was plenty of work to be found. My father had made enough money for passage from working in the shipyard.

Childhood Memories of the Manongs

When my parents landed on Angel Island in San Francisco Bay, their friends were in the Delano area working in the grape fields. My parents did not know where Delano was. A Japanese grower from Stanford decided to hire

*Connie Tirona (center) singing Christmas carols with members of the
San Diego Aklan Association, San Diego, 1991*

them. (Part of Stanford at one time was all a nursery owned by this Japanese
farmer.) So my parents had a place to stay.

But their friends from Delano contacted them again and asked them to
join them there, where they could earn more money. So my parents decided
to move to Delano to be near their *kababayans* (countrymen) from Hawaii.
My father said there was a lot of Bombays (East Indians) but not as many
Mexicans in Delano. However, the Bombays were moving on to El Centro.
My parents stayed in that area for quite some time, until I was born, and
then my father decided to move the family back to northern California.

I was born in 1929 in Selma, which is right next to Fresno. I remember
many Filipinos as I was growing up. They still had their cockfights. The
cockpit arena was really the gathering place for all the Filipinos. Even if some
didn't like to bet on the cockfights, everybody was there. I remember the
women having little stalls, with their little tables filled with individual special
delicacies they had cooked. And of course, the men who were single at the
time were so happy to have Filipino food because they lived in these bar-
racks, while the families lived in cottages and could prepare their own food.
These cottages were really dilapidated shacks, but they were always kept neat
and immaculate.

Even when they were following the seasonal crops, all of them—there were three families in my parents' group—would pitch in to buy a car so they could travel from camp to camp. And we would all go in that car, and I can remember sometimes there was not enough work for everyone, and the ones who got the work would buy the groceries. And everyone would pitch in to get a small place where we all lived together. It was somewhat crowded, but we always kept it clean. Everybody would cook and help.

I can remember one time, they were down to their last fifty cents. They were going to another place where there was an opening for pruning grapes. So, the other two families would stay behind in the place that they had rented, while the rest would go seek jobs. Well, they only had fifty cents. Two chickens crossed the road. Let me tell you, those chickens did not stay alive for very long. They plucked them and cleaned them that night. They gathered vegetables from their garden; they always had a garden wherever they went. They threw everything in a pot. Those two chickens fed three families that night. Soon they were able to get jobs again. Not one of us ever went hungry.

When I was about four or five years old, my parents moved up to Oakland. With his experience working in the shipyard in Hawaii, my father eventually got a job at a shipyard. So he was able to leave the agricultural job environment. He was a rigger and retired from the Mare Island shipyard after twenty years. And guess what? He went back to work as a foreman in the fields again. I think he was one of the first who wanted to organize a union against the growers. He was always fighting for the rights of workers.

In the 1930s, most of the *manongs* were still on the farms. The *manongs* were those men who came here from Hawaii without any families. They were bachelors. And they were the best dancers, the best dressers. There was just something very suave about them.

There was an antimiscegenation law in California then. So if the *manongs* got caught talking to a white woman, gosh, they were beaten up. I can remember one incident in particular. It happened in Watsonville. I remember it so well—when some white men came into the labor camp. I thought they were the Ku Klux Klan. They were on horseback, and they took two Filipinos and tied them with a rope. Then they rode up and down the camp, dragging the two Filipinos after them. They wanted to show the "brown monkeys" that they could not speak to the white women.

I was horrified. I could not understand why people do such abominable acts. My father and mother, the priests and the nuns, they were always saying that we are all human beings, children under God. Then why did they do this? Was it because we were of a different color? And my father said to me, "Yes, and that will always be. Hopefully, when you grow up it won't be as bad. But there are also many good people on this earth to make up for the ones who are so narrow-minded."

It hurt me deeply to watch the Filipinos being beaten up. We were called "brown monkeys"; we were "ignorant"; we were "savages." I just felt a sense of betrayal, because my parents came to this country for the opportunity to improve their life style, and they thought that Americans were kind people.

In my father's case, he was in the Philippine Scouts, which was under the Americans at that time. And he said there were so many kind Americans who helped him so much. Americans were very giving, he said. But of course, these were the missionaries that he met, and the army officers were always trying to encourage him. They told him what good books to read and tried to help him with his English, because they saw that he was really interested. That was what was in his mind. But he saw the difference after he arrived in Hawaii. He always said to me, "In order to change things, you have to be educated. Use your brains. I made a better life here. With God's help, you will be able to do something to give back to this country." That really made an impression on me. I will always remember it.

There were about thirty *manongs* in the labor camps in the Sacramento–San Joaquin area that we would visit. Sometimes the *manongs* would come and visit us. They were so homesick for family. They always looked up to my father because he had a "government job" in the shipyard. We went to see them almost every week or every other week. My mother would bake all her delicacies all week long for such visits, and the *manongs* enjoyed eating them.

It was so beautiful there when we visited them. They built what looked like a Japanese bathhouse. They installed a huge metal tub with hot coals underneath to warm the water. Of course, you had to bathe outside first. That was the biggest treat! And the *manongs* would fix up their rooms immaculately. They scrubbed their place because "the families were coming!" They picked fresh corn and cooked good, wholesome food. Their big thing was fishing in the delta's rivers. We would go up there and fish, and they would be roasting pigs.

After eating they would play guitars and mandolins, and we, as little children of the families, would sing and dance. The *manongs* liked to hear the little kids sing. They had a small makeshift stage for us, and we would go up there with our curly hair and cute little dresses. And they would throw coins at us. It was the biggest thing for them. You could just see tears of joy on their faces. They would come up and hug us. And I was thinking, "Gosh! Just a little joy that we brought to them." But they were so happy.

I especially remember when we sang the Visayan songs. You could see the tears on the faces of those grown men. Usually, Filipino men are not like that. I don't think Asian men really show their feelings. I remember my younger sister had a beautiful soprano voice, and she would sing this one Visayan song that said something about how hard life was in a strange land. It was like a love song. As they listened to her song, tears would form and slowly flow from their eyes. They would drink their wine and cry softly. They would say to my parents, "Thank you for teaching your daughter to sing that song."

Soon it was time for us to go to bed. As I was drifting off to sleep, I could hear them laughing as they started to sing nostalgic songs from the Philippines. Lying on a small cot, it just lulled me to sleep. The next morning, we would go fishing again and do the same thing. Breakfast was prepared and served. We would leave for home on Sunday evening. After such weekends, the *manongs* prepared for another grueling week of hard work.

The *manongs* bought me my first bike. They wanted to have snapshots taken so they could send them back to their families in the Philippines. When they received mail from the Philippines, they would ask me to read it to them. Some of them did not read well. Their families probably had someone write the letters in English for them. One of the letters said, "Thank you for the picture of your adopted daughter with the bicycle you got her. Thank you for the money that you sent." And I would end up writing back to them. The *manongs* would keep the mail they received until it became so frayed and torn because of so many readings. You could tell that they read it at night when loneliness overcame them.

I wish for those days again. If I could relive one day in the past, I would love to see them again.

Growing up in the 1930s and 1940s

At this time, Filipinos were experiencing much prejudice and discrimination. We could not buy homes in certain areas. My parents bought a home in Vallejo on the other side of town by the waterfront, where all of the people of color lived. We would take walks on Saturday nights to pass the time away. We could not afford anything else. We just wanted to see people. We could see all the Filipinos all dressed up with no place to go, except the dance halls. My mother would say, "No, no! We don't go this way," as if I didn't know what was down there.

Where we lived there was one certain block that you could go up to and feel comfortable. You could go to this one theater, and that was all right because that was where all the people of color would go. But if you went beyond to the next block, people would stare at you. They would look at you when you went into a department store. My father would say to us, "Well, we don't have to go there. Things are so expensive up there anyway."

Being foolhardy, I told my sister, "Well, I am going up there." She told me that I should not. When I asked her why, she told me what had happened to her. She had gone into a department store because it fascinated her. The manager told her she did not belong in there and to get out. She told the manager she was just looking around and was not doing anything wrong.

I guess that when you are a child and curious, you would do anything. Since I could not go into that department store, I remembered that there was a Sees candy store in the same block. So I went there to buy a piece of candy. The lady in the store asked if I had any money. When I showed her my money and pointed to the piece of chocolate candy I wanted, I remember her taking double pieces of paper so she wouldn't touch my hands. Being the child that I was, I purposely dropped the money on the floor. She had to come around the counter to pick it up. I was about eight at the time.

Then I decided I would be more adventurous, so I went down to another block and into another department store. Again, I was kicked out. Then I went into a Chinese-owned store, and they welcomed me with open arms. They asked me what I was doing at that end of town. I told them I was just curious and wanted to find out what it was like, since we were told that we could not go there.

Of course, I got a spanking afterward because I disobeyed my parents. My father sat me down and asked, "Well, what did you learn?" I replied, "Everything you said was true, Papa." He said, "I just wanted you to know that you can do these things. You can go anywhere; it's just that you may not be treated as good as other people. So you have to learn how to respond and react in that situation." I told him about dropping the money on the floor in the candy store, and he laughed.

I went to a Catholic school. The reason we were able to attend this school was because the sisters said that we only had to pay so much. Our home was five miles away from the school I attended. But that was all right, since I had many friends that I picked up on my way to school. I can remember walking to elementary school and being taunted at times.

My sister and I were the only ones of color in the school. But that never bothered me because I thought I could play just as well as anyone could, and I was equally as bright as the other students, if not brighter. I used to bring rice and fish to school for lunch because I love to eat both. It was a great meal for me. The little girls would not sit by me, and I wondered why, because their lunch was not as good as mine. The nuns would come over and say, "They don't understand."

In high school, some of my friends were Greeks and Italians. They were white people but never thought about color. The only problem that I had was when they had a school dance. They did not allow people of color to attend. My friend, who was the captain of the basketball team, invited me. I told him I could not go, and he said he would not go either. All my friends said they would not go also, but I told them it was the rule and rules are not made to be broken.

In the late 1930s, war clouds were already forming in Europe, and Japan was starting up something. I remember the *manongs* leaving agriculture, because more money could be made in the shipyards because of the impending war. So my parents decided to buy a bigger house, which was a two-story one, so they could rent out rooms to the *manongs.*

My mother, I think, was very lonely. It was a good thing that there was a support group of about four or five Filipino wives who had met each other in Hawaii. These women would get together and do some embroidery. They usually met in our house and embroidered pillowcases, which were sought after by the *manongs.*

My mother took care of us, and she always encouraged us to go to school. She would take over some of our chores if we had a lot of homework to finish. I think she regretted the fact that she was not able to finish school. But I told her not to feel that way as we, her children, have learned a lot from her. I think she envied women who worked in offices, who were able to be out with people and carry out conversations with them. She was not ashamed of herself, but she felt that her life could have been more fulfilling. She really encouraged me to do more, and I did more. Even in her last years she was always proud of what I had done.

When I was a teenager, in the late 1940s, I was Miss Philippines of this particular fraternal organization in northern California. We were chosen for our intelligence and personality, and also on the number of tickets we could sell. Since I had made many friends among the *manongs* and I was their adopted daughter, I had little trouble selling tickets. The *manongs* usually bought them by the fistful.

During the pageant and gala dance, the contestants had to wear a *terno,* which was the native dress of Filipinas. Generally, the town mayor or police chief would act as the judge in these pageants. The pageant was one of the ways for Filipinos to get together. It was a big night for the *manongs* to see the families, to see a favorite adopted daughter, or a niece or goddaughter. That was something for them to look forward to. It reminded them so much of home.

Through the years, at birthday and baptism parties, I would listen to my parents' friends talk about discrimination and prejudice. They knew that they could only go so far in their jobs and that they would never be promoted, no matter how hard they worked. There was just so much prejudice back then.

I still remember the time that we went to Santa Maria, Pismo Beach. My father was hungry, so we stopped at this restaurant. But the owners told us that we could not be served in the restaurant but that we could get food in the back. As far as obtaining part-time work while in high school, there were a lot of jobs that I couldn't have even though I was well qualified, much more qualified [than the whites]. The only jobs they would offer me were as a stock girl, where they put you in the back.

Once there was a Filipino doctor in Stockton. My mom and dad thought he was the next thing to God. When my father was working in the shipyard, we would drive from Vallejo to Stockton, which took about an hour and a half, to see this doctor. On the way we would stop by the roadside to admire the scenery and the wild flowers. My dad knew that I loved flowers. He would pick a bunch of them, and as we stopped to see friends along the way, we would give them the flowers that he had picked.

My father was one of the most feminist Filipino men. He wanted his daughter to do the things that a man could do. He took me hunting with him and taught me how to shoot a rifle. What he really wanted me to do was to join the service. But I was not cut out to be in the service. His grandsons were. When my oldest son, Michael, graduated from the Naval Academy as an officer, my father cried because he was so proud. My father was a military man. I always felt that if he had had more education, he would have been one of the generals in the Philippines.

He also wanted me to learn. I remember him telling me, "Okay, we can't afford to buy books, but I will take you to a place where books are free." So he took me to the library. He told me, "You start on the first floor, and you go all the way to the top floor." There were three floors. And he said, "You read everything." My father was an avid reader. He would read all kinds of newspapers, although it took him a while to do so.

I remember when he went for his citizenship [test], that was in the 1930s, he was able to get his citizenship because he was in the Philippine Army under the U.S. Army. My father was well read, and he was very military minded. He saw that war was impending. So he decided to become an American citizen. That was a big decision, because at one time he had wanted to go home to the Philippines because of the mistreatment here. And he thought that when he became a citizen, things would be different. Isn't that something?

I can remember when he was studying for his citizenship exam, he would study the words, and he would ask me to spell them and pronounce them for him. It was like each day was a lesson. At that time, becoming a citizen was much more difficult than it is today. You practically had to take a political science course.

When he did get his citizenship, he was so proud. All of his friends came to celebrate, and the next thing you know, he was teaching classes to the other Filipinos. And I would be with him, and he would say, "My daughter will pronounce these words for you and spell them for you." Because of this, I learned to like political science and history.

I want to cry whenever I think of my father and my mother. They were immigrants, and they had to come to a strange country, not having a friend to meet them or greet them. They had to fend for themselves with limited English. They spoke English but with a heavy accent. I did not mind interpreting for them when I was growing up. I thought it was wonderful walking into an office and feeling that I was somebody because I was doing this for my parents.

I was always proud of my parents. Unfortunately, some of my friends were ashamed of their parents. They couldn't handle the kind of prejudice that they encountered. I thought my parents were extra-strong people who taught me how to cope with it. And I hope that I have given that to my children.

A U.S. Navy Wife in the South and in the Philippines

I met my husband when he first came here with the U.S. Navy. He is a mestizo, a mixture of Chinese, Spanish, and Filipino. His great-grandfather was a Spaniard, and his great grandmother was Filipino Chinese. He was born in Cavite, which is in Luzon. It's across the bay from Manila and at one time had a U.S. naval base. He attended a Jesuit school in the Philippines.

My father at that time worked in the shipyard. And the Filipino sailors were traveling up and down the coast. So my father would bring the sailors home because they were lonely. They hadn't had Filipino food for a long time. Of course, my mother was so happy. She was cooking again. And we would meet these Filipinos who were from different places in the Philippines. It was good because we would get to know more about the culture. A lot of them traveled from Pampanga and joined the Navy at Sangley Point.

It was very interesting because the first time my husband met me, he had heard so much about me already from the other sailors, who called me "the rambunctious one." So he told me, "I am going to marry you." I told him, "You are so conceited."

My husband was a hospital corpsman in the Navy. After his corps school in San Diego, we went to Charleston, South Carolina. Now here, on the West Coast, we had encountered discrimination. We weren't allowed in restaurants and things like that. That's what I grew up with. So when we moved, I said to myself, "Oh, my gosh, Charleston. That's even worse."

Now, when I go to a new city, my first act is to get on a bus so I can see all the sights and meet the people. So, in Charleston, I got on this bus and I sat in the back, because it is easier to get off the bus from there. I was sitting with blacks, but I didn't think anything about it. Then I saw the bus driver coming toward me, and the blacks were all looking at me. The driver told me to come up to the front of the bus. I asked him why. And he said, "Because you're considered white." I asked, "Really? What if I choose to sit back here?" "Then I can't go on," he replied. So I had to move.

And then, when I got off the bus, I just went to the first water fountain to get a drink. This black lady told me, "Ma'am, you can't drink at our water fountain." I asked her why. And she told me that I had to drink at the water fountain for whites. I am not white, but in Charleston, I am considered white.

When I went to the dress shop, it was the same thing. Blacks had a special place in the back. I go to the back because that's usually where the bargains are. But they told me, "Ma'am, you need to go up to the front."

My husband was stationed in Charleston for almost two years. My oldest boy was born there. Then he was transferred to northern California. After we had our first two sons, we were looking for a home in South San Francisco. This was around the early 1950s. I was pregnant with my third child, and I lost that child. So my husband went by himself to look for a place for us.

He came back and told me that there was a nice little house in South San Francisco, big enough for us. So we went to look at it. I was still weak, but I wanted to see the house because my husband had put a down payment on it. We parked across the street so we could get a better view. I saw people looking out their windows. See, my husband is very fair skinned and tall. He doesn't look like a Filipino. Two women came out and called the real estate agent over, and I could see them talking animatedly. Then the real estate agent came over and said, "I am sorry, but somebody else has already bought this home."

I was so angry and hurt. And I could see my husband's face. He really wanted us to live there. He was commuting from Vallejo to San Francisco at the time, and this would have been a shorter commute for him. I have seen this look before. This had happened to my father when I used to go with him to look for homes, and we always ended up on the other side of town. We could never live near the schools. Only whites could buy homes there. After a while, you sort of get these vibes about people. You just sense it.

I was so angry. I felt that my husband had joined the service to fight for this country and that we had the right to buy homes there. So, I told the real estate man, "This house hasn't been sold. They saw me, and they don't like my color." You could see that he was getting all flustered. I said, "I am a Filipino. My color is brown, and it is going to stay that way. It will never change." He was trying to make all these excuses. And I said, "It happened to me as a child when my father was trying to buy a house. I can see it, and I can sense it."

Then I walked over to the two women, and I said, "You know, I don't want to live in a neighborhood where I am going to have to deal with people like you. You can sell it to whomever you want. But there will come a day when we can buy a house in any neighborhood." When we got into the car, my husband said, "We will have a home." I said, "We will. It's going to happen." And we did. This house, the one that we live in now, is our fifth house.

When my husband received his last orders for transfer to the Philippines, we chose to travel by ship because we had always traveled by plane in his past transfers. So we went first class, and the ship was the *President Cleveland*. My father was so excited, because my parents came to California from Hawaii on the *Cleveland*—but in steerage class. So I told him to come and see us off.

We got the red carpet treatment. My father just stood there. He looked at the ship, and, of course the captain greets you as you come aboard first class. So my father went up to the captain and said, "Sir, I am so proud. I came on this ship steerage class, and my daughter is going back first class." I tell you, I just started to cry. And the captain shook his hands. My father asked where the steerage class was. The captain said, "Sir, that's like the basement of our ship where we keep all the storage." This was really something for my father. He had all his friends with him. They all came to see us off. And he told them, "You see! Here they are—traveling first class."

In the Philippines, I was discriminated against not only by the Americans but also by the other Filipinos. I was shocked and hurt. If it weren't the Americans thinking that I was one of the local bar girls, it was the Filipinos saying that I was too fat, too Westernized, and too aggressive. When I first arrived there, I spoke English without an accent, and they would look at me strangely and say, "Oh, you're not Filipino, you're Hawaiian." I replied, "Well, I am Filipino, but I am also American." And so they said, "Oh, well then, you don't eat rice. You eat bread; we'll get you bread." I think I was so Westernized in their eyes.

When we went to gatherings and family parties, I didn't like sitting with the women. I just didn't want to talk about diapers and children. There were other things to talk about, and so I went over to talk to the men. But then I was told, "No, no, women stay together over there." And I thought, "In this day and age?"

The other thing that really made me very angry was that I was an American but I was not allowed to have an A-card [reserved for U.S. citizens] for shopping in the Navy commissary, because they said there was too much black-marketing being done by Filipinos.

My first son had a bad allergy. We had to give him this special milk called Similac. Of course, I didn't know that it was one of the big black market items. I told the commissary staff that I needed Similac for my son. They told me I couldn't buy it. So I said, "I am an American citizen, and I have as much right as any American here to go to the commissary at any hour of any day it is open." So I went to the American embassy in Manila and spoke with the vice consul. I told him that if I did not get an A-card for the commissary, which gave me the privilege of other Americans, I would call my senator. They finally gave me an A-card, which was the big talk on the base among the Filipinos. I was dubbed "Miss Troublemaker."

Also, being a Filipina and being married to a military man, I walked aboard the base to go shopping. There had been times when I was whistled at and derogatory remarks were made within earshot. These military guys think that you are there to make money or that you married an American for the purpose of going to the States.

One day, I went to the base dispensary, where my husband worked, to pick up his paycheck. I was dressed nicely, and as I walked by the fire station I heard catcalls and snide remarks being made by some of the firemen. I said to myself that I should just ignore it, but I was fuming inside. I saw my husband at a distance, standing by the dispensary door, and I waved at him.

The next thing I heard was, "How much do you charge?" I kept on walking. "Hey, are you deaf or something? How much do you charge? You have a good body." I stopped and looked directly at the man making the remarks and said, "I want you to come down from whatever you are standing on and give me your name." He refused, so I went to the fire chief and reported him. I told the fire chief that if he did not do something to reprimand that individual, I would report the entire matter to the legal department.

Needless to say, the entire fire department personnel lined up and apologized to me. I told these men, "Look, I am an American of Filipino descent, and I am a woman. As Americans, we come here as ambassadors of good will. This is not your country. You are the foreigner. I don't want a forced apology. I just want you to think before opening your mouths. I don't know how old you are or if you have a wife or a girlfriend. Would you like the same thing to happen to her?" That was an incident that I will never forget. After they apologized to me, the captain said, "It won't happen again." I said, "But it will, because I am one who can stand up and say something. The other women will take it, because they are afraid of the military."

I didn't feel a sense of belonging in the Philippines until our third tour there, I think because by then, I was involved in many things. While I was there, I went out to the different barrios and provinces and read to the schoolchildren. They had a reading hour. I would get all the military wives together because they were bored. All they did was go to the beauty shop and get their hair done and their pedicures.

When I was the president of our Navy wives' club, we did a lot of things. One of the wonderful things that I was very pleased with was when the Vietnamese children that were napalmed came to Subic on a hospital ship. We were able to entertain them and bring them things. We went aboard, and it was the most touching scene I could remember so I cried. So did the rest of the wives. Poor children!

And you know, these children loved flowers. So I had all the gardeners bring bouquets of gardenias aboard the ship, and the children loved them. We would hand out a little bouquet to each of the little girls. There was one girl in particular, she had no legs and only half an arm, and when she took it, she started to cry, and she started saying something in Vietnamese. The interpreter told us that she said the flowers reminded her of when she was home, when she had her family. And she would smell that gardenia. We just stood there and cried. That was one of the nicest experiences in my life—that I was allowed to go aboard the Navy hospital ship and be with these children.

Discrimination in San Diego

When we came back from the Philippines in 1970, my husband was stationed at Camp Pendleton. We bought a house here in Carlsbad. I think we were among the first Filipinos to move to Carlsbad. It's still a very white community.

When we first moved here, my son would always go jogging. One time, he was running through the neighborhood. A police car stopped him, "What are you doing in this neighborhood?" "I live here." "No, you don't." He said, "Well, I live at this address. But I am not going to ride in the car with you. You can follow me home." So they followed him home to make sure that he lived there. I always tell my children, "It's going to happen to you. Don't ever resist the police."

In the last fifteen years, I think things have simmered down. I don't run into prejudices or people looking at me cross-eyed that often any more. But it still happens. My daughter, Lori, when she was giving birth at Tri-City Hospital, was having a difficult time, as it was going to be a breach delivery. And they were just waiting for the baby to turn.

The doctor was in another part of the hospital. Well, another shift of nurses had come on. I knew the first shift, because some of them were friends and classmates of our children. Before the first shift left, I asked them to get the doctor, because I didn't think the baby was going to turn and Lori's labor was nearing almost thirty hours. I said, "I think you should get that doctor or let me find him."

A nurse from the incoming shift came in. She looked at my daughter, and she looked at me and said, "Do . . . you . . . speak . . . English?" I was very tired and very angry so I said, "Much better than you." And I said, "I would like to speak to the head nurse." I told my daughter she was going to be all right, as I was going to get that doctor right away.

I went to the head nurse and I said, "My daughter has been in labor for almost thirty hours, and I don't appreciate having someone come up to me and ask me if I speak English. I want that doctor right now!" And they got that doctor so fast. I told her, "Is it because we are of color that you think that we are like rabbits that give birth? I think that nurse is prejudiced." Now, all you have to do is say that word. So, apologies were given. And I said, "You should take a sensitivity course on how to deal with people of color."

The head nurse was a friend of mine, she said, "Oh, gosh! I am so sorry." I said, "It's only because you know me. Why is it that you have to know me? Why isn't everybody made aware?" And so after that incident, they started sensitivity courses there at the hospital. So you have to complain. If you sit back and don't say anything, they tend to walk all over you. And I think for the most part, Filipinos have a colonial mentality. They tend to not do anything. But you don't have to scream at them. You can be calm about it.

Sometimes, I am not sure what it means to be an American. I am not equal to anyone. My color is different and that has mattered all of my life. I feel that not all Americans are equal; they are not. I think when I went to the Philippines, that's when my feelings probably started. I found out that I had to tell these American servicemen that I was an American, and even then they questioned how I became an American. Did I live with an American to become an American? And I think that's when I felt that the word "American" really didn't mean anything if you were a person of color, you know, it really doesn't. I don't know, maybe a lot of people would disagree with me, but that's how I feel. I probably have people say, "Well, then, why doesn't she go back where she came from?"

Chapter 4

"My Dream Is to Be Able to Give Something Back to My Country and My People"

Luz Latus

"I Am a City Girl"

I was born in 1934 in Manila. I know a lot of people who would not admit to their ages but I do. I will be sixty this year [1994], and I am proud of it. I am a city girl, and I am a Tagalog by birth. My ancestors are all Tagalog. They are all from Manila and the surrounding areas.

My mother was a housewife and an embroidery designer. In our town, Santa Ana, the only industry that was there was an embroidery industry. It was huge. They produced baby dresses with all these intricate designs. All of the women in our family were employed there. My grandmother worked there first, and then she passed it down to her four daughters.

My father was a merchant and a landowner. He owned land in Cavite and had a *copra* [dried coconut] business. Before that, he worked under the Manila Health Department as a market inspector. The *copra* business gave my dad extra income to send us to school. We were not rich, but we were not poor either.

There were ten children in our family, but two died in infancy. Out of the eight that were left, five were girls, and three were boys. All of the girls came to the United States at different times. I was the first to come through an exchange-visitor program for nurses. My other sisters came as nurses and accountants. All three boys stayed in the Philippines with their families and our parents.

During my childhood, everything was within walking distance in our town. The church was there, the kindergarten, the elementary school. Everything was conveniently located. Everything happened in that little community. We all knew who our neighbors were.

At that time, Manila was not Americanized yet; it had a lot more Spanish influence. You could see the Spanish influence in the church designs, the buildings, as well as the homes of the very well-to-do along the famous Pasig River. Also the clothing, the foods—a lot of recipes from Spain—the language, and most of their family names were Spanish names. My father had Spanish blood in him, and his name was Martinez. Catholicism was very important. There were several Friars Seminaries in our town, and our lives seemed to revolve around church activities.

Manila is a melting pot. Everybody in the Philippines wants to go there to study because it has the best universities, such as the University of Santo Tomas, the University of the East, and the University of the Philippines. So we had people from different regions living there.

As I got past my elementary school, I became more aware of regional differences because some of my classmates were from Ilocos or Cebu or Mindanao, and they spoke different dialects. Sometimes I could understand them; sometimes I could not. I spoke only Tagalog, the national language. Most of our help—I would not call them "maids"—came from the provinces. These people came to Manila because they needed jobs or because they wanted their children to be educated in Manila.

Becoming a Nurse

My high school, Araullo High School, was about five miles from my house, so I had to take a jeepney there. This high school sat across the street from a nursing students' dormitory. One day my best friend said to me, "What are we going to do when we graduate?" I replied, "You know what? I've always watched nurses—their caps, their uniforms. They always look so clean. So I am going into nursing." I also was influenced by my youngest aunt, who was a nurse. She was one of the pioneers at the Chinese General Hospital in the Philippines. She was my role model, and I wanted to be like her.

At that time, in the 1950s, nursing was not considered prestigious. When I told my father that I wanted to become a nurse, he said, "Why can't you be a teacher? Why can't you get another profession where you don't have to be the servant of the country?" As a nurse, you are the one who takes care of the patients: you give them a sponge bath, a bedpan. My father did not want his daughter to just be serving bedpans to sick people. He would have liked to see me become a teacher, a doctor, or a lawyer, but he did not suppress my desire to become a nurse.

In 1954, my best friend and I were accepted into the prenursing program at the University of the Philippines [UP]. We had to commute a long way

Luz Latus (left), then president of the University of the Philippines Nursing Alumni Association of California, presenting an award to a fellow member, Anaheim, 1992

from our home to UP. We would leave early in the morning, take the bus there, and come home when it was almost dark. Depending on the traffic, the trip would take from two to three hours each day. It was hard on us, but we finished the program.

After one year, we enrolled in the Philippine General Hospital School of Nursing, which is the training hospital for the University of the Philippines. If you are in medicine, you have to go there for your hands-on training. For three years, we studied and had nursing duties. Sometimes, I had one whole month of night duty, from eleven to seven, then I had to attend classes the following day. It was quite a sacrifice. It was not easy, but we also had so much fun. All of us lived in the dormitory for nursing students for the whole three years. We had dances, outings, talent shows, so many different programs. Those fun times made up for the hard work that we had to do. I graduated from the School of Nursing in 1958.

After graduation, I landed a job right away as a public health nurse instructor for the Manila Health Department. My father helped me to get that job because he used to work there. I loved that job because I loved teaching. Soon after, I decided to get a bachelor's degree in public health. I went to school at night, to the Philippine Women's University College of Nursing. Since I was already working in public health, the school gave me some credit toward my course work. So it only took me one year to get my B.S. degree in public health nursing. I graduated in 1959.

An Exchange Student in the United States

After getting my public health degree, I decided to go to the United States, because it seemed like everybody, all my friends and even the teachers in the school, wanted to come here. We were always having farewell parties for people who were leaving for the United States. Now that I think about it, that was a brain drain from our country. Everybody was leaving, especially the health care people. They are not only coming to the United States; they are going all over the world. If they ask me, "What is your advice to the people in the Philippines?," I would advise them to stay home and take care of our own people. But that is hard to do. The reality is that people in the Philippines need jobs and money, and that is why they continue to leave.

I wanted to experience life in America, but I did not intend to stay permanently. At that time, U.S. hospitals were recruiting nurses in the Philippines, so a whole group of us decided to go ahead and apply. We all got accepted! We came to the United States as exchange students for additional training.

Another Filipina nurse and I were sent to John Sealy Hospital in Galveston, Texas. Can you imagine that? From the Philippines, I went straight to Texas. The only information I had about Texas was from the movies and from an American patient at the Veterans Hospital where my sister worked. He was a Texan and gave me a little orientation about the state.

When I first got to Galveston, I was shocked because not all the Texans were tall. Not all of them wore cowboy boots or cowboy hats, and they were not all riding horses. There were no horses there! It was not at all like how it was in the John Wayne movies. What impressed me was how kind the people there were. But it was hard to communicate with them, because we had accents and so did they! We eventually got used to it. Later on, other nurses from the Philippines joined us at this hospital. We all worked together, and we formed a tight-knit group.

In 1963, after one year in Texas, I moved on to Chicago. There was a large group of Filipina nurses in Chicago before I got there. Beside the other

Filipina nurses, I befriended all kinds of people, from the pastor of our church to all the diverse people of the world—English, Lithuanian, Haitian, Jewish, you name it. We were always being invited to birthday parties, and I learned so much about the different cultures. It was a very enriching experience.

I worked at two hospitals in Chicago for another two years, learning more about medical surgical nursing. I was trained in coronary care. My specialty was taking care of the heart. During those times, having a specialty was good. But now the trend is caring for the *whole* patient. You don't just take care of someone's heart and forget about his teeth, his eyes, his lungs.

Getting Married and Moving to San Diego

I never returned to the Philippines because I married my husband Bernard. He was an American in the U.S. Navy, and I had met him seven years earlier in the Philippines. During my first year as a nursing student, Bernard's ship had just docked in Manila. Because the sailors were new to the Philippines, they wanted someone to show them around and tell them about the country. So all the nursing schools were invited to participate, and the nursing students were asked to be the sailors' hostesses. All of us were very excited, because we seldom were allowed to leave our dormitory.

We were picked up by these big buses and driven to Manila Hotel, the biggest hotel in the city. All these well-dressed and clean-shaven Navy sailors were there. There was entertainment—folk dances and all kinds of floor shows put on by the USO. That was where I met Bernard.

After that, we went our separate ways. Sometimes, he would write. Sometimes, I would write. Sometimes, we would forget. But his mother kept on writing to me. She knew of me because her son would talk to her about me. But I really was not interested in a serious relationship. In 1963, when I was in Chicago, Bernard tried to get in touch with me again to let me know that his parents had passed away. I was getting ready to go back home at that time, and he asked me not to leave. He wanted me to come to San Diego to meet him.

It just so happened that I had a friend in San Diego that I wanted to visit before I went home. One day this friend and I went to get a blood test. It turned out that the doctor we went to was the co-owner of Doctors' Hospital [now Sharp-Cabrillo Hospital]. When I told him that I was an RN, he offered me a job right away at the hospital. So I decided to stay in San Diego for a while. I had to live close to Point Loma, because that is where the hospital is.

Bernard came to visit me at my friend's house. Very soon after that, he gave me a ring and took me to meet his relatives in Pasadena. We got married in 1964, when I was thirty years old. We have stayed in San Diego ever since. I would not want to live anywhere else.

My husband got out of the Navy because he did not want to be away from home too much. At first, he worked at Doctors' Hospital as an assistant engineer. After that, he worked for the Department of Defense as a naval training specialist and an audiovisual equipment specialist. He retired last July [1993] after thirty years there. So he is very aware of the military community because he worked for them. Many of our friends are other Navy families.

I worked at Doctors' Hospital for five years, from 1964 to 1969, specializing in coronary care. At that time, not many Filipina nurses worked there. I was alone with all the white nurses. But that was okay. I didn't feel uneasy with that. They were like my family, very nice to me and my husband—my three children were born at that hospital. In 1969, my last child died, so I left Doctors' Hospital and did not work for a year.

When I decided to go back to work, my younger sister was a supervisor at the Casa Blanca Convalescent Hospital—Genesee Mental Health, so she asked me if I wanted to work there. I told her I would like only a day job; I did not want rotating shifts or anything. I worked there for a year and a half, and I gained experience with geriatrics, which is useful because everybody is going to get old some day.

In 1972, when the Veterans Administration [VA] Medical Center opened in La Jolla, I applied for a job there. During the interview, they asked me where I would like to work. I told them my specialty is public health nursing. They said, "We have a position for you. We are going to open the ambulatory care department, and we would like a public health nurse there." So I got hired right away. There were no problems. I was a U.S. citizen, and I had graduated from an NLN [National League of Nurses] accredited school. I have worked at the VA ever since.

I developed the first "nurse-run" clinic in the ambulatory care department at the VA. Right now, I am in charge of the anticoagulation clinic and manage four other clinics. I also teach a class for all inpatients and outpatients in the facility who are on short-term and chronic anticoagulation therapy. It is a lot of hard work, but it pays well.

Organizing Filipina and Other Asian Nurses in San Diego

I think the job situation has gotten worse for Filipina nurses today. Because so many want to come to the United States, they often got exploited by the recruiting businesses. Once they are recruited here, instead of working as a professional nurse [RN], they become a nurse's aide, or a licensed vocational nurse [LVN]. That is not right. Some even end up in nursing homes doing menial tasks.

Our organization, the San Diego Chapter of the Philippine Nurses Association of America, investigated a couple of local recruiting businesses because we were told that they were exploiting some of the nurses. I think the situation might be a little better now because we hear the recruits are encouraged to attend refresher courses and preparation seminars for the board. As a professional organization, we would like to protect our profession and our nurses. That is why when the nurses run into problems, we tell them to contact us right away. We have received complaints from nurses being denied promotion, being told not to speak Tagalog at work, or being physically abused by other co-workers.

Our organization is very strong. Right now, we have twenty-four or twenty-five chapters all over the United States. California has the most active and the largest number of chapters. Just the other day, I received a phone call from a nurse who wanted to start a chapter in Brawley, [a town next to] El Centro. I told her to go ahead. In the San Diego chapter, we have more than three hundred paid members. The smallest chapter that I know of is Fresno, with seventy-five to a hundred members.

When I first came to San Diego in 1964, there was no Filipina nurses association. The organizations that existed were mostly Navy-related or military-related, like the Filipino American Veterans Association. There also was a Filipino American Women's Club, so I joined it because all my friends were members. I am the type of person who wants to be involved. I don't want to stay in the corner and just sit there and listen. I want to be active.

In 1974, a group of us nurses decided to organize the Filipino Nurses Association. We had our first meeting in the Paradise Valley Hospital basement, and we elected our first president there. There were about seven or eight of us at this first meeting, but we grew and grew. I believe the fastest growth was during the 1980s.

In 1990, Carmen Galang, another Filipina nurse, and I founded the Asian American Nurses Association of California [AANAC]. Both of us have served as presidents and advisers to the Filipino Nurses Association. We wanted to move on. We looked around and saw that Filipinos were not the only Asian nurses in San Diego. So we decided to form an association that would include the Japanese, the Koreans, and other Asians. Initially, we were accused of trying to divide the Filipino nurses, but that was not our purpose. Our purpose was to incorporate the other Asian groups, because it is important to network with them. There is something unique about each of the Asian groups, and yet we could come together and share what we have in common—our Asian culture. Currently, the organization has approximately seventy-three active members. I served as an AANAC president for two years, and now I serve as an adviser.

In May of 1993, I was nominated to be the nurse of the year by the Hospital Council of San Diego and Imperial Counties. I also received a letter from the Sigma Theta Tau International Honor Society of Nursing, informing me that I was the recipient of the excellence in clinical practice award. Then my alumni association from UP nominated me for the nurse of the year award for the Philippines. So I had a very busy year.

In 1993, I was in charge of coordinating the reunion for our alumni association, the UP Nursing Alumni Association International. Our class celebrated our thirty-fifth anniversary, but nurses from other classes also attended. The climax was a dinner-dance at the Anaheim Hilton. About five hundred people go to the reunion every year. They come from all over, from Canada, the Philippines, the Middle East. More than half of my classmates live and work outside of the Philippines. Not many stayed in the Philippines. If you take a look at our roster, you would see that we are scattered all over the world.

My high school fortieth reunion was also in 1993, and the celebration was held in the Philippines. There are fifty-six of us in our class, and we also are scattered all over the world. I was unable to attend the reunion, but a classmate of mine who went brought back pictures and souvenirs for the five of us who live here in San Diego. We had a picnic last week at Shelter Island with all the families.

Regionalism Among Filipinos in San Diego

When Filipinos immigrate here, they try to maintain regional or provincial ties by setting up their own organizations. The Cavitenos, the Pampanguenos, the Ilocanos—they all do it. Now they even have hometown organizations. For example, the Legaspians have their own group, and the Nabuans have their own group—and yet, they both are from Bicol.

I do not belong to any regional organization. The people from Manila never formed our own group, even though there are quite a few of us here from my hometown Santa Ana. Maybe city people are not as regionalistic as people from the provinces. In 1979, a group of us founded the Nayong Pilipino Association. We do not segregate. Nobody really cares if I am an Ilocano or I am a Pampangueno or I am a Bicolano. That's why we called it Nayong Pilipino because it is *"nayon"*—all of us! We also have minority members who are the American husbands of Filipinas, like my husband.

The members of Nayong Pilipino are like brothers and sisters. We get along very well. We help each other. We have social events. When our children reach the age of sixteen up to eighteen, we have a cotillion ball where we present them as debutantes. The teenagers are proud to be included in this affair, because it is really in their honor to be presented to society. They get to dress up: tuxedos for the guys, and long white gowns for the girls. It is a chance for them to be recognized by their parents, siblings, relatives, friends, and the community. All my children went through that. Most of the parents tend to join the organization when their children reach that age group, because they want them to be presented to the community. We also have a picnic, a Mother's Day, and a Father's Day celebration every year.

It is a family-oriented association. When we have our yearly picnic, the kids come, eat, and then leave. Later that day, they come back and eat some more. We bring lots of food and spend the whole day together. We have games and prizes for the children.

Culture, Identity, and Child-Rearing

From Point Loma, we moved to North County six years ago. Our house is about three miles from the ocean. When I passed through this area in the 1960s on my way to Washington State, I fell in love with it. I told myself that if I stayed in the United States, I would like to live here. And my husband did the same. He said that he has always liked this area of San Diego. When we first saw this house, we got scared that we wouldn't be able to afford it. But we decided to be brave, to take a chance. There are not many Filipinos in our neighborhood. We don't really know our neighbors because we all work. You know how it is, you have this big house, and nobody stays in it.

I have lived in the United States now longer than I have lived in my country. I am an American citizen, and I am very much interested and informed about what goes on in this country.

But I think as you get older, your ethnicity becomes more important to you. In my nursing practice and in my dealing with people, I still go back to my roots. What I learned from home in the Philippines is still what I do here. I will never lose my Filipino traits. I still believe in my heritage, my religious beliefs, my traditions, and my family values.

We have three children, two girls and one boy. Our older daughter, Lisa, graduated from San Diego State University and now owns her own business. Our son Victor is in the U.S. Army. He married a German girl and lives in Germany. Laura, the youngest one, is still in college on and off.

My children do not always agree with my ways of doing things. When they were small, we used to take all three of them to church every single Sunday. They were not allowed to miss church. And they all went to Catholic school. We put all our money into their education. But when they got older, they did not want to go to church any more on a regular basis. So now, it is just my husband and I going to church together.

I want my children to have respect for the elders. I feel bad when they talk back to me. I guess in the Philippines we were raised not to talk back to our parents. And I want them to value education, to be ambitious, to work hard, and to save. Our children have never experienced hard times, so it is hard to teach them about some of these values. I am frugal, because I grew up in the Philippines and I saw so much poverty there. My older daughter is the only one of my three children who has visited the Philippines, so she has seen the poverty. I feel that Americans waste too many things. They waste water, utilities, food. Sometimes when I see my children throwing food away, I tell them, "Remember those hungry kids in the Philippines."

I used to compare my children to other Filipino children and said, "So-and-so knows this and that about Filipino culture." But I do not do that any more, because I cannot compare my children to a pure Filipino person because they are only half-Filipino. In fact, they are a mixed lot, because I have Chinese and Filipino blood, and my husband has Irish and Italian in him. So what does that make my children? I think they mostly refer to themselves as American. They are very Americanized in their habits and their tastes. They are very independent, opinionated. They love sports, and they are very conscious of how they look and dress. They like pizza; I don't.

Sometimes, I wonder what could have happened if I'd married a Filipino? Then maybe all my kids would be lawyers and doctors and nurses. My children are not that ambitious. My daughters don't even want to become nurses!

I always tell my children that Filipinos are very ambitious people. In the Philippines, we finish our education first before we think of the other stuff like dating. When I was in nursing school, we were not even allowed to have visitors. The only ones who could get us out of the dormitory were our parents. Otherwise, we did not leave the dormitory. I remember that when one of our classmates got pregnant, she was kicked out of school. So she never finished her education. But in the United States, it is just the opposite. People date liberally, and they take their time with their education. They are not as focused.

I try to see to it that my children know something about my country. Because I am so involved in the Filipino community, they know about the folk dances, the music, the culture. They also know some of the history. I tell them about our national heroes, about the good things that come from there, like the different kinds of food, the arts, and crafts. I try to inform them so that they are not ignorant about my country. Both my husband and my children eat Filipino food, even the most unusual dishes like dried fish. Whatever I cook, they eat. All three of my children understand Tagalog, but they don't really speak it. I did not purposefully teach them the language, but they picked it up when they overheard me talk to my friends and my family.

I now have a grandson and a granddaughter. They are even further removed, because my children did not marry Filipinos. When you look at them, you cannot even tell that they have Filipino blood in them. But that is okay. Maybe it is an improvement of the race. But they know that they are Filipino. They know that their grandmother is Filipino. I am not sure what will happen if we continue to marry outside of our race. But there are still so many Filipinos in this world that I don't think we would ever be removed completely.

Ties to the Philippines

If things improve in the Philippines, my husband and I would like to return there to live. We are not interested in making money, in getting rich. What we'd like to do is to help the country and the people. I want to go back to my hometown and volunteer in the health centers to promote the health of the people there. I'd also like to offer my services to my school of nursing, the hospital where I graduated, to serve in any capacity that they can use me. My dream is to be able to give something back to my country and my people.

When I visit the Philippines now, I notice a lot of changes. One thing I notice right away is that the people who used to live there are not there any more. And it seems like life is harder there now than it was when I left. When I left in 1960, there were only twenty-three million people in the Philippines. Now it has more than doubled. When I go back home, I am the same person. I am a Filipina. I go to the market. I sit there and order my food. I talk to the people in the street. I walk to the church. I walk to the market. I walk everywhere.

Although I have lost a lot of my family, the Philippines is still home to me. I also consider the United States home, but if you ask me, it is more my children's country than it is mine.

Chapter 5

"My Experience Is Atypical"

Paz Jensen

A Family of Scholars

I was born in Manila in 1940, but I grew up and I had my elementary school and high school days in Davao, Mindanao. We went to Mindanao right after the war, because my mother felt that it was a good place to open up a private school. We had a private school and a bookstore. There were some stockholders, but it was mainly family owned. It was our money that was used to open up the school. So I was always in an environment of education, helping with the school.

Both my father and mother were among the first American-educated scholars. In fact, my mother was one of the students of the Thomasites.★ She was one of the favorite students then. Because of that, she had many American books, and I read every book. I learned about *Nancy Drew* and *Little Women* and all that when I was in elementary school. When I first came to the United States, I was surprised that I knew more about U.S. history and U.S. literature than most average Americans.

We were raised in a family that had books. English was our first language. It is typical of families in the Philippine, especially in Manila, that from the time they are little kids, they have been speaking English with their parents. Because the cultural thought is to get the child prepared for going to the United States, he has to be able to speak English.

In the Philippines, one of the ways to advance is not to be a businessperson but to be an educated person. We believe that with a college degree, you can go anyplace, so education is a priority. I think almost every family in the Philippines has two major goals. Number one is to get a college de-

---

★The Thomasites were the first group of Americans who came to teach in the Philippines. They arrived in 1901 on the S.S. *Thomas,* hence the name.

93

gree, to have a profession. And number two is to play music. You can see families all over the Philippines—they would be poor, they would have a *nipa* hut, with the grass-thatched roof, but they would have a piano or another musical instrument.

My dad started out as a mathematics high school teacher at a Jesuit school. But when one of his friends became a senator, he got a job working as a budget preparer in the budget office of the Philippine Senate. So we were separated; my mother and the children were in Mindanao, and my father was in Manila.

My dad died when he was only fifty-two. The reason that he died early was because he was a gourmet cook. One day, when he was visiting us in Mindanao, he asked our houseboy to catch a frog that he saw, not realizing it was an orange and brown variety—the most poisonous. So within an hour after he ate that frog, he was dead.

Women Role Models

My family was matriarchal because my father was always away from home. But my mother's family and my grandmother's family were also matriarchal, because during the time that my great-grandmother was raising her family, there was a big epidemic and almost every man died in the town where they lived. So my great-grandmother raised the family by herself. And so, that tradition was carried on and on.

But even on my father's side, it was very matriarchal, which I believe is the case in the Philippines. For example, while her husband was president of the Philippines [1935–1944], Mrs. Manuel Luis Quezon was head of the Philippine Red Cross, and she ran the health and welfare system of the Philippines. So when I came to the States and I heard people talk about Susan B. Anthony and the fight for women's rights, it was a surprise to me that it was a big thing to have to fight for women's right to vote, because it was assumed that it was there in the Philippines.

I think that's what makes us different from the typical Asian. Our society is not a patriarchal society. It has always been women dominated. You notice that there's a lot more Filipino women in politics and in philanthropy in the Philippines. More women actually than men.

When I was growing up in the Philippines, women were already represented in almost all high positions. We read about them. In fact, my mother co-authored a fourth-grade reader, and in this book, most of the contents were women role models: Eva Kalaw Katigbak [a Philippine Senator], and Mrs. Quezon, and so on. There were so many role models of women in politics, in philanthropy, and in society. It was nothing new.

I think that was why it was easy for Corazon Aquino to go from being a housewife directly to being a president, because even when she was still the

*Paz Jensen on the steps of "Cheers" in Boston during a
break from the annual meeting of Community College
Mathematics Teachers, 1993*

wife of Benigno Aquino,★ she was running the whole household. She ran the farm while Benigno Aquino was running for mayor and for governor.

Coming to the United States: The Peace Corps and the Ford Foundation

Right after high school, I went to the University of the Philippines [UP] on a scholarship. Davao is one of the developed cities in the Philippines, so there was not much difference for me going to Manila. The standards of living were about the same. I didn't feel like I was lost or that I was a country girl. While I was at UP, I was so involved with student government. I was an honor student, and I was valedictorian and number one in every class. I studied mathematics and physics and also education.

At that time, this was around 1965, the Peace Corps was just beginning to come into the Philippines. They used UP as one of the centers for training. Because of my interest in education and because I'd been in Mindanao and traveled all over, the people at UP asked me to be involved in training the Peace Corps volunteers before they went to their sites. I was twenty-five years old.

My main job was to train the Peace Corps volunteers how to teach mathematics in the elementary schools. I went around and visited every island in the Philippines where the Peace Corps volunteers were. I did that for about two summers. Then the Peace Corps asked me to come to the United States to train the volunteers before they went overseas. So they sent me to the United States, where I got involved with training Peace Corps people who went to Fiji, Samoa, Indonesia, and the Philippines.

At the same time, I was working with the Ford Foundation writing elementary math textbooks for Filipino children. The Ford Foundation also wanted to send me to the United States to get my master's degree. So, both of them together, the Peace Corps work and the Ford Foundation scholarship, started my being here in this country. Prior to that time, I had no intention of coming to the United States. Everything just happened.

When I returned to the Philippines, the Peace Corps called me again, and I got sent to Hawaii and then to San Jose State University and to Stanford University in California to do more training. My job was mathematics coordinator. I had a house and a car. I had the use of a four-seater plane that flew me from island to island in Hawaii to supervise the Peace Corps volunteers in their practice teaching. I lived an exciting life.

★Benigno Aquino, Marcos' chief political rival, was assassinated in 1983.

Getting Married and Moving to San Diego

In Hawaii, I met the person who became my husband. (We are now divorced.) He was a Peace Corps volunteer, but he quit the training and went
back to his old job in San Diego. His family is from San Diego. I followed
him to San Diego when my Peace Corps contract ended. This was in 1967.

He [my former husband] is not Filipino. His background is Norwegian,
Danish, and German. I think that his family was fairly happy about the marriage, because I was a professional. But at first we had a bit of friction with
his grandmother. When he said goodbye to go to Peace Corps training, his
grandmother told him not to bring back "those dirty Filipinos." She always
thought that Filipinos were second-class, that they were dirty, and that they
were always fighting. So she warned my husband about them. But I warmed
her heart by doing some handicrafts for her and cooking for them. Whenever we had parties, I would bring Filipino dishes, and so that changed her
outlook and attitude about Filipinos.

We got married in San Diego, and then I just sent the announcement to
my family. If my [former] husband had to go through the kind of scrutiny
that my mother would put every suitor of my sisters and myself through, he
would not have passed. My family would not have approved of him. After I
got married, I didn't go back to the Philippines. It was too expensive, and I
was on my own. During our whole marriage, my [former] husband never
visited the Philippines.

I did not face any difficulty when I first came here. That's why I say my
experience is atypical. It is not the same as that of other Filipinos who come
over here directly from the islands.

When I first came to San Diego, I lived in La Mesa because I was supposed to be teaching immediately at San Diego State University. I was lucky,
because I had a job waiting for me. What happened was the chair of the
math department at San Diego State at the time was a woman that I had met
in Hawaii during the National Math Conference in Honolulu. When I told
her that my fiance was from San Diego, she said, "Come on over. I have a
job for you in San Diego." It happened to be that one of the members of
her faculty was pregnant. Because my husband was finishing up his bachelor's degree at the same university, I did not want to have such a big disparity
between the two of us, so I did not take the job.

In the meantime, there was a job at Grossmont Community College. So
I went and put in my application. It was my first job that I would have to
be interviewed for. But it turned out that there was only one other person
who wanted that same job, and he was the chairman of the mathematics
department at Grossmont High School. He gave me a call at my house, and
he said, "I hear we're the only two competing for this position. I'll tell you
what, my high school principal will release me only if I find someone to

replace me. And I want to go to college teaching. So can we make a trade?"
So he got the college position, and I was in the high school position. And I
didn't even have to interview!

I taught math at Grossmont High School from 1969 until I moved over
here to Cuyamaca Community College in 1985. After four years of teaching
mathematics, I became both teacher and chairman for the rest of the time.
And then, in the evening, I was teaching math as a part-time instructor at
Grossmont College. So when Cuyamaca College had a vacancy for a full-
time position, I applied and got the job here. And I have been here since
1985. So, from 1969 to 1985, it was Grossmont High School, and then here
at Cuyamaca College. And that was it.

Helping the Aquino Administration

Immediately after Ferdinand Marcos left the Philippines in 1986, my sister,
who was then one of the assistants of Vice President Salvador Laurel, asked
me to come home to help Corazon Aquino. I was always interested in helping the Philippines because I am a Filipino. Also, Corazon Aquino's husband
was my father's cousin. So we really have strong connections. And then her
son is married to a former student of mine, who also contacted me for advice
and help. And her physician was my classmate in college. You see, I had
such contact with the Aquino administration, and so I was very interested
and very much involved.

I took a year's leave of absence and went back to the Philippines to help
the Aquino government. But it was very difficult because she did not have
policies. I am not surprised that she did not progress the way she could have,
because she did not have a long-range plan.

I had many meetings with the World Bank and International Monetary
Fund to try to get money for the Philippines, to get business investments. I
got involved in the shoe, shrimp, and fish business. But everything that I
tried to do failed. The small-business Filipinos just do not have the foresight
and effort to be entrepreneurs. They want immediate harvests, and they are
not willing to go on a long-range plan. Even now, I am still trying to help.
I have a shrimp business, and am trying to get the shoes of the Philippines
sold here.

The Filipinos are excellent craftsmen. They are very artistic, bright and
good in handicrafts. But because the government will declare a holiday just
almost any day, the people will miss work the day before and the day after
the holiday. The workers cannot be relied upon to meet deadlines. So the
U.S. investors that I contacted to do business with the Filipinos just gave up.
The Philippines could have had a good opportunity at that time. But Aquino
herself lost opportunities for economic growth by declaring religious holiday

after religious holiday, and there was no discipline for work. I feel very sad about this.

I had a lot of contacts with businessmen and educators. For example, Harcourt Brace Jovanovich was ready to help with books and textbooks, but the government would not repeal the plagiarism law that Marcos brought into effect. See, Marcos wrote a bill where any Filipino company, by submitting an application through the public library, could copy copyrighted materials that come from the United States. Marcos gave them protection. So I worked toward getting this bill repealed. I went to every senator and to the president and the vice president themselves. But they would not or they were not strong enough to repeal it. So what happened? There was so much plagiarism going on that the U.S. businesses did not want to get involved.

I believe Korea was able to have a strong hold on copyright products now, so that people there who copy Nike, copy books, et cetera, are now being punished. But they wouldn't change the copyright law in the Philippines. It is pretty sad.

A lot can be done to help the Philippines right now. They need electronic generators, roads, and telecommunications. Those three. Once those three are in place, they will need people who would be dedicated enough, who would forget about the "quick harvest" idea, and work and plan long just to get the country out of these terrible economic situations.

When I took a year's leave of absence to help the Philippines, I think that was the cause of my divorce. Because I was away for a whole year, my husband said, "You can't be there and be a wife." Which meant I had to choose between him and my country. And at that time, I was so idealistic about helping my country that I chose the Philippines. So we had a friendly divorce. It's sad that it happened, especially because my efforts in the Philippines failed.

Another reason why we were divorced was because my husband never saw me as an individual or as a person. He saw me as a representative of the Filipino culture. And therefore, I must behave as such. Everything I do, if I do it well, it's for the good of the Filipino race. And if I do it awful, I am such a bad representative of the Filipino culture. So he never saw me as me, as a person. I was hurt when I found out about it. I was really hurt. But this works the same way in every other culture. Even among Caucasians. How many of their husbands marry them but don't really know them as a person? That's the same thing.

The Filipino American Community in San Diego

I am not that connected to the Filipino American community. When I first came to San Diego, I heard about the existence of the Navy base, and I was told that lots of Filipinos lived in National City and that there was a growing

Filipino community in Mira Mesa. But we decided to live in La Mesa because it was closest to where I was going to teach. Most of the people here
are businessmen. There are about twelve chambers of commerce in the area.
So it is a middle to upper middle class area. La Mesa is far from where the
main Filipino community is. If I miss Filipino food, I would have to drive
twenty miles to get it.

I have two children, a boy and a girl, who are now twenty-two and
twenty-three years old. Both of them are seniors at San Diego State. I never
really got involved in the Filipino community, except when my children
were growing up and I wanted them to learn about the Filipino culture. So
I joined the board of directors of Samahan Philippine Dance Company. I
was pretty active with the company. I used to give fund-raising dinners at
my house, and I was involved in other fund raisers so that the dancers could
buy new costumes and other things. But that was way back then, from 1978
to 1985. I am also a member of the Filipino American Educators Group, but
I am not a very active member. Other than that, I really have had not much
involvement with Filipinos, other than once in a while when I get invited
to some parties and things like that.

I think Filipinos in the Philippines and here in San Diego lack unity. That
was developed from way back in the Spanish period, because the only way
that the Spaniards could keep us as slaves and keep us ignorant was by the
"divide and conquer" tactic. That was the philosophy that they used. They
developed each community to be different from the others. We have different languages. Ilocano is different from Tagalog. Tagalog is different from
Cebuano. The Spaniards made sure that people kept to their languages.

Then when Filipinos come to the United States, there's always these
regionalistic clubs. Cavite Club, Pampango Club, Pangasinan Club. So it
fosters the same kind of regionalism. The language that they speak and the
food that they eat, these are seen as very regionalistic. So it won't go away.
I don't think it would change. However, people from Manila and the main
cities like Davao and Cebu and Baguio, they are more cosmopolitan.

Regionalism is beginning to be less and less among the young people. So
I see that there is hope. The young people speak a common language, English. And the thing that binds them is the fact that they have ancestors who
are from the Philippines.

But among the older folks, I don't think regionalism will go away. That's
their only hold on home, so I really don't blame them, because that's their
only way to get involved. I myself don't join these organizations because
number one, it's so expensive, these dances and the balls. I mean, I added
them up one time, and it just ran into hundreds of dollars. And clothes too.
I also don't join because this is the way these people show off, you know,
their clothes and their finer things. And I am not for that. It's all a very
materialistic sense of prestige, and that is not for me. And I don't miss it.

But I am not totally out of touch with them. Through telephone contacts, I have friends that I call regularly, and I can go to any parties and enjoy them. For a long time, my best friend was my husband. Then my second best friend was my business partner, and he married somebody else. So right now, I would say my best friends are the people I work with here at the college. There also are a few Filipino friends in the area that I can call on, and they would lay their lives down for me.

I still go to a Filipino hairdresser in National City. And I do it for a purpose. Number one, only a Filipino can cut my hair the way I want it done. Plus ever since I was going to college at UP, I'd purposely go to a Filipino hairdresser and a Filipino store. And stay there. I just listen. I like doing that. I just listen to gossip without being involved, without being in the middle. I am an outsider.

I also read the Filipino newspapers to find out what is going on in the community. When there are conferences that involve Filipinos, I go. I just don't like to be an active person. I don't like the social life. Plus I am very busy. Right now, at work, we are trying to incorporate high technology into our instructional programs. I wouldn't be able to do that unless I spend the time experimenting with them. So I spend my free hours doing those.

Here at Cuyamaca College, we have a Now Program where we encourage high school students to think about postgraduate and postsecondary education by actually taking a college course after a full high school day. I am coordinating that program.

Some high schools send a lot of Filipinos to this program. So I know what goes on in these communities because I have to know the students' background and their family background. I find out if they are in gangs or any type of club. So, I am on top of the community tempo, or temperature, however you may put it. I also have to know all these things for the Mexican Americans, the blacks, and the Vietnamese. So, because of my involvement with this project, I am very aware of the different minority communities.

Discrimination in the United States

Although I have had a good life here, I feel that discrimination does exist. For me personally, the only time I experienced it was in 1969, when I was traveling with an American family across the country. We rented an RV and we were driving from California to New York. I don't think this would happen now, but when we were in South Dakota, we went into a roadside cafe and we wanted to have breakfast. They refused to serve us breakfast because I was with this family.

The second time that I experienced discrimination was also in 1969, when my husband and I went to buy our first house in a new development here in La Mesa. We'd talked on the telephone first, and over the phone the salesman was all pitches and et cetera, et cetera. When we got there to look at the houses, he just said, "No, there are no houses for you." He said that as soon as he saw me. I still remember this man who just said, "No, there is no house for sale." Other than that, I have not felt any discrimination for being an Asian or a woman or whatever.

But I think things are much different now. In fact now, at the college, we are pushing diversity hiring. Let me put it this way, my standards will never change. It will always be who is best qualified for the job, whether the person is black, brown, male, female, or whatever. I would hire the one who is best qualified. And if I interview a Filipino and he is not qualified, I will not hire him. So even though there is this push for minority hiring, I get telephone calls from qualified minorities who say, "I just want to make certain that I am not being hired because I am a minority."

For the Asians, here is where they have difficulty getting a job: their accent. The oral expression is where they lack expertise. If they have to teach in the high school, the students are often not tolerant of their accent. And you can tell that. But I have always been lucky because I teach high-level math classes, so my accent does not matter. But if you go down to the lower remedial classes, and you are a minority teacher, a Filipino, Chinese, Japanese, Iranian, or whatever, you will often have a difficult time.

I think the minority teachers suffer the most in the high schools. In the elementary schools, the students are still children. They think the accent is cute, and they have the patience for that. In the high school, the students give the minority teachers the worst times. They make fun of their accent. Many are not tolerant or understanding.

I have been approached by a lot of former teachers in the Philippines to give them a recommendation to teach in the public schools here. But most of them don't have or they don't know the discipline that it takes to be in an American classroom. In an Asian classroom, such as a Philippine class-room, the children obey. The students sit and put their hands forward on the desks and listen. Next to God, you know, it is the teacher.

But here in the United States, it is not that way. And to make that teacher come over here to teach can be really difficult, since the American kids can get out of hand sometimes. You really need to have a good amount of class-room discipline.

Again, my case was different because of my experience working at my mother's school. I was trained to be a school administrator back home. So I had a very different attitude. I was raised with a management background ever since I was in high school. So it was quite easy for me. Right now, I am an instructor at Cuyamaca College, and my position is also as administrator of the math, science, engineering, and liberal arts division. I do not find it difficult to be an administrator, since I had the training.

Culture, Identity, and Child-Rearing

Even though I have lived in the States a long time, I am still very Filipino. My way of eating has not changed. I still have rice in the morning. I love rice, fish, vegetables, and fruits. And I think I have retrained most of the people that lived with me and had been involved with me to like fruits and vegetables.

Most of my traditions, my way of dressing, I think, is very Filipino. I have not changed. And part of my management method is very Asian. Among my colleagues, when a male is making a mistake, and he is my superior, I can make him see how to do it the right way without making him feel embarrassed.

I think the diplomatic attitude is very cultural, very Asian. I go out of my way to make sure people are comfortable. I don't like confrontations and the like. That's not how I solve conflict and crisis. If there's a pleasant way to do it, I'd rather do it that way.

Also, how I raised my children is very Filipino. But it is less now. For example, when my daughter says she is staying with her boyfriend at their beach house, I have to close my eyes. That's not Filipino, but what can I do? I mean, she's got her own life. She is an adult. And that's what she wants to do.

As I said earlier, I became active in the Samahan Philippine Dance Company for my children, so that they would be involved in the Filipino community. But then they told me point-blank, they didn't want to be involved. They had their own lives, so I didn't want to mess around with that. But now the tendency for them is to go and meet with Filipinos. When they meet Filipinos at parties, they are just so proud to be Filipinos too.

Because there were not too many Filipinos in La Mesa, where my children grew up, they didn't learn how to speak the Filipino language. But now, as adults, they are asking me to teach them the language, so once in a while, at home, I give them lessons, and they are learning it fast enough. In 1985, I took them to the Philippines, and we stayed there for two months, and they learned the language pretty quickly. Both of them are linguists anyway. They speak fluent French, which I do not, and Dutch and Spanish.

I would say that my children, although of mixed heritage, are very happy second-generation Americans. They both are talented in music, fine arts, and writing—but unfortunately, not in math. Both will have earned their college degrees this term, 1994.

Chapter 6

"I Sacrificed My Five-Year College Education to Become a Steward"

Leo Sicat

Childhood Years in the Philippines

I was born in the Philippines in 1942 in the town of Santa Rita in the province of Pampanga. My mother and father were farmers. I remember once, when I was about five or six years old, my dad took me with him to harvest watermelons to be sold the next day at the market. I had so much fun going with him; the sky was bright blue and the moon was full.

I remember my dad as a six-footer gentleman. He was quite good looking, kind, and very soft-spoken. He used to bring me ripe sugar canes from the fields. He died when I was quite young. At that time, I could not understand why he was gone, but as I grew older, I realized that I would not see him again. We did not even have a single photograph of him.

The family was devastated by my father's death. Each day was difficult to get by. With the small property that my father left us, the elder boys tilled the lands so that the younger ones could survive and continue with their schooling. The days seemed much longer when you were trying to make ends meet.

There used to be ten children in our family. But my eldest brother, Edison, died at an early age, and my younger brother Alfred drowned and died when he was in the first grade. At the present time, there are eight of us in the family. I have two brothers and one sister in the United States right now. I sponsored one brother, and the other brother was sponsored by his daughter in Sacramento. My sister came here through marriage to a U.S. Navy man. And the other four are back home.

Life in the U.S. Navy

I grew up for seventeen years in Pampanga. After graduating from high school, I went to Manila to study chemical engineering at the University of Santo Tomas. I went there for five years, and I was about to take the board exam for chemical engineering when the United States Navy came along.

It was a common thing there in the Philippines to join the Navy, partly for adventure but also to make more money and upgrade our standard of living. Many of the Filipinos from Cavite were able to join the U.S. Navy simply because they had very close access. The recruiting office was right there in Cavite City. For the people who live in the provinces, they have to keep sending applications, hoping to be called for an interview.

In our case, we read in the *Manila Times* newspaper that the U.S. Navy was recruiting. So me and my friends wrote a short application letter responding to what was asked in the ad. The Navy did not call us for a year and a half. When they finally called me, I was just about to graduate from college.

It was a very competitive process back then at Sangley Point in Cavite City to be accepted into the U.S. Navy. The day of the exam, there were about 350 people in my group. The processing itself, calling the names of the people and checking their requirements, disqualified many people. By the time we went to the examination room, there were only about eighty of us left. Then we took the exam. Only thirty-five of us passed the written exam. It was a simple exam: arithmetic, fractions, and division, subtraction, and decimal points. At the end of the day, only seven of us made it—out of 350. We were so proud!

In my case, joining the Navy was probably a sacrifice, because I went through a five-year college program already. It was confusing for me to have to choose between being a chemical engineer and being a U.S. Navy man. At that time, I didn't have much idea what the U.S. Navy was all about. It was a fad at that time. Most of my friends had joined the U.S. Navy, and they talked about the good life in the United States. To me, it was exciting, although I was not very fond of the military. I decided to join the Navy in October of 1966.

When we were recruited, we were promised to be only a steward. We told the recruiting officers about our experiences and that we wanted to become a personnel manager, a hospital corpsman, a yeoman, or an ocean mate. But they told us that we were not going anywhere but straight to steward school.

Leo Sicat (far left) leading the Philippine Independence Day parade in Balboa Park, San Diego, 1992

There was no promise of promotions, no promise of increase in pay, no promise of being able to work other than becoming a steward. But at that time, we felt that those things did not matter as long as we could join the U.S. Navy. Perhaps we thought that we could fight for what we wanted once we were already in the United States. So we ignored the contract that bound us into not being able to do other work besides stewardship work. We took that gamble.

In my case, I sacrificed my five-year college education to become a steward in the U.S. Navy. But I have no regrets. Even if I had become a chemical engineer, there was no guarantee that I would have been able to get a stable job in the Philippines or to come to the United States eventually.

From the Philippines, I came directly to Treasure Island in northern California. Then they flew us straight to San Diego. That was October 1966. We had about three months of military training. The training went well for me. I put my heart into it, because I was already there.

We had an international group. We had the anglos, the blacks, the Latinos, the Samoans, and the Filipinos. We had very few Chinese and Japanese there; out of a thousand you might see one or two. We interacted with everyone, although there were some language barriers. Slowly, after a month or so, we were able to adjust, to catch up with the Americans—at least for them to be able to understand us. Once we got adjusted to the weather, and the people, and our ears were able to cope with the language, we were okay. But I was homesick. I missed the folks back home and my friends of many, many years. You know how it is when you leave your homeland. You still love the place where you came from.

After the training, they sent us to steward school—all the Filipinos and the blacks. At that time, there was not a single white guy in our class. At the school, we were taught how to cook and bake, how to set the table, and how to position the silverware, and the glass and the cup. They basically taught us the job of a waitress. Personally, I was so insulted. I was almost a chemical engineer, and I came to the United States just to become a steward.

But I didn't really have any choice. I was here already, so I might as well put my heart into it. Putting modesty aside, I got very good at my job. I became a steward, and very quickly I became a cook. It's an expertise that not very many can achieve. Only the rated people, those who were third-class petty officers, were allowed to cook at that time. I got so interested in cooking that I even mixed the Betty Crocker book with the Navy recipes. I think that is why so many Filipino men can cook. We learned how to cook in the Navy, and we brought it home. The Filipino women are very fortunate because the husband does the cooking. In our household, I do the cooking, and my wife does the washing.

At the beginning, I was content to be a steward probably for the rest of my military life. But after three and a half years, I got bored. If it were not for Admiral Elmo Zumwalt, I would have been a steward for the rest of my Navy career. He was the chief of naval operations at that time. He noticed that the Filipino stewards were very bright. He found out that these guys were not just high school graduates and that they probably went to college. So he opened the doors for the Filipino stewards, allowing us, if we wanted to, to change our specialty. Most of us took the opportunity to change our rating.

I thought of how I could move out of the steward rating. I converted into becoming a commissary man, because the promotion was tight in the steward rating. I took my exam three times in the steward rating for third class, but each time I was unsuccessful. I wanted to advance but I couldn't.

When I changed my rating to commissary man, I made second class. I earned two ratings advancements right away in one year. But I was still a cook.

Later, during our deployment in the western Pacific during the Vietnam years, I thought of changing my rating again. So I looked at the possibility of moving out of the "food industry" and into some other areas where I could practice what I studied back home.

First I chose to become a personnel man, but I was already second class petty officer [E5] at that time. They would not accept me into personnel school because my classmates would be one-stripers [E1 or seaman recruit], and two-stripers [E2 or seaman apprentice], while I was a second class. I was way up there compared to them. But they would accept me if I wanted to become a hospital corpsman. So I put hospital corpsman as my second choice.

In July of 1972, I went to hospital corps school in San Diego for sixteen weeks of training. In my class, there were three Filipinos who were already doctors in the Philippines, and one of them never even made chief or E7 [chief petty officer]. This guy joined the Navy because he wanted to become a military doctor, but the Navy never allowed him to do that. So he remained an enlisted guy. He's got so much hate for the Navy because he lost a lot of time and money.

In corps school, I learned how to become a nurse. I did not like it at first. Actually I was going to back out because I didn't like the smell of the hospital, and I didn't like blood. But then when I was going through the course, my vocabulary and my knowledge changed. As I got into the books I told myself that this was challenging. This was something where I probably could make use of my chemical engineering background.

After I finished basic hospital corps school, I was stationed at Balboa, where I became a supervisor of the admissions office there. It was a very good learning experience. At that time, in 1975, the prisoners of war from Vietnam were just arriving, and we were the ones who treated them.

As a hospital corpsman, I made first class very quickly and got rated [advanced to E4 or third class petty officer] in six and a half years—something that I can be proud of. My other contemporaries, they were still stewardsmen, three stripes [E3], not even rated people. I felt bad for them. Some of them had been in the Navy for ten or fifteen years, and they were still E3s and E4s. In the other ratings, some hard-working Filipinos were advancing so fast that it only took them five to six years to become a first-class petty officer and probably eight or seven years to become a chief petty officer. On the average, it takes eight to ten years to make first-class and ten to fifteen years to make chief.

When I made first-class petty officer, I went through six months of preventive medicine school in Oakland. I earned my associate degree there.

When they allowed Filipinos to change ratings in the early seventies, we were advancing so fast that we became the middle managers. I made chief in less than twelve years. Then I was a chief petty officer for a long, long time in the Navy and no place for advancement. No matter how hard I tried, because of the specialty that I went into, the promotion process was so close-ended. It [the chance for promotion] was from slim to none. I had no place to go. So I had to wait for the proper time to throw in the towel. In 1990, after twenty-four years in the Navy, I retired. I don't have any regrets—only in the beginning.

Right now, I do real estate and insurance. I am a loan officer. I am also busy doing community service.

Marriage and Family

Six months after I joined the Navy, my ship sailed to the Philippines. I kept it a secret, not telling anyone that I was coming home. I wanted to surprise my parents, my friends, and my girlfriend Norma, who is my wife now. So in April 1967, exactly on the day of our town fiesta, I returned home.

At that time, we were constantly going back and forth from the Philippines to Vietnam. So every four weeks, I was in the Philippines. I kept meeting Norma, so we decided we should get married. We got married in July of 1967.

All three of my children were born in the Philippines. I was going back and forth from the Philippines to the U.S. and also to Vietnam for five or six years. But I couldn't take my family with me because I was not yet rated. That's another area where the U.S. Navy deprives you. If you wanted to bring your family, you have to be rated first. If you are not rated in ten years, that is just too bad. That's why I wanted to get rated real quick. I finally was able to bring my family to the United States in 1973. My children still speak Pampangan, even though they grew up in this country.

In the Philippines, my wife was a schoolteacher for six years. When she came over here, I would not let her work until after one year, because the kids were small. That's our custom—you want to take care of the kids. In the Philippines, we had a babysitter. Norma's mom took care of the children. In the United States, we had no childcare.

When all of the children were in school, my wife tried to find a job in the evenings. I told her not to find work, and she just called me up one day and said, "Pick me up over here because I have a job interview." Maybe she was bored just staying home.

She tried to work as a substitute teacher, but she could not handle the kids. The kids here are different than the kids in the Philippines. They say to the teacher, "I don't want to do this. I don't want to do that." In the Philippines, if the kids say that, you spank their butt. And they behave. You can't do that here. So she didn't want to teach any more. Right now, she works in an engineering firm in Carlsbad as a mini-supervisor. She loves her job.

When I made chief, I went to all the different places. The traveling was good, but it was very punishing for the family. We went to San Diego, to Oakland, to Okinawa, Japan, for five months, to Oceanside. After my tour in Oceanside, we went to Glenview, Illinois, where we enjoyed my three and a half years there. I was happy with what I was doing, and I was the leading chief.

In Glenview, I became active again in community service. I founded the Philippine American organization. They had a very good school system there. My three kids did not even have time for television because they had so much homework to do. They were busy, and they got accustomed to that, studying and being competitive. They finished their junior high there.

In 1982, we moved back to Oceanside because I was transferred to Camp Pendleton, which is a Marine base. Because the Marines don't have their own medical personnel, they rely on the Navy for medical support. Most of the Filipinos who work in Camp Pendleton would be hospital corpsmen.

When the kids started school in Oceanside, they said it was boring. As parents, our mission is to get our kids to excel and to get them to study. So I kept prodding them to give me straight As. We Filipinos are like that. I was not able to enjoy the luxury of an education in the United States, so I wanted my children to try their very best. Education is their license for a better life. All three of my children finished high school with honors, and my oldest son and daughter were CSF [California Scholarship Federation, an honor society]. Now all three have graduated from college.

We never argue as to what course the children were going to take. We let them choose what they want to do. Some other Filipino parents, they want their children to be this and that, and that puts so much pressure on them. If they don't enjoy what they are doing, what will happen? They will fall. They will stop. They will get discouraged and disappointed. I think the Filipino parents are making a mistake by requiring their children to be what the parents want them to be. I think some parents find it hard to give away some of the power of being a parent. They are so demanding of their children, even when the children already are adults.

In the area of marriage, of course, we cannot dictate what their hearts and their feelings are. But naturally, being Filipinos, we would like to see our children pick a partner with the same identity. But not necessarily Filipino. If they choose an Asian American, Vietnamese, Chinese, or Singaporean, I would really have no preference, because their partner would be in a similar race and would appreciate our culture.

I raised my children the Filipino way but also the American way. The Filipino way is probably the closeness in the family and the values that we carry. We want our children to grow up and be good, law-abiding citizens.

We want them to excel in education so that they can be an asset to this society.

We also want them to know what the American customs are so that they can blend with both customs. If you live in this country, you are not a Filipino only, although foremost you are a Filipino. You cannot change that—your skin, your hair, your eyes, and your name. But you also have to be American—American in a good way, not in the other way. The good American is the one who is patriotic, loves this country because he lives here. I don't like the other way of being American, which is burning the flag and cussing the government. If you want to get what you want, you have to be a part of the system, to make this country a better place to live. But some people don't get involved, and then they badmouth the people who serve.

I also don't like people who become a liability to the government. I try not to be; why can't others try? At least clean the streets. It's a big space out here in America, where they can do something and get paid, but they don't want to. Some of the people don't want to work, like the homeless people and those guys who carry signs "Work for food."

Ties to the Philippines

I got my citizenship in 1974 in order to enjoy the life of a U.S. citizen. That did not take anything away from me being Filipino. We visit the Philippines whenever the opportunity comes. All of us were able to go home, to Pampanga, in 1990 and 1991.

It is a family reunion whenever we go back there. When you go home, you have to spend a little money. Your relatives expect that from you. Also we cannot get away from sending money to the Philippines, because the people back home always need that support. The only time you receive a letter from home is when they need money. They are not going to write you a letter just to see how you are doing.

I used to think that I would go back to the Philippines and retire there. The Philippines is the land of my birth. That's where I grew up, and some of my childhood friends are still there. What I miss most is the slow pace of life there. It is not a "rat race" everyday like it is here. I miss waking up in the morning, taking a walk on the riverbank under the morning sun, napping in the afternoon, and visiting friends in the evening. Most of all, I miss the closeness of the family, when everyone gathers together and has fun in the old house.

But now I don't think I could retire in the Philippines, because the kids do not want to live there permanently. Also they have been telling Norma and me that we have to stay here to babysit their children. So we will probably stay and die here, especially since our property there was destroyed by the Mount Pinatubo eruption. But I still pay close attention to Philippine politics. I watch it very closely through newspapers, television, and through friends. I was in constant contact with the consul here in San Diego, because they talked directly with the people there. The consul is the sister of Philippine President Fidel Ramos. [The Philippine consulate in San Diego was closed in September of 1993].

Life in Oceanside

I enjoy living in Oceanside. I don't want to live in south San Diego, because it is so saturated already. I like country living.

When we went shopping for a house, we stopped by one of these new developments, and the guy who was working in the office didn't even want to talk to us. He was not very receptive. He warned me that these houses were expensive, ranging from $135,000 to $145,000, and that they needed 20 percent down, or $30,000.

Because of his unfriendly attitude, I became bad. Perhaps he didn't like Filipinos, or maybe he didn't like the way I was dressed. I told my wife in Pampangan that I did not want to buy that house. But then I turned to the real estate guy and said, "If you require $30,000, what if I give you a $45,000 down payment, will you sell me the house?" He became very helpful then. I let him do all the paperwork, and then I told him that I will be back soon with the down payment. Of course, we never went back. Then we went to the valley, the area close to Camp Pendleton, and bought this house.

In this neighborhood, there are not very many Filipinos besides my in-laws who live down the street. We have a Korean here, a Japanese there, a black guy here, and a Filipino over there. And those are the only people I see. In this country, you don't really socialize with your neighbors. It's not like the streets of the Philippines. There, you walk down the streets, you talk to everybody. But in this neighborhood, you try to walk around, and you don't see anybody. They are all inside the house. You cannot just knock on their doors and say, "Hey, how are you doing?" That's how it is here.

One of our neighbors is a retired admiral in the Navy and currently the mayor of Oceanside. When we first moved into the neighborhood, he welcomed us and invited us to his house. That's why we became friends. These are the kind of people that we want to talk to; they do not discriminate. I feel that the people who discriminate are those people who have not been exposed to education. They cannot understand what it is all about. But if they are highly educated, I think they understand what life is all about and how not to hurt other people.

I do not prefer to live in a place with more Filipinos. We just want to live in an area where it's safe and peaceful and decent. We do not want to live in a place where it is too saturated with one ethnic group. I notice that the community becomes cheaper when it becomes saturated with one ethnicity. It has to be mixed. Otherwise, it's too close for comfort. A lot of Filipinos want to live in a place where there are many Filipinos. Maybe because there is pride in ownership for them, like, "This place belongs to Filipinos." National City comes very close to that; about 35–45 percent are Filipinos there.

Community Involvement

The Filipino mentality, you may have heard it from other people, is when someone is up the ladder, they try to pull him down. I think everybody does that, but it is worse among Filipinos. We are not like the Chinese, the Vietnamese, the Japanese—they support each other, especially the Chinese; when someone is going down, they bring him up. That's why in the Philippines, the Chinese are very progressive and very successful in business. But the Filipino is not going to help you. He wants to be the number one guy out there. I don't know why we are like that. I guess we keep blaming Spain for it. But I don't see what Spain has to do with it; those four hundred years are gone. This is now. We might as well work together. It will probably take time or somebody like José Rizal or Martin Luther King to get us to work together. Until that time, it's going to be very difficult.

In San Diego, for those of us who are in community service, our main objective is unity. But when it comes down to it, we tend to go our separate ways. We put our personal feelings on top of what we want to achieve. And that breaks unity. This happens all the time. Maybe it is because of regionalism. The Philippines is composed of seven thousand islands, and every one of the regions has different customs and traditions. In the U.S., when the British and Europeans came here, they threw away the Indians and the Spanish, and brought the same culture. In the Philippines, there were the Pampanguenos, the Tagalogs, the Ilocanos, etc.

Because we speak different dialects, when we go to another province, we don't understand each other. When I was growing up, I could hardly speak Tagalog. Even when I was graduating from high school, I spoke only English and Pampangan. We had to study Tagalog in my second year in high school, and that was it. How much can you learn from that? I learned Tagalog through conversing with people when I went to Manila. In Manila, they speak English and Tagalog, so you have to speak Tagalog there in order to be understood. In Manila, you become a Filipino because you speak Tagalog. In the U.S., every Filipino we meet, unless we know that he is from Pampanga, we speak to him in Tagalog.

A good example of factionalism is in our local Pampangan organization. Our main goal is to unify the township organizations. We want to bring all the people from Pampanga in San Diego into one big group. Every town has its own attitudes, its own personal goals, and its own ways of doing things. So unless you have a strong leader, unification is probably not going to work. We tried to unify but it did not work out, because we did not get along with each other. It takes a lot of hard work in order for every one of us to understand that unity is what we are trying to achieve.

We want to unify because we want to be a stronger force. It's important because we want to be involved in this country; that's part of being a U.S. citizen. If we are unified and we are strong, then perhaps we will be able to either vote for a Filipino who will look after our interests or at least vote for someone who will listen to us. If we are not strong politically or if we are not unified, nobody is going to talk to us.

We Filipinos don't get the respect that we deserve. We are not being heard. I'll be honest with you—the Vietnamese have been very fast in getting the respect that they deserve. The Japanese too. And the Koreans are building it. But we Filipinos have been here for a long time, and we have never been able to do that. That's one of our main problems.

When it comes to politics, Filipinos are number one. They will talk and talk until the next day without sleeping. But yet, when you start organizing and trying to unify the groups, nothing happens.

I guess people still see themselves as coming from this particular town, this particular region. For myself, yes, I am a Pampangueno, but publicly, I would not consider myself that. I consider myself as a Filipino first. That is my primary identity. I am in another country—I *should* be a Filipino. Like you are not a Californian or a Texan—you are an American. If I say I am from Pampanga, the Americans will ask what is that. But if I call myself a Filipino, they know I am from the Philippines. It's more simple that way.

Right now, I identify myself as a Filipino American. There are two kinds of Filipinos in the United States: one is a Filipino, and the other one is a Filipino American. A Filipino American is the one who is of Filipino ancestry, and then becomes an American citizen and speaks both English and Tagalog. And then the other one is a Filipino who cannot speak the American language, and until he is more adapted to the American way of life, he is a Filipino.

We [the first generation] carry the customs and the attitudes that we have from the Philippines. That is something natural that we cannot change. We just have to live with it. I am counting on the next generation to be able to work together. They are the ones who will probably understand the American society. Regionalism is not important for my children. They see themselves as Filipinos. Perhaps we all have to die first, and then the next generation will get it right.

Chapter 7

"I Only Finished First Grade"

Nemesia Cortez

Running away from Home

I was born in 1943 in Bulag Bantay, Ilocos Sur. My whole family, my father's side and my mother's side, came from there. My parents were farmers. I only finished first grade, and then I worked on the farms.

In the old days, whatever your parents wanted to do with you, like if they wanted you to marry somebody, whether you liked it or not, you got to marry these people. It was the old style for them. I guess they just wanted us to be somebody when we grew up. They didn't know our feelings. So when my mother met this man that she thought I will be okay with, she wanted me to marry him. I was nineteen years old. But I said no, because he already had three kids. I said to my mother, "There is no way I am going to take care of somebody else's kids. I want to take care of my own."

When my mother forced me to marry that guy, I ran away to my auntie's place in Pangasinan. But my mother didn't know that I went there. When they could not find me at home, my mother went to the highway and stopped all the cars. She called up the radio stations. She stopped all the buses coming by from the highway to look for me. But I was not there. They could not find me.

What happened was that I was so late going to the place to take the bus that there was no more transportation. But there was one pickup truck which had all the *bagoong* [salted fried shrimp]. I asked the people in the truck if I could ride with them. They told me that they were not taking passengers. But I explained to them that I had to run away from this guy that my mom wanted me to marry because I didn't want to marry him. So they let me sit down by the *bagoong,* and they hid me there.

I saw my mother on the highway. I saw that she tried to stop all the buses.

117

But when she stopped our pickup, the lady who owned the *bagoong* said that she hadn't seen anybody. I was so relieved then.

We left my hometown maybe around 9:00 in the morning, and we reached Tagupan around 3:30 in the afternoon. When we reached Tagupan, I stayed with the lady who owned the *bagoong* at this place. There was this old man there who had a son. He saw me and he wanted me to marry his son. I told him, "Hell, no." I said to the lady that I was with, "This man wants me to marry his son. I don't like it. Can you do something about it?" She told me, "Yes, he talked to me about it last night. So why don't you pretend to go and sell something? Just put your clothes inside those five-gallon cans." That's what we did. She put my clothes inside those cans, and then we pretended that we were going to sell something. Then I went to Pangasinan to my auntie's place.

When I arrived at my auntie's place the next day, my mother was already there looking for me. I told her that I was not going home with her. My oldest brother was also there. He was mad at me because I was giving my mother a hard time. They didn't understand my side, so I just didn't say anything. But when my uncle arrived in Pangasinan from Manila, I asked him to let me come with him, because I did not want to go back to Bulag Bantay with my mother.

Getting Married

I went with my uncle to his place in Manila. When I was in Ilocos Sur, I did not know how to speak Tagalog. I only knew Ilocano. When I went to Manila, I had one week to learn Tagalog. Thank God, I learned. I learned by ear. I practiced Tagalog with the kids, because kids don't know that is not the way you are supposed to speak. So they tell you how to pronounce the words. So I learned Tagalog the same way that I learned English when I came here—by ear.

In the meantime, my auntie went to San Francisco to visit her husband, who was in the U.S. Marines. After six months, her husband passed away. So she brought her husband's body back to the Philippines. Her brother-in-law came with her. Of course, the whole family went to Pangasinan to attend the funeral, and they wanted me to go too. I told them that I didn't want to go and that I wanted to stay in Manila. But my auntie called me from Pangasinan and said, "You just come. You don't have to do anything." I was surprised that they were so nice to me again. They came to Manila and packed all my clothes. So I really didn't have any choice.

When I got to my auntie's house, they locked me up in the room. They cornered me again. They wanted me to marry my auntie's brother-in-law. I told them that I didn't want to get married yet. The thing was I already had a boyfriend in Ilocos Sur. We wrote letters because that was the only way

Nemesia Cortez (far right) posing with family members at Manila
International Airport prior to leaving for Hawaii, 1965

that we could do it. We could not see each other. When I was in Manila, I wrote to my boyfriend that we had to save some money before we got married. When I told my family that I already had my boyfriend and that we were already sending letters for seven years, my uncle said, "Did he kiss you?" I said, "No." So my uncle told me, "Well, if he didn't kiss you, then you can marry this guy. I want you to be somebody later on." So I didn't have any choice.

We got married at the U.S. embassy. I really had a hard time when we got married. Of course, I didn't love this man, and he was older than I was. When they asked, "Do you love this man?," my aunt had to pinch me in the back for me to respond. So finally I said yes, because I didn't have any choice. They all surrounded me. I said to them, "If this is really what you guys want, I want him to take care of me. That's all I want." So that's what happened.

Life in Hawaii

My husband was a civilian worker at Pearl Harbor. He was a sandblaster. He was originally from Bulag Bantay, where I came from, but he grew up in Pangasinan. I don't know what year he went to Hawaii, maybe in 1945 or something like that.

Three months after we got married, he brought me to Honolulu. I arrived in Hawaii on July 10, 1965. My husband wasn't making that much money. So in 1967, I started working. I worked for the pineapple factory. I made $1.45 an hour at that time. We were doing okay. The rent was only $45 a month. So we saved little by little.

After three years in Hawaii, I got my citizenship. God was helping me, because, like I said, I only finished first grade. I did not go to school for the citizenship. Somebody gave me a home-study card, and I tried to study from that. Thank God the questions that they gave me were not so hard: Who was the first president? How many states? How many senators? I wanted to be a citizen because I wanted to bring my family here, and I wanted to vote. I vote, but I don't belong to any party. I want to vote for people who can help the poor people. I wish Kennedy were still alive.

I learned to love my husband because he was so good to me. He took care of me and the children. If you really respect marriage and respect what your husband gives you, then you learn to love him. We have two daughters. My oldest was born on January 4, 1966, in Hawaii. I had a hard time delivering her. It took me one week. So I told myself that I was not going to have any more babies. But then my husband said, "If you don't want any more babies, I understand. But I want a son. So if you agree to adopt, we can adopt, because I don't want to push you to have another baby if you cannot." I told him that I had to think about it. It took me five years to think about it. I said to myself, "Why do I have to take care of somebody else's kid? Why don't I just have my own?" So we had a second baby. It was a girl again, but we love her just the same.

We stayed in Hawaii for nine years. We lived close to a lot of Filipinos. We were poor but we were happy, because on Saturdays and Sundays, we always went to the beach and had picnics. It is not like it is here now, where everything is so expensive and everybody is so busy making money. When some people from Hawaii came and visited me last week, I told them, "We are not happy any more. It's not like before. We don't even see each other."

In 1973, my husband passed away. I was thirty-two years old. I think that's when I grew up, because I had no one else to take care of me. I didn't even know how to cook. When I was single and lived with my mother, I liked to work in the fields better than inside the house. It was more fun working outside. There was fresh air and everything. When I got married, my husband cooked everything. It's when you have nobody to cook for you that you learn how to do it.

When my husband passed away, I tried to go back to the Philippines. I had some money from my husband's life insurance. But the president of the union came and talked to me. I told him that I was going back home because if you had money in the Philippines, you could have a maid, and you could have this and that. But what he told me was, "Okay, you have money right now. But if you go back to the Philippines, once you spend all your money, what if you and your kids want to go back to the United States? Who is going to sponsor you then? I want you to think twice before you even go." What he said was true. I had to put things together, and decide what was best for me and my children. If I go to the Philippines, of course, I would have a good life while I have that money. But what happens when the money is all gone? So we stayed in Hawaii. I still appreciate what the president of the union did for me and my children.

Moving to San Diego

In 1974, a friend of mine applied to buy a house here on the mainland, and she encouraged me to also. I thought to myself, "Why not?" All of us who wanted to buy land here went on a tour of the West Coast. We went and saw all these different places so we could decide where to settle down. We went to Oxnard. We went to Washington State, which I didn't like because it gets too cold there sometimes, and it rains so much. We went to Los Angeles. Then we went to San Diego. When we reached Oceanside, the breeze was so nice. I decided to stay in Oceanside. I like the weather here.

I didn't know anybody in Oceanside when I made the decision to buy a house here. Because I didn't have my husband any more at the time, I told myself and my kids that God was with us and that we were going to make it. We came over here alone, just me and my kids. We didn't have a car then. We just rode the bus until I got tired of riding the bus and bought a car. At that time, this area was all farms. They were selling a place over here, two and a half acres for only $25,000. If my mind before were my mind right now, I would have bought that piece of land.

When I first came here, I had some money. Not much, but good enough to get by. First, I worked in the tomato farm. I had a friend who worked there, and she encouraged me to go and work with her. My kids were in school already, so I went to work. I made pretty good money then.

When my kids were in the first and eighth grade, I met this Filipino lady, Mrs. Peachy Ribaya, at a party. She was running a boarding home then for the old people. I asked her if I could go and watch what she does. Then I asked her if she could help me to open a business from my house, because I needed to be home when my kids came home from school. I didn't know anything about the business then. So Mrs. Ribaya brought me to San Diego to these seminars so I could get a license. Before it was not so hard to get a license. Now, you have to spend many days going to seminars and things like that. It's much harder now.

I started my own boarding house in 1982. I believe a lot of Filipinos are in this business now. Before, I didn't have any problem getting people [boarders]. But now I only have four people. They are all white. Filipinos don't need boarding homes, because their family takes care of them when they get old. It is a difficult business, but no matter how hard the job is, if you enjoy it, you don't feel how hard it is. And I enjoy helping people.

Ties to the Philippines

I have gone back to the Philippines about five times already. I went to three places. I went to Manila; then I went to Pangasinan; and then I went to Ilocos Sur. I love to go back just to visit, because my family is still there. But things have changed. When I drink the water there, I get upset stomach too much. My stomach cannot take it any more. There also are a lot of mosquitoes. When you go to the store, the meat doesn't look clean. And when you walk through the streets, you cannot take a breath any more. My children went to the Philippines once, but they didn't like it at all. As a matter of fact, when my oldest one arrived in Manila, her whole face was swollen from the pollution. She was allergic. So she never even wants to hear about going back to the Philippines. I am not trying to put my country down. I love the Philippines. I was born there, but things seem totally different now.

I was twenty-two when I came to the United States, and I am forty-nine years old now. So I have lived here longer than in the Philippines. I don't want to go back there to live, especially now that we don't have the Americans to guide us any more. A hundred times I want to stay here, ten times I want to stay there. But it is not really that important for me to go there any more because my kids are here. I don't have any business there any more. My brothers and sisters have their own families, and I have my own family here. So they understand.

I have seven brothers and sisters. They all married people from Ilocos Sur. When you don't go anyplace else and you don't meet anybody else, I guess you tend to marry the ones you already know. You don't have much choice. Three of my siblings are in Ilocos Sur, and one is in Pangasinan. I have one brother in Washington State right now. He is in the U.S. Army. And I have one brother in Honolulu. I sponsored both of them to come here. What I did was I ordered my mother first. Then I used my mother's name to sponsor my two brothers. It was pretty easy to order them before.

I brought my mother over here because I wanted her to taste life in the United States. I believe that we have a better chance over here than in the Philippines. But she went back to the Philippines. I send money home to support her. But once she is gone, me and my children have to be on our own. My family in the Philippines has to know that I am a single parent supporting my kids. Sometimes they think we pick up money under the tree.

Community Involvement

There are not many Filipinos in my neighborhood, but it really doesn't matter to me. I am okay here. Right now, I'd rather be alone than to be around so many Filipinos. I am not saying that I don't like Filipinos, but I have learned that the more you know somebody and the more they find out who you are, the more they talk about you. No matter how much you help people, still they talk about you. So I am trying to avoid that. That's the sickness of the Filipinos; they are very jealous. No matter where you go, still they talk about you.

The only time that I see other Filipinos is when there is a gathering like the Filipino cultural events or the Filipino parties. But because of my business, I cannot just go anytime that they invite me. I have to stay here. What's really important to me is my business. I don't trust other people to take care of my people [the boarders]. My people are the most important to me right now.

I used to be a member of the Fil Am [Filipino American] Cultural Association but not any more. I tell them, "Just ask me what kind of contribution I could give, and I'll be happy to give." This way, they cannot pressure me to do whatever they want me to do. I don't have to be involved so much. I figure that if you are a member, they are not going to stop pressuring you until you say yes. But if you are not a member, they cannot force you.

Culture, Identity, and Child-Rearing

When people ask me who I am, I say I am a Filipino. I never tell them that I am American, even though I have lived here longer than I have lived in the Philippines. Even though I am a citizen of the United States, still I am a Filipino. I guess Americans are people who were born here. But even if I were born here, I am still a Filipino, because my blood is still Filipino.

Being Filipino is important to me because I respect my father and mother. To respect them, I still am a Filipino. Just the way I respect my husband, even though he passed away already, still I am using his last name. Even though my husband was older than I was, I am so proud that he came to the Philippines, married me, and brought me to the United States so my children and me now could have a good life.

When my youngest daughter was five years old, I asked her, "Who are you? Are you a Filipino?" She told me, "No, I am an American Filipino." The oldest says she is a Filipino but that she was born in Hawaii. My daughters have never told me that they didn't want to be Filipinos or that they only wanted to be Americans.

My children were born and raised here, so they do pretty much what they want. They think they know everything. I can only do so much as a parent. It's tough sometimes to be both a mother and a father. Like when I taught my daughter how to drive, I told her to slow down but she pressed on the gas instead. So I said, "Help me, Lord."

I tried to raise my daughters the Filipino way. To me, the Filipino way is to respect other people. When you go to their house, you don't have to run all over the place, jumping on top of their beds. Sit down nicely and respect people. When they talk to you, you have to talk to them. When I was young, when we had visitors, my parents only had to look at us and that meant we had to get away, because this was for adults only. And if you didn't do that, when the visitors went home, you were going to get it.

When I try to teach my kids these things, they tell me that I sound like an old record. They even talk back to me sometimes. In the Philippines, when my father said don't do this or don't do that, you listened to him. Not here. But you just have to stand beside the children. You can only do so much. Even if the kids are nice in the house, when they go outside, you don't know what they are doing. I'll be happy, even when I am not here any more, if they can learn to respect people. That's the most important thing.

My problem right now is that my children don't go to church any more. When they were kids, my oldest one even went to Catholic school. And now she doesn't even want to go to mass. She says she doesn't have time but I don't believe that, because it only takes an hour of your time.

The first time that my daughter brought her boyfriend to the house, she was eighteen years old. I almost passed away, knocked out. Lord, tell me what to do? My oldest daughter is already married with two kids. She lives two blocks away. She married a white person she met at work. He was her manager. I wish she'd married a Filipino. I tried to stop my daughter's wedding because I wanted her to finish school first before she got married. But I did my best for her wedding. To Filipinos, a wedding is the last happiness that you can give to your kids. So you try to do your best, especially for your oldest one. My daughter got everything she wanted for her wedding. Her in-laws—they live in Chicago—didn't help me at all with the wedding.

Filipino funerals are also different, because to show respect, we wear black clothes for nine months. And then we do the prayers for nine days. After that, we do the prayers again on the forty-fifth day. I haven't seen any American do that yet. I hope my children will do this when I die. I really hope so, or I'll have it in my will.

Honest to goodness, I don't mind whom my daughters marry, I just hope that it is not going to be colored *baluga* [black] people. I am not saying that I have anything against them. I don't know why because I can make friends with *baluga*. I know that it is not only *baluga*; in any nationality, there are some bad people. But I keep praying to God, "Don't let my kids marry *baluga*."

I prefer for my daughters to marry Filipinos, because I know that Filipinos can save money. There are Americans who also know how to save money, but I believe that the Filipinos can take care of their money better than anybody else. We Filipinos know how to value money. We appreciate what we make. We appreciate how hard we have worked. What I see here is that the Americans like to go out, they don't like to save. And once their kids are eighteen, they finish their responsibility as parents. Filipinos don't do that.

My oldest one likes to be Americanized. She doesn't save money like we do. She just wants to go out and have a good time. That's what I call Americanized. I know that they want to give some gifts to themselves, but what about tomorrow? They don't have the tomorrow, they only have the today. But I like some American ways. For example, when the old Filipinos get mad, they don't want to talk to you, period. But the Americans, when they did something wrong, they would admit that they were wrong and say that they are sorry. Filipinos don't do that.

My oldest daughter, she spoke Ilocano until she went to first grade. When we came over here, she stopped speaking it. Now she understands Ilocano, but she doesn't speak it. The youngest one grew up here, so she doesn't even understand it. I speak to them in English.

When my grandchildren come over here, I try to teach them how to speak my language, Ilocano, One is eight years old, and the other is five years old. They could pronounce the words, but they told me, "Nanny, I have a hard time pronouncing these words sometimes. So is it okay if I memorize some words and not all of it?" I said, "Well, as long as you can say a couple of words." They understand maybe two or three words. That's all. I teach them how to eat Filipino food. I told them, "You will be beautiful if you eat Filipino food."

Discrimination

I don't see much discrimination here. Not yet. Thank God. But I don't see people that much. I don't bother them, and they don't bother me. The only thing that happened to me was when I was working in the tomato field and I went to a store that had a sale. I went straight to the store from work. Of course, I was not clean. I kept asking this salesperson the price for one of the items. I guess he thought I didn't have any money, because he kept ignoring me. No matter how many times I tried to talk to him, he just ignored me. So I came home, changed my clothes, and came back to the store. Of course, I put all my rings on, you know.

When I got to the store, I didn't even open the door, yet this same salesperson opened the door for me. He asked me, "Can I help you?" And I said, "Do you remember me? I was the one asking you five times how much this price is. And you ignored me. You even walked away from me. I understand if you had somebody talking to you, but you didn't. Now you come and talk to me?" I went and complained to the manager, "It's not right. How does he know that I don't have money?"

"I Am Happy with My Life"

I am happy with my life here, with my business. The only thing that bothers me is that I don't have any education. Sometimes when people ask me what college I went to, I just smile. It bothers me when they ask me, but at the same time I am not ashamed to tell them that I only finished first grade. I tell them the truth.

I want to end my story with a happy ending. Last August [1993], I got to go to Europe. My granddaughter came with me. She was nine years old. I always wanted to go to Europe. I worked so hard and saved little by little to get there. I landed in Frankfurt, Germany, and my brother met me there. He is in the Army and is stationed there. After Germany, we went to Austria, then Rome, then London, then France. It was so beautiful, especially the castles and the churches. Castles and churches—that's all I went to see. My favorite place is Paris. It was so amazing. The buildings are so beautiful. I just hope I can go back again. I would like to go to Spain someday. I want to go visit Saint Lourdes, the big church there.

Things are going well for me. I believe that my husband must still be praying for me.

Chapter 8

"International Medical Graduates Are Tested Every Step of the Way"

Edgar Gamboa

Family History

I was born in Cebu City, Central Visayas, in 1948, the second of nine children. Cebu was where the Spanish conquistadors, led by Ferdinand Magellan, first landed in 1521. It was also the island where Magellan was killed by the natives led by the first Filipino hero, Lapu-lapu. So the Spanish influence in Cebu is strong.

My father's father was a Spanish *haciendero* [landowner] from northern Spain, and his mother was a mestiza, or half-Filipina and half-Spanish. My mother's father was a very successful businessman and the foremost importer of American-made products in the region. My wife Lucie's family is one of the oldest and wealthiest families in Cebu. Her maternal grandfather, who was educated in Spain, was the city's first physician. He also started the island's still-existing electric company, a shipping company, and several other establishments. Lucie's father was a family physician who practiced for at least fifty years.

My father was a self-made man. His father died at an early age. As the only son, my father had to work very hard to support the family. He wanted to attend medical school but he couldn't afford it, so he settled for accounting, attending evening classes while working full-time. Later, married with four children, he attended and graduated from law school.

An Anti–Martial Law Student Activist

The reason that I came to the United States was mainly political. I had been accepted to medical school, the Cebu Institute of Medicine, in 1970. When the Philippines was placed under martial law in 1972, I joined the Christian Social Democrats, an organization of political moderates, founded by Senator Raul Manglapus. I was president of the Medical Student Government and a member of the National Council of Medical Students, and we used to regularly demonstrate in the streets, protesting extensive government abuses.

Fred Dimaya, one of my best friends in med school, was an active underground student activist for the KM [Kabataang Malcabayan], a student Marxist-Maoist group. In 1972, he actually left for the hills to join the Communist movement. He served as a volunteer medic for the "people's army." He was later captured, imprisoned, and tortured. I had the chance to see Fred again soon after his release from prison. He was a broken man. I heard later that Fred was able to put his life back together. He had met his wife, a student nurse activist, "in the hills," and they had been captured together. I understand that he is now a religious minister.

I graduated from medical school in 1974. At the time, my intention was to stay in the Philippines. But I also fell in love with surgery. I saw how significantly one could help others by being a good surgeon. I wanted to work with the rural and urban poor. I did my postgraduate internship at the Veterans Hospital in Quezon City, where surgical technology and science fascinated me. After that internship, I went back to Cebu to specialize in general surgery.

Many medical graduates and friends were leaving for the United States en masse, but I still felt it was not right to leave behind a country in disarray. Ironically, med graduates from the University of the Philippines, a hotbed of nationalistic fervor, were the first to leave for the United States in droves and contributed more to the "brain drain" phenomenon than those from any of the other six medical schools in the country.

I vividly remember one incident, when med students were demonstrating against the administration, the dean of the medical school remarked: "All you idealistic students. Your concerns about the poor and about the national state of health, these are all well and good. But soon after you graduate and start your own families, you will quickly grow up and decide to leave the country. I guarantee it." Then he challenged the student body, "Those who are *not* going to leave the country, why don't you stand up so we can see you?" I remember only three of us stood up out of a group of fifty or sixty students. We boldly said, "We can promise you, sir, that we are not going to leave and abandon our homeland. We have a responsibility to care for it." As it turned out, out of the three who stood up, I was the first who left.

Edgar and Lucie Gamboa with Philippine Foreign Affairs Minister
Raul Manglapus (center) holding his godson Michael Joseph
Gamboa, San Diego, 1988

Leaving for the United States

I was the first to leave because my dear father, who had more wisdom than
I had, on his own, asked his staff to send applications to different internship
programs here in the United States. One day, he beamed as he handed me a
two-page contract from Yonkers General Hospital and said, "Ed, you can
start your internship in New York in July."

I was fascinated by the thought of traveling and working in the United
States, but it really was not in my plans. However, my papa, who was a very
patient man, explained, "Look at it this way, Ed. Why don't you go to New
York, do your surgical residency, and then by the time you finish the five-
year program, Marcos would have been history. Then you can return to the
Philippines as a well-trained surgeon and a more effective physician for your
countrymen." My father wanted me to leave because he was concerned that
my student activism would eventually get me in trouble. The government
kept our names in secret files. Being older and wiser, my father put things in
perspective for me, "You have to fight your battles, but more importantly,
you have to know which battles to fight. If you stayed here and kept demon-

strating against the government, you'll end up in prison, just like your friend Fred, and you won't be able to achieve your goals."

So in 1976, I left for the United States on the week of June 12, Philippines Independence Day. I remember feeling elated as the Pan-Am jet lifted off from Manila International Airport. I was at last free from the tentacles of Marcos's repressive government. But I also felt sad about leaving behind a beloved and wonderful homeland. It was an emotionally wrenching period in my life. I was not just leaving my country and family behind, I was also leaving Lucie, my bride of one month, behind too!

Problems with the Immigration and Naturalization Service

Lucie and I were classmates in medical school, and we got married in a small chapel in the mountains of Baguio—the most romantic place in the world. Our wedding took place a month before I left for the United States. If we had not gotten married, my wife would not have immigrated to the United States. She could have easily practiced with her father. In fact, all of her brothers and sisters have stayed back home.

When I presented my papers to the American embassy in Manila, I had expected that my J-1 graduate student visa would be processed expeditiously and that Lucie would be granted a dependent's visa. However, after a quick interview, the clerk handed me my visa but said that Lucie could not be given a dependent's visa. Why? Because she was a doctor! It did not matter that she was my wife. With mounting pressure to restrict the entry of physicians into the United States, Lucie could not get a visa unless she had a hospital contract. They were afraid that once she entered the U.S. as a dependent, she would seek work as a physician. Sarcastically, I pointed out that perhaps America would welcome her with open arms if she were a plain housewife with no skills and below-average IQ.

I was ready to tear up my visa and throw it back at the embassy clerk when an official spotted the confrontation and took me aside. He acknowledged that the policy did not make sense. But he told me that since the doors were closing fast on foreign doctors, I should not tear up my visa in protest—no matter how angry I was. The more reasonable approach would be to go ahead to New York and secure a contract for Lucie. It turned out to be sensible advice, because in less than two weeks I was able to obtain a contract for Lucie to work in a hospital in Brooklyn.

But the problems were only starting. Once I sent the contract to Lucie, all sorts of new requirements came up, and her papers got bogged down at the American embassy. The Philippine Labor Department also came up with their own bureaucratic processes. This dragged on for about four months. We were getting concerned that the opening at the Brooklyn hospital for Lucie would be gone and that we would have to start all over again. Finally, in desperation, I wrote to the First Lady, Mrs. Betty Ford. She understood the predicament and wrote back that she would direct her staff to look into the matter. In a week's time, Lucie's visa magically appeared. She arrived the week before Thanksgiving. This episode demonstrated for me the best and worst of America.

The Movement for a Free Philippines

Once' I got slightly settled, I joined the Movement for a Free Philippines (MFP), which was organized by Raul Manglapus, then the most prominent Filipino leader in exile, who was based in Washington, D.C., and later in Boston. When martial law was declared in the Philippines in September 1972, Senator Manglapus had just left Manila and was on his way to a speaking engagement in California. He remained in self-imposed exile and led the movement against the Marcos dictatorship from outside the Philippines.

As members of the MFP, we mostly did propaganda, lobbying Washington against sustaining the Marcos regime with foreign aid. The MFP was very effective when President Jimmy Carter was in the White House, because Carter was genuinely concerned with human rights. Unfortunately, his successors were not as concerned. We in the MFP also financially supported the grass-roots antigovernment movement in the Philippines.

As activists operating outside the Philippines, we did not want to take so much credit, because, after all, we were not in harm's way and did not risk our lives, unlike our *kababayan* (countrymen) back home. The government media called us the "steak commandos," meaning that we generally enjoyed life, dining on steaks, in the United States while fighting the regime from across the Pacific. But we liked to think of ourselves as José Rizal's resurrected propagandists, who had attacked the Spanish repression also from abroad in the 1880s.

The day after the brutal assassination of Senator Benigno Aquino in 1983, I was among the very first who marched in front of the Philippine embassy in Manhattan. Nothing had been formally organized. A few of us just showed up at the embassy carrying placards denouncing the assassination. Peter Gabriel, my eldest son, was two years old at the time. I carried him on my shoulders as we walked up and down Fifth Avenue. Lucie and my parents (who came to the U.S. in the early eighties) joined us. The network crews came and taped the impromptu demonstration. It was shown in the evening news. We had more formally organized marches later, particularly in San Diego, toward the fall of Marcos and the triumph of the People's Power in 1986. But for me, the demonstration in Manhattan was especially poignant and memorable.

In 1981, two years before his assassination, Lucie and I had a chance to chat with Ninoy [Benigno's nickname] Aquino at a conference in Detroit.

He was a different person then from the young, aggressive senator who had ignited us with his wit and charisma when he visited our medical school in 1971. In Detroit, out of prison finally and barely recuperating from heart surgery, he spoke about laying down his life for the Philippines: "The Filipino is worth dying for," he reminded us. Dr. José Rizal felt the same way a century before. Little did we realize Ninoy would undergo the same political martyrdom two years later.

The Whole Family Leaves the Philippines

My move to the United States was primarily political, but the decision of my entire family to subsequently emigrate was more complex. As martial law bled the country, my father, ever the wise man, began to realize how dire and gloomy, not to say how dangerous, the future had become for his children. My younger brother was enrolled in engineering, my sister was taking accounting, but my father wondered, "Well, what are all these degrees going to add up to if the economy is totally controlled by a dictatorship? The children will have a better and more predictable future if we left for the United States or for Canada." My mother agreed. She was even more convinced than my father that this was a painful but necessary move.

So my father started to seriously plan on moving the whole family out of the Philippines. It was a tremendous sacrifice on my father's part. He had raised his family in Cebu City and had established firm roots in the community. He had a thriving law practice and a comfortable life. But he always placed the welfare and future of his children first. Many of his friends and clients thought he had made the wrong decision, but in retrospect it was the right one.

The planned emigration was accelerated when my father was detained by military authorities. It did not matter that he was a prominent citizen, a respected lawyer, the manager of a reputable airline company. The local military command just snatched him from his office one morning, without a proper warrant of arrest, and kept him for interrogation without notifying his family for more than twenty-four hours. This episode convinced our family of the urgency to leave the country. My father realized that if the military can do this to him, they can do it to any citizen.

My father came to the United States to work out the necessary papers for naturalization, since he was a U.S. Army veteran, having served with the guerrilla forces and the USAFFE [United States Armed Forces in the Far East] in World War II. At the same time, he pursued the possibility of immigrating to Canada under the sponsorship of my sister, who had migrated to Toronto in 1976. My father's Canadian papers were processed more quickly than his U.S. naturalization application. He could never understand how the U.S. government could be so insensitive to its own veterans, because it took a long time before his U.S. citizenship, which he had earned during World War II, was finally granted.

When our entire family finally emigrated to Canada in 1979, my brother Andy had one more year left to finish with his engineering degree, while my sister Chona had one semester left of her accounting course. Unfortunately, they both lost their college credits, since the Canadian educational system did not recognize their Philippine college education.

A Foreign-Born Physician in the United States

One of the myths I would like to dispel is that doctors from the Philippines, or from other countries for that matter, are not well educated or qualified. "60 Minutes" once featured a news report about an unqualified foreign physician in New York. From that single anecdote, the reporter generalized that many, if not most, foreign physicians come to the U.S. with questionable credentials and do not undergo adequate screening and testing. So I wrote to CBS stating that "you should realize that for the last ten years that I've lived in the United States, I have taken no less than twelve major examinations. If I were not foreign-born, I would probably only be required to take half of those exams."

International medical graduates are tested every step of the way. Before entering the United States, we were required to pass the ECFMG [Educational Council for Foreign Medical Graduates] exam and the VQE [Visa Qualifying Exam]. If you passed these exams, you were then qualified to enter a residency program.

Regardless of your medical background, you are required to start with first-year residency. In my case, I lost a little over a year, which is relatively not that bad. Some people wasted five, seven, ten years. After completing a year of family practice, I pursued general surgery, which took another five years of specialty training and testing. In the interval, I had to take the FLEX licensing exam, even though I had already passed a licensing exam in the Philippines. Later, when Lucie and I moved to California, we had to take the California state licensing exam, regardless of our valid medical licenses in New York and Pennsylvania. Then I had to pass the specialty board certification in general surgery. So it is wrong to think that international medical graduates are below par. If anything, these physicians in general are above average, because they have surmounted the difficulties in their homelands and the rigorous screening and testing in the United States.

It is a very difficult process for a foreign-born physician to establish himself in the medical profession here unless he is extremely determined. For instance, when I arrived in 1976, it was next to impossible to get into a decent surgical program. I could not even get past the door for an interview. The best that I could do was to concentrate on surgery during my family practice residency. Since I was only assigned two months of surgical rotation, I frequently switched call schedules with other residents so that I ended up spending five or six months in surgery. I also got to know the attending surgeons well enough to secure good letters of recommendation. None of my letters of recommendation from the Philippines carried any weight with the program directors.

So the following year, I got into an average surgical residency program in New York. It was a brutal struggle, but two years later I finally was accepted to a good university program, the State University of New York at Buffalo, where I eventually finished my surgical residency.

From there, I was accepted at Downstate for Pediatric Surgery chief residency. I also joined the faculty at Nassau County/SUNY-Stonybrook for two years. Then I received a transplant surgery fellowship at the University of California at San Diego, where I was the only Filipino in the surgical faculty. It is true that I did eventually get a faculty position and earned a fellowship with the American College of Surgeons. But I believe I could have progressed much quicker if there were no extra barriers in the way.

What I resent is the implication that foreign medical physicians are either poorly trained or a burden to the system. There is no way that I could set up an office here [at Scripps Memorial Hospital in La Jolla] and work in the trauma system if I had not gone through the same rigorous examinations that American graduates have gone through and more. As a foreign medical graduate in a competitive university program, you have to work extra, extra hard to prove that you have earned your position. Graduates of American medical schools do not have to face these culturally related barriers.

I would not categorize the situation as blatant discrimination. It is a more subtle form of racism, where people feel that an individual who does not carry the right genes, whose skin is a tad darker, or who comes from an unfamiliar university, somehow could not possibly be as qualified and talented and educated. If it is any consolation, I have noticed that as one goes higher in his or her career, discrimination diminishes proportionally. Now that I am an established surgeon, for instance, people accept me as a colleague, no longer as a mysterious foreign doctor.

But like resistant viruses, subtle forms of discrimination keep coming back. Sometimes, I wonder if I am too sensitive to discrimination. It's very interesting, because if I am wearing my lab coat and am readily identifiable as a physician, I can go make my rounds and be greeted at every floor with respect and collegiality. But if I were to wear denims and a sweat shirt and shopped at the mall, I would not receive the same courteous reactions. Now, if I spent a lot of money, then I might get some attention. Even then, people wonder if I can truly afford the items I am interested in.

By the way, the only time that I don't detect this subtle xenophobic apprehension is in a religious gathering. In a spiritual or religious conference, it doesn't matter whether you look black or yellow or red or whatever, you know you are accepted as you are—a human being.

Deciding to Stay in the United States

In 1985, a decade after I first came to the States, I reminded my wife that "it's probably time to pack up and return to the Philippines." We had originally planned on staying only for five years.

We actually returned to the Philippines for a visit, soon after our green cards were processed. I looked at the possibility of establishing a surgical practice there but Lucie had her reservations—despite the fact that she had never wanted to leave the Philippines in the first place and the fact that her father was eager to hand his practice over to her. I think that without question, women in the United States, native or foreign born, enjoy the highest status, in terms of independence and potential for personal or career development. Lucie, as a pediatrician, wanted to achieve her own success, independent of her family background. If she were to stay in the Philippines, she could literally stay home, do very little, and still be considered successful. She didn't want that. She wanted to make something of herself rather than sit on the family laurels, so to speak.

Eventually, our discussion centered on what was best for the children. We reviewed the pros and cons of raising them in the Philippines or in the United States. It was a difficult choice to make, but we concluded that educational opportunities, at the university level, were far superior in the U.S. So we decided to stay, even though we knew that it would be difficult for us to impart on the kids the conservative values of the old country because of this country's liberal milieu. On the other hand, we felt that it would be good for the children to be exposed to a more international culture.

Starting over in San Diego

After we decided to settle in the United States, I convinced Lucie that we at least should choose a place that is similar to the Philippines, in terms of weather, topography, and culture. Just about the same time, I heard about the transplant fellowship opening at the University of California at San Diego [UCSD]. San Diego reminded me so much of home—the ocean, the seaport, the hills, the weather, the Hispanic influence, the sizable Filipino population. And I liked the transplant program at UCSD. So San Diego seemed to be the perfect place, after eight moves in ten years! That move in 1985 was definitely the most difficult. Lucie was reluctant to leave her practice in Rockville Centre in Long Island and start all over again in San Diego. Michael, our second child, was only a month old when we traveled across the country; Peter was four. We left an unsold house in Baldwin, Long Island, and rented one in Paradise Hills. We spent all our savings, and Lucie needed a bank loan to start a new practice. It was back to square one.

In 1987, when I decided to leave UCSD to pursue private practice, I was looking to setting up an office in an ethnic Filipino section of the city. Lucie has established her practice in Mira Mesa, because according to the latest census, that area had the most children in San Diego. Mira Mesa happened to have a large percentage of military families because of its proximity to Miramar Naval Station and a large percentage of Filipino American Navy families. But Lucie actually had a mixed group of patients, which she preferred. We had talked about ethnicity in medical practice, and while I tended to prefer to direct my efforts to ethnic minorities, Lucie had a more sensible philosophy. She pointed out, "You should open your practice to everyone, not just to Filipinos, or to ethnic minorities. You have to be a physician to all men, women, and children. Otherwise, you may be practicing a subtle form of discrimination." Although I did not intend to favor one race over another, I felt that I should practice some sort of "preferential option for the poor," as stated by Vatican II. I guess in a way it was an immigrant's undying passion to stay bonded to the Third World. I initially went to Mercy Hospital partly because it was the only Catholic hospital in San Diego and it served the city's poor community. But then, Scripps Memorial Hospital had a very reputable staff, which interested me.

Lucie and I are the only Filipinos on the medical staff at Scripps. Sometimes, I wonder what I am doing here, in this predominantly Caucasian "country club." Other times, I think that perhaps there is a point in my staying here as the lone Filipino surgeon. Many of the Filipino nurses, the maintenance personnel, the ladies who work in the cafeteria, they are happy and proud to have me here. Somehow, I have become a symbol of ethnic success in a predominantly Caucasian arena. At least, my presence contradicts the impression that foreign physicians can't practice outside of an ethnic community or a small, second-class hospital. The surgical competition in sunny San Diego is tough, and it is even tougher here at Scripps. Since I've practiced here in 1989, at least three or four American surgeons have departed, deciding that the place was too competitive.

As I get older, I realize that we control very little, if any, of our destiny. When I look back at what has happened in my life through the years, I see that Divine Providence has benevolently led me on, regardless of my own convoluted plans. For instance, I did not think I would be a physician, much less a surgeon, since I used to faint at the sight of blood. And I thought I would be a student activist working with the poor in a Philippine barrio, but instead I am a trauma surgeon in affluent southern California.

Straddling the Fence: Between the Philippines and the United States

Like most immigrants, I still have strong ties to my original country, despite the fact that all of my immediate family members are either here or in Canada. I went home last year [1992] when my grandmother died, and I enjoyed the chance to visit with relatives and friends.

Through the Pilipino Medical Association here in San Diego, we sponsor an organization of seventy-plus physicians, we sponsor scholars in the Philippines, and we participate in medical missions yearly or every two years. We maintain contact with med school classmates and manage to send them used equipment, medical supplies, and educational materials. I think expatriates just have a natural tendency to want to help their own people. When Mount Pinatubo erupted, for instance, there was a flurry of fund raisers from the more than one hundred organizations here in San Diego alone. Monetary aid and relief goods and packages were eventually sent to the local bishops, rather than to government agencies, so that hopefully most of the relief went to the needy and those affected most by the catastrophe.

For me, there's always this deep-seated, lingering desire to help the Philippines, while at the same time there is the growing desire to develop the emerging Filipino American community. In talking to friends who have resided in the States from five to twenty-five years, there exists the feeling of "straddling the fence," placing one foot in the Philippines and the other here in the United States. There is that constant tension between how much of one's efforts should be directed back home and how much toward one's present community. Sometimes when you channel so much of your efforts to the Philippines, you necessarily neglect your work or career here. And then you try to balance things out again. And I wonder whether time eventually pushes the immigrant to one side of the fence or the other. I do know of some immigrants—a cousin of mine who's been here since the 1960s is a good example—who never get out of this "straddling" position.

When we were in New York, steeped in our residency training programs, we had very little time to pursue extracurriculars. My time was totally controlled by the university schedule. Now in private practice in San Diego, I am more involved with the community, having attained some measure of stability and having finally achieved some reasonable control over my time. Currently, my community efforts revolve around my being president of the Pilipino Medical Association. There is always the opportunity to extend my activities to the other Filipino American organizations, since there are over a hundred in San Diego. But I have to budget my time carefully, since my surgical practice and community involvement can easily snatch those precious hours away. With four young children, ages five to twelve, spending time with them and my wife is top priority.

The Filipino Community in San Diego

The issue of unity is typical for practically any emerging ethnic group. Fortunately, San Diego has the Council of Pilipino American Organizations (COPAO), an umbrella for all the local social and political organizations. COPAO has been effective on some issues, but I wish that it would become more efficient and influential and assume a broader agenda. Part of the problem is that it is an evolving organization which tries hard but cannot keep pace with the rapidly changing Filipino American community.

When COPAO was started in the seventies, most of the pioneers were so-called old-timers or Navy retirees. So naturally their interest and focus were on Navy-related affairs. Thus, COPAO's level of perception was necessarily limited. Furthermore, the elder generation, through no fault of its own, harbored the vestiges of a colonial mentality. Most Filipinos, including myself, suffer from that malady, which takes a while to overcome. We stand in awe of colonial power and authority. Thus COPAO prefers to avoid confrontational issues with city hall. Its agenda remains cautiously conservative, focusing on community growth, youth education, welfare and health care of senior citizens, and employment. Unfortunately, at this point, as a community, we have yet to develop the audacity to pursue vigorous and wide-ranging political and economic objectives.

In the 1970s, the influx of Filipino professionals injected new blood into the community. Their level of education, their relative affluence and independence, broadened the community's vision. The problem with professionals is time constraint. The old-timers have the time to sit and discuss issues around the fire, but they are reluctant to march off to city hall. On the other hand, the professionals are eager and ready to march, but they do not have the time to sit by the fire.

Now there is the third group: the emerging second-generation Filipino Americans. These young men and women, born and raised here, are very highly educated, dedicated, and aggressive. They do not have a colonial mentality, and they are well schooled in the intricacies of the American political system. But their drawbacks are youth and inexperience.

I think we have begun to recognize these diverse community talents and resources. And I can already see the oncoming waves generated by an increasingly influential and progressive Filipino American community.

Culture, Identity, and Child-Rearing

Since I've been fortunate enough to have traveled around the world, I no longer tend to tie myself down to any particular group. When there is a need to be identified as a Filipino, I am proud to identify myself as one. When the need is not there, I do not see why I should not assume an international identity. In other words, if there were a natural disaster in the Philippines requiring massive assistance, I would plead for funds from all quarters and identify myself as a Filipino. Or when the community gets bad press from the negative activities of Filipino gangs, in my own way I counter that by projecting my positive image as a Filipino physician. But I believe that the development of a broader, international outlook is what our generation demands.

When you start sinking deeper roots in this country, especially when you start raising children, you harbor second thoughts about Western cultural and social values. You can say to yourself, "Well, we'll raise them here in the States because they'll be much better off economically and academically, but we're going to make sure their values come from the old country." That's exactly what I adhered to for a long time, until I gradually learned more about the real American culture, the culture behind the culture, and its underlying spiritual and religious foundation, despite its advertised amorality. My previously pessimistic views on Western decadence have gradually changed.

Let's take attitudes toward sex, for example. Brought up in conservative and religious Philippine society, Filipino immigrants experience a cultural shock when they enter the U.S. because of what appears to be widespread sexual permissiveness in this country. But then the Good Lord has a way of directing you to meet and get acquainted with deeply religious and spiritually mature individuals, whom I would call "modern saints," right here in the United States. America, I found out, is actually more religious and moral than what the popular media give it credit for, and Americans are just as concerned about the pro-life movement, about liberation theology, about lay involvement, about the ill effects of affluence, about prayer, and about morality.

I have become very selective in the sense that I want to give my children many of the treasured values from my culture, like respect, fellowship, introspection, resilience, acceptance, prayer; and some from the West, like independence, healthy aggressiveness, planning and organization, focus; and even some from an international mix, like discipline, spirituality, sacrifice, humility. I would love to come up with an ideal mixture which I could just hand over to my children like a family treasure, but I know that it is a lifelong struggle which they will have to undergo individually. That is, after all, part of life's great adventure.

But as parents, we do what we can. An example of my achieving a balance of cultural values is the way I hold open and democratic discussions with my children. As you know, like most Oriental cultures, Philippine culture is strictly disciplinarian: the children are not supposed to talk back to their parents. It's considered good manners, despite your strong feelings, to stay silent, especially in family discussions, where the father is the tribal king.

When you come to the States, you see these brats arguing with their parents in supermarket aisles, so you quickly remind yourself, "We better go back to the old system. Keep the kids' mouths shut!" But then you begin to realize that the old system, while important, invariably represses children's personality development, their self-esteem and self-confidence. You begin to appreciate the benefits of appropriate self-expression. I now blend the old culture of respect for parents with the new culture of freedom to engage parents in fair, argumentative if you will, but healthy and constructive discussions of issues.

In terms of language, we speak primarily English at home, unfortunately. I guess it has become more natural for us to speak in English. When I realized that, I insisted that we speak Spanish, Filipino, and English, by rotation, at the dinner table. The kids had fun, but we eventually reverted back to English. I've tried teaching the children the Visayan dialect. They do understand, but they can hardly speak it.

What my wife and I really want to give to our children is the closeness of our family and enduring religious principles and values. We pray every evening with the kids. When we were growing up, our families always prayed together in the evening, especially the Holy Rosary in honor of our Blessed Mother, before bedtime. And we always had our meals together. Here we manage to get together for breakfast half of the time, but we usually get everyone together for dinner and prayer. We always attend mass and receive the Holy Eucharist. Jesus Christ was a smart psychologist. When he instituted the sacraments two thousand years ago, he knew it had the power to keep families together.

Last year [in 1992], when my son Peter was assigned to write an essay about his summer vacation and what made him most happy, he wrote that "one of the things that I liked best was when all my family got together for my grandparents' fiftieth wedding anniversary." My parents, all of their nine children, with their spouses, plus twenty-four grandchildren and five great-grandchildren, got together for a grand reunion. It was a lot of fun for everyone, and the kids loved every minute of it.

Today, I believe the children would be more successfully balanced if they were brought up as "international citizens," rather than as strictly Filipinos or purely Americans. I would prefer that they understood all cultures, studied all philosophies, tolerated all races. Until the kids came along, I did not appreciate the benefits of a multicultural environment. I was just this Filipino immigrant, who enjoyed his American venture, but longed deep down to return to his native Philippines. As a father, I have changed at many levels. Now I would like my children to be in a mixed group as much as possible, socially and educationally. The diversity of this country is such a blessing, if we recognized its many positive aspects, rather than bemoaning its disadvantages. The United States, as a melting pot, has the potential of forming a truly international society and serving as a cultural role model for the rest of the world.

"A Third Culture"

When I think about these cultural interchanges, one of the writers who puts it in clear perspective for me is the Jesuit Father Thomas Green. We've corresponded for years now, by the way, because as I read his books, I simply had to write to him. Father Green grew up in upstate New York, was ordained a Jesuit priest, and was supposed to be sent as a missionary to Japan but ended up in the Philippines. He was thirty-something when he started missionary work in the Philippines and now, in his late fifties, teaches there at the San Jose Seminary and Ateneo University.

So half of his life was spent growing up in the United States and the other half working in the Philippines. And his cultural values, he says, are all mixed up, but with favorable results. To paraphrase Father Green, "I love the Philippines. I consider myself part of this beautiful country and its people. I love Filipino food. I have many Filipino friends, yet I cannot honestly say that I am Filipino. My heart still goes back to New York, where my family is." He regularly visits his mother in New York every year. When he is in the States, he says that he feels American again, especially when he finds himself back in his old home, and gets to meet his relatives and old buddies. And yet somehow, he says he no longer feels "fully American." He observes poignantly that "I have really become part of a *third culture*—a culture which is neither American nor Filipino." Instead of being lost in an identity crisis, one can pick up the good things from each culture and jettison the bad.

Since I stumbled on to Father Green's idea of a "third culture," my loyalty now really belongs to both countries. Previously, my loyalty was 100 percent to the Philippines. I delayed my application for U.S. citizenship precisely because of that loyalty. But now I care deeply about American society. I vote. I write letters to the editor. I call the White House comment line. I worry about what President Clinton says and does not do. I worry about what happens to California. I am deeply bothered by Governor Wilson's political rhetoric against Mexican migrant workers. I support my wife's efforts to run a charity clinic for migrant workers and their families.

I think this happens once you cross the threshold and make the decision to settle in this country. As the kids grow up, you get involved in their school activities and then in the more serious problems of the American school system; you get involved in your local church and community, and then in the wider political and social arena. Prior to arriving at this threshold, I was merely curious about U.S. politics. My focus was on toppling the Marcos dictatorship. American politics for me was merely Washington's continued support for Marcos. Now, I call the White House to push Mr.

Clinton toward a more aggressive policy in Bosnia-Hercegovina. I am concerned that America sits back while the holocaust rears its ugly face again in the form of Serbian ethnic cleansing. News of a downturn in the economy used to affect me but only on an intellectual level. Now I have become very sensitive to recession and the fact that thousands of Americans are losing their jobs and homes. America has become a part of me, or I have become a part of America.

But you don't become more sensitive to this country at the expense of losing your sensitivity to the Philippines. I think you just become a little bit richer, more fully human.

Chapter 9

"PASACAT Became My Whole Life"

Anamaria Labao Cabato

Family History

I am Anamaria Labao Cabato. People call me Ana. I was born in San Diego in 1955. My parents are both immigrants from the Philippines. My dad is from Baliuag, Bulacan, and my mom is from Santa Ana, Manila.

My dad joined the U.S. Navy in 1930, when he was nineteen years old, and that's how he came to the United States. I think he faced a lot of discrimination in the Navy, but he doesn't really talk much about it other than to say that Filipinos could only be stewards. My dad was fortunate enough and had the wherewithal to become a chief petty officer. After twenty-eight years in the Navy, he worked with the civil service for another eighteen years. Today, at the age of eighty-two, he is as feisty as ever and is one of the best cooks around.

My dad's family was very poor. His father was a policeman, and his mother worked at a tailor shop. It was a hard life. There was no money to pay for school. My dad would talk about not having any shoes, not having the means to even go past the seventh grade in school. That is one of his very big disappointments in life. He feels inadequate because he doesn't have the education that other people have. Nevertheless, he is filled with much wisdom, and he appreciates education tremendously.

My mother came from a family of nine. She lost her father at the age of thirteen, so her mother had to raise the nine children. Fortunately, her two uncles, a lawyer and a doctor, helped and guided her mother in the rearing of the children. They taught them discipline, family and religious values, and the importance of higher education. All nine of them went through college. Music and songs, as well as helping the poor, were part of their family.

My mother, who is the eldest of the family, was always with her mother, doing charity work in their church as well as attending masses daily. That's how she was exposed to religiosity and community service. Her lawyer-uncle trained her in office work, and later she was employed at Philippine Air Lines International Division.

There are only three girls in our family. No boys. My mom had twins, but they died. My dad said that it was a blessing in disguise, because he did not know how he would have been able to support five children. So we were boom-boom-boom, one right after another. I was born in '55, and '56 and '57 came the other two.

When we were kids, my dad would always say to us, "Sit up like a young lady," and "You got to have a good education." He'd say it just like that, to all three of us. He always instilled in us the importance of education. And we all finished college; my sisters from the University of California at San Diego, and I am from San Diego State University.

The Filipino Community in San Diego in the 1960s

In the 1960s, after my dad retired from the Navy, my parents started getting involved in the Filipino community in San Diego. They always went to these dances sponsored by Filipino clubs. I think they met these people through the Navy, and they just started networking that way. Filipinos are such a social bunch of people. They like to party, to be with the people from where they came from, you know—their *bakadas*. It's like their gang. So our upbringing was primarily around all Filipinos—the social gatherings, the dances.

At that time, we could fit the whole Filipino community into one small building called the FAVA Hall, the Filipino American Veterans Association Hall. That was the place to hang out in the sixties. But in the seventies, when so many Filipinos started coming into San Diego, the community grew and grew, and pretty soon, there were just so many people that you didn't even know who was who anymore.

Before, we didn't have the same kind of regionalism like we do now, because there were fewer Filipinos. Then when more started to come over, they began to say, "Oh, you're my townmate; you're from my same province, let's stick together." It's unfortunate. I wish somehow we could move away from that, because I think it prevents the positive growth of the Filipino community. It hurts our ability to move forward as a whole community. We don't have a voice.

I hear that the Filipinos are laughed at because we can't come together. There are so many factions that no one group can represent the Filipinos so that we can be heard. There's about 150 Filipino organizations in San Diego. Isn't that ridiculous? I wish that they would just condense or categorize them. They compete with each other too. People would say, "Oh, we have the best ball." "No, we have the best ball." "We have the best cotillion."

*Anamaria Labao Cabato surrounded by PASACAT performers at
the troupe's annual New Year's Eve dinner, San Diego, 1991*

"No, we do." Who cares? I mean, get on with more important issues that
are for the future of the community, like helping the youth.

Getting Involved in the PASACAT Dance Troupe

My parents, especially my dad, have always been very active in the community. That's how we got involved with PASACAT [Philippine American
Society and Cultural Arts Troupe]. At the time—this was in 1969—my dad
was president of the Filipino American Community Association of San
Diego, and he organized a three-hour dance program that featured Philippine folk dancing. The original dancers were just a small group of families.
I was one of the original dancers. I was fifteen years old when I started
dancing.

From that point on, there was an enthusiasm to continue it. In 1970,

PASACAT was formed as a separate organization. Since then, we have been trying to promote and propagate the Philippine culture by exposing the young kids, as well as the community at large, to the culture of the Philippines. Hopefully, the people in the audience are going to get a better understanding of and appreciation for the differences in culture, and for the people themselves. In that way, you are the peacemakers, people of good will.

I grew up in National City. There were a lot of Filipinos where I went to school. We were all Navy children. I don't think any of my classmates were the children of professionals. Maybe their mothers were nurses, but it was the Navy that got them here.

In school, I wanted to be accepted but I just could never fit in, because I couldn't wear stockings and I couldn't wear make-up. My parents were so strict. I remember being really hurt because I was not accepted. In the sixth grade, what left an impression on me was that I wanted to be part of this gang composed of African Americans, Filipinos, Guamanians, and Mexicans so that I would be respected. There weren't any Filipino gangs at that time. So the Filipinos hung around with the Mexicans and with the black people. It was white or "colored."

At Sweetwater High School [in San Diego], I felt inferior because I was a Filipino. If you weren't white, you just didn't fit in. They separated you from the majority. I think that's where the most pain came as far as my being Filipino. I was a "wanna-be," but I could never fit. I felt that I was too Filipino-ish to be a part of the popular group. The only way I could overcome that was by feeling proud of who I am.

There were Filipinos who were part of the popular clique, but I felt that they were—I don't like to use the word—but that they were "whitewashed." They denied and perhaps ignored their Filipino heritage, and they even showed themselves to be more American than Filipino. I said, "Boy, they're missing the boat." They were like "coconuts," brown outside but white in the inside, a derogatory term for "whitewashed" Filipinos. How can you deny who you are? You are trying to be like them when we are who we are. So I didn't care for them. They turned me off, and that's probably why I didn't hang around my high school classmates. I'd rather hang out with people in PASACAT because I could relate to them more. And you know, to be dancing, to be performing, it is a real high.

In high school and in college, all I could think of was Philippine dance. I was a loner by choice because I focused all my energy on PASACAT. I didn't hang around school and network with the other students. I wasn't accustomed to befriending classmates. But in college you need to develop this support group, and I didn't have one at SDSU [San Diego State]. That's one of the reasons why it took me fifteen years to get my college degree. I felt more fulfilled doing PASACAT things. I enjoyed the camaraderie—being with a bunch of people. Most of the dancers were from the South

Bay—from National City, Chula Vista, Imperial Beach area. And all of them were the children of Navy families. It was like being in a gang; those people were like family to you. You do things together. Every weekend, we'd have rehearsal. After rehearsal, we'd either go bowling or go just anywhere. Then we'd do the shows together. It was fun!

And I was proud, because I felt that I knew more about our culture than other Filipinos. I was exposed to the tribal dances and the dances in the South. I was in awe of the diversity when I realized that the Philippines is the only place in the world where every continent is represented. The tribal dances look very African. The Maria Clara dances look very European and Spanish. The dances from Mindanao look very Asian, and then the country dances look South American with a little bit of Western flair in them. Even to study the development of the Catholic faith and how the religious traditions are practiced, you can see its roots from the tribal rituals.

I would say the Philippine culture is the best of so many worlds because it has been blessed with an abundance of beauty from all over. I'd love to go to the Philippines. Just visit, not live. I would like to go to the mountain provinces, because the tribal dances are intriguing. Go to Mindanao and see the Muslims there, and look at the actual instruments and the costuming and the jewelry.

Back then, when PASACAT was first started, it was the girls who more or less liked to do the dances, and the guys were just doing it because they were forced by their parents. We only had about twelve girls and maybe four or five boys. But then, as the years grew, around 1973, people wanted to do it because they enjoyed it. They enjoyed the camaraderie—the sense of belonging. So PASACAT continued with a steady flow for about seven years. And then in the 1980s, it dropped a little bit. We still got more people, but we didn't grow.

Professional Immigrants and PASACAT

Then the big growth in PASACAT came in the 1990s. I think in the past Filipino Americans, whether it's the Navy families or the professionals, they shunned their culture. They said everything was going to be American because to be successful, you have to be American. Don't speak the language. Don't practice the cultural traditions. Now that their kids are in junior high school and high school, some parents have evaluated this and are now anxious for their children to learn about their cultural heritage. They want to expose the young Filipinos to the culture.

But the big growth in PASACAT came primarily from the children of professional immigrants. In 1990, our choreographer, who had been with us for five years, left to go to Samahan, another Philippine dance troupe in San Diego. When he left, we felt lost, because we depended upon him so much.

Because we were already happy with the level of quality that we had reached, we felt that the only way we could step up to another level was to expand and gain more exposure.

We decided that we had to go to the North County because in our area, the South Bay, there were already three dance troupes. The market was saturated here, but the North had nothing. It's virgin territory. People in the North County really hungered for something. They wanted to join PASA-CAT, but they couldn't come all the way down to National City. So we decided to go to them. We were trying to hit Rancho Peñasquitos, Mira Mesa, Rancho Bernardo, and Poway.

The first thing we did was to perform for the area schools. We told our college students to make their mornings available, to schedule their classes in the afternoons, so that we could book them for school performances in the mornings.

One day, after our performance at the Deer Canyon Elementary School, the principal was so elated, he told us, "This is the very first time that I have ever seen my Filipino students' eyes light up. You couldn't believe the joy that they showed when they saw Filipinos performing their culture." Then he said that if we could connect with these students, we would be able to prevent them from joining gangs. So in 1991, we received a $3,000 grant from the San Diego County Public Arts Advisory Council for an outreach project to the Filipino students in the North County. We received another $2,000 in 1992 to continue the program.

We send a team of dancers up there once a week for three hours to teach, to carry the spirit, and to give the students the nurturing of what PASACAT is all about—the camaraderie, the respect and appreciation for their cultural identity, and the support. We want them to feel that they can talk to anybody in the troupe if they've got problems. These kids need a support group. They need guidance. They need nourishment. One thing we make sure of is that our dancers get enough rest and that we feed them after a performance. Somebody told me that the best way to bond is by breaking bread together. So we share our meals together.

I want to make sure that our ties are strong, because that's very important to the success of our shows. I think the key ingredient in the success of PASACAT is the spirit of oneness that draws the audience into our show. And because of the love that's outpoured by everybody as a whole, the audience can feel that. I don't want to ever lose sight of the oneness and the love that is there. Plus equality. If you do a solo dance, or if you do a group dance, or if you go out there as a bamboo clapper, for the *Tinikling,* a dance with rapidly clapped bamboos, your role is equally important. It doesn't matter. You are all part of this company. And when you say company, it means one.

Here in National City, we have about sixty to seventy students. They range in age from about six to eighteen years old. The majority of them are junior high students. In the North County, we started off at about thirty students. That has grown to about sixty to seventy. And it's still growing. But because they live so far away, I think some of the dancers from the North County don't feel the oneness. They feel they're not a part of PASA-CAT, but we open the house to them. And they want to come. But it's too far to come down here. It is a 30–40 minute commute, and parents don't approve of the drive, because rehearsals end at 10 or 11 p.m. That's one of our challenges. We realize that it is a very, very sensitive issue, and we have to continuously monitor it so that they don't feel this division.

But they go to rehearsals together—north and south are under one roof rehearsing. The parents are there, waiting for their kids, so they are bonding with each other. And the kids are bonding. It's only after the performance that they might not have the opportunity to bond even further. After a performance, you are on a high, and you want to hold on to that high. And the way you hold on is to be with the people who created the high.

But it is working out. For instance, when we went to go see Samahan perform at Poway, after the performance, one of the North County parents opened their home to us. So there's a give-and-take there. And sometimes the North County dancers do come here and stay overnight at my house. When we had our show last September at the East County Performing Arts Center, they all spent the night here—all thirty-five dancers and musicians. I didn't even sleep in my bed because three of the dancers were sleeping there. So I slept in my huge walk-in closet. And it was peaceful. They wanted to savor the high for as long as possible. The majority of them slept over. The group included about six or seven people from the north who even stayed or came back.

Filipino parents in the North County are very involved in their children's education. So they are looking at PASACAT as an extension of their educa-tion. It's their way of exposing their children to the Filipino culture. They realize that it needs to be done, because if their children are proud of who they are, then they can stand up on their own in a predominantly white school. One of the parents from the north said to me, "This is the only thing I have to give my child—by being involved in something like this, getting them involved."

I think the parents up north are more enthused because they are profes-sionals. They value education tremendously. On the other hand, the people down south are just trying to make ends meet. They are not as educated. They want their kids to be involved, but they don't take an active role in helping the organization.

Our North County board members are doers. They don't just talk. We've got a financial adviser on the board, a senior financial analyst, an accountant who has his own business, a mechanical engineer, an auditor working for the Department of Defense. That's a strong and talented board! Here in the South Bay, the board members are Navy retirees, civil servants, a couple of nurses, maybe one or two teachers. They do not have the business skills that the North County people have. Our North County outreach project doubled our revenue in 1992, from forty-six thousand to almost eighty-six, eighty-seven thousand. They have the knowledge. They have the skills to get a project going, and they have more connections.

1992 was the best year that PASACAT ever had. But in 1993, things started to get worse. Some of the parents of the North County performers questioned the competency of the organization, how PASACAT spent the money. One of the members of the board of directors created the PASACAT budget for 1993. This member criticized our expenses, especially the artistic staff fees. As a result, those same enthused parents pulled their children out of PASACAT. One went to the executive director of the San Diego City Commission of Arts and Culture, our funder, and questioned many things. The board was upset by this, and decided to keep a low profile for the remainder of the year. We didn't recruit. We didn't book too many performances. We just backed down.

Also, on the personal side, my eighty-year-old dad was having heart problems. He was in and out of the hospital. Finally, at the end of August, he agreed to have a by-pass. He had a quadruple by-pass and is doing well now. That drained me and my family emotionally. Since I am the catalyst behind PASACAT, what affects me affects the group.

But 1994 looks better. We had a board of directors retreat and decided to make some changes in the structure of the organization. I want to change it so that I can do more of the administrative work, like working on developing grants and increasing performances. Currently I am managing the group instead of doing the job of an executive director. But we are moving slowly, because the older members of our board do not like changes and they resist them.

I see my life as a journey. PASACAT led me to my journey and helped strengthen my faith. I always pray to God to help our performances; he is the source of everything. PASACAT gives me an appreciation for what gifts the Lord has provided me, and now this is my apostolate. My ministry is helping these kids. I'm making some money from this, but it's not going to cover the cost that I have of the troupe using my house, watching my TV, cleaning out my refrigerator . . . . But I can help these young people, keep them on the right track, or at least try to guide them in the right direction, to be positive influences in the community.

I've known some of the dancers for about eleven or twelve years. And some of them used to have this hardheadedness, stubbornness, and you just can't talk to them. But now, they have softened up, because they are friends with the other dancers, people they would have never met otherwise, and they hang out with each other. They talk about their problems. They've become a support group for each other. They cry with each other. They laugh with each other.

Marriage and Child-Rearing

I lived with my parents up till the time I got married, which was in 1978. I was twenty-three years old. When I started with PASACAT, my husband's mother was my teacher for the first four years, until I took over as dance director and artistic director and choreographer. That's how I met my husband. So, everything was convenient for me, because he was just there and I didn't have to look anywhere.

Usually, when dancers get married, they fade out of PASACAT. But PASACAT became my whole life. My mother-in-law was the president of the organization. I was the artistic director. My mom was the secretary. My dad was the PASACAT building manager. My sisters were dancing. It was truly a family affair!

When I had my first child, Joyelle, I told myself that I was going to get on with my life. It's time for somebody else to take over. But I couldn't let go, because they wouldn't let me go and I didn't want to go. So I would leave Joyelle in her car seat, place her in front of me, and continue to teach. Joyelle was only eight or nine months old then. She couldn't even walk.

PASACAT was fortunate to have this Ph.D. student from the Philippines, Bayani Mendoza de Leon, cross our way. He was here on a Fulbright scholarship at UCSD. He's a composer and very nationalistic about the Philippines. The music that he writes expresses the beauty of the Philippines and its struggles for freedom. In order for him to make ends meet, he worked at PASACAT and Samahan to develop a choral ensemble, the rondalla [a string instrument], and the percussion. He taught us how to sing. He wanted Philippine music to thrive in San Diego. When I told him, "Bayani, I have to get on with my life," he said, "Ana, you have to continue. This is the only way the Philippine culture will stay alive here in San Diego."

So I am now committed for life—for as long as I can nurture it and contribute to it. It's part of my ministry. I devote twenty to thirty hours a week to PASACAT. That's a lot. And I have a full-time job beside that—another forty hours a week. My weekends are all for PASACAT and the church.

Now I am a single parent with two kids. My husband was from the Philippines originally. I think because he's from a broken home, he never had the foundation to withstand setbacks in life. His business was affected by the economic recession, and it was difficult for him to catch up financially. That affected his self-worth.

His mother left him to be raised by his aunts and uncles. So he felt like he was abandoned. And yet he abandoned his kids. When his business failed, he just said, "I'm going to Ensenada for a week," and he never came back. We separated two years ago, but I haven't divorced him. Now he is wasting away in the Philippines—gambling—that's another one of his vices.

But I survived him. It's still very painful, but I feel that it is a small cross that I have to bear. I feel grateful, because even though it is a loss to me, I have been compensated. PASACAT has grown. It's doing well. We received a great review from the dance critic of the *San Diego Union Tribune*. I cried when I read it because, after all these years, we're finally being recognized for our professionalism and artistry. I think that the Lord has compensated me.

My daughters, Joyelle (fourteen) and Gemma (ten), attend private Catholic school. Joyelle's best friend is African American, and she's a nice girl. Because of our involvement in PASACAT, my children's close friends are other Filipinos. I want my children to be proud of who they are and to know what their roots are. So I involve them in PASACAT. I record the music for performances so they hear the music. And we watch the videos of the performances frequently, especially when the dancers hang out at our home.

The dancers have become our extended family—uncles and aunts to these girls. They take care of them. They'll drive them to places if I am not here. Sometimes I feel like I don't have enough time for my children. I have a full-time job at Pacific Bell, then I have PASACAT, then the church. Gemma has not been doing well in school for the last three or four years. But I just don't have the time or the patience to sit down and go over her homework with her every night. And I don't have my husband here to help me out with her.

I think my parents were stricter with me, and I find myself a little bit more lenient with my children. For instance, slumber parties. I allowed my older daughter to go to a slumber party at her African American friend's house. I let her go because I never had that experience; I could never sleep over at a friend's house. Boy, my mom and dad were ballistic when they found out that I let Joyelle go to a slumber party. Can you imagine that? I have my own family, and my parents were lecturing me for letting my *own child* go to a slumber party! They were upset, because they don't like the idea of slumber parties. But they're also prejudiced against blacks. They call them "colored." I said, "Mom and Dad, that's so wrong. We're colored people, too."

Race, Culture, and Identity

When we were growing up, my mom and dad wanted us to be exposed strictly to Filipinos. You couldn't associate yourself with blacks, Mexicans, or Caucasians, in that order.

I think their views have influenced my views. For example, before, I was against interracial marriages because of the cultural differences. I felt strongly that if two people had the same background, there was less to contend with as far as what is the common ground. But now my view is changing. I think that if the [non-Filipino] person can embrace the Filipino culture and respect it, then that is okay. It doesn't matter what color they are. Why the change? Probably because of my own marriage. My husband I are both Filipinos, but look, it didn't work out. Now I look more at the person and what their background is.

When I was younger, I used to question my identity. I remember asking mom or dad, "Am I Filipino? Am I American?" Even my kids ask me that today, because you don't know what you are. "American Filipino" is what I would say now. American because I was born here, and Filipino because I am of Filipino descent. That's my interpretation. I discovered who I was, what it meant to be a Filipino, through PASACAT. Before that, being Filipino to me just meant going to lots of parties and dances, and eating lots of food.

I never learned to speak Tagalog. I guess my parents were trying to prevent us from having an accent. And plus we had to conform with the majority. I can sing many songs in Tagalog, and I can understand about 95 percent of what is being said, but I just can't speak it.

I wish I could speak it, because that would have made my work with PASACAT easier. Here I am, promoting the Filipino culture, and then the people who contract us to do performances, they are usually Filipinos. When they ask me if I speak the language, I have to say no. That makes me feel inadequate. Somebody was telling me that the best way to handle that is to answer in Tagalog that I do not know how. Do that much. That way, it shows them that you are attempting to speak it and that you are not rejecting them. Then they will speak to you in English.

My youngest sister doesn't have a deep appreciation of Filipino culture. I think she resents it. And the resentment must be because me and my mom were involved in the same things—PASACAT and the Filipino community of our church, Saint Rita's. When we have a family reunion, all we would talk about is PASACAT and the church. But my sister didn't want to get involved in these things. I think she wanted to make a place of her own.

She has the highest position careerwise out of the three of us. She's the general merchandise manager for the Marine exchange at Camp Pendleton. She started her merchandising experience at the age of thirty. She's got clout, making lots of money. She also is divorced and that broke up our family. But that's one of the things that's never discussed. We just don't address it. In the Filipino culture, these problems are tucked away. You just sweep them under the carpet. There's a lot of pain, because my mom and dad were very hurt. Well, we all were.

After college, I went to work for Pacific Bell. This was in 1981. When I walked into my first workplace, I said, "Oh, my gosh, I need sunglasses. There is so much white here." I wasn't accustomed to being surrounded by white people. It took a while for me to adjust.

It was a culture shock for me because my upbringing was totally all Filipino—even in our church. When I was with an all-white group, I felt insecure and out of place. But I also felt proud of who I was. My involvement with PASACAT helped me to develop myself and gave me the confidence that I could stand up to anybody because I have some deep roots. The people at work were very nice and helpful to me. But sometimes I felt uncomfortable because I was not able to understand what they were saying. It's not that I couldn't understand the words, but my thought processes interpreted what they said differently. I attribute this to our cultural differences.

I know that discrimination exists, because I hear people talking about it. And I see people being discriminated against—African American people, Mexican American people. They are treated differently. I think with Filipinos, it doesn't happen to us as much as it does to the African American people. But if the African Americans weren't there, the Filipinos might be the next target. See, that's the thing about discrimination: the next time, it could happen to you. I think that's what a lot of people feel. Even though they may not have been a victim directly, it doesn't mean they are not ever going to be. But I don't let it bother me. Maybe I tune it out. It has not made an impact on my life.

When I was an account executive at Pacific Bell, I had to do some heavy selling, and part of my pay was based on commission. Being in the sales environment, you have to be aggressive. But that goes against my nature, the pushing and selling—being too aggressive. It's against my faith too. I'm an easygoing person, and I felt that the upper management's concern was to make the quota. I couldn't fit into that sales environment. I was not meeting quotas. I am not saying that this was discriminatory, but the job called for me to be something that I was not. Why can't they accept me as I am and accept my efforts in the sales environment? Luckily enough, my sales manager saw this and helped me to find a different position. He was sensitive to my cultural and religious values.

I don't see Filipino women as subservient. I see them as strong women. I see Mexican American women with demanding husbands who walk all over them. My mom is strong. I think all Filipino women are strong. They are the ones who hold the family together, even in the Philippines. I think being a woman, you have the sensitivity, the knowledge, and the ability to make things happen. And even in your budget, making things work in the household.

I think there are different roles for men and women. There's some things that men do, and some things that women do. For example, I can't stand doing my car stuff. I just learned how to put gas in the car when I was thirty-four years old, when my husband left. And you know, the trash, the yard work. But cooking, cleaning, and raising the children, it should be both husband and wife sharing responsibility.

Chapter 10

"I Knew
that I Wanted
to Be
a Naval Officer"

Daniel Gruta

Childhood Years in the Philippines

I was born on April 5, 1962, in Manila. My parents' families were not from Manila. My maternal grandfather was from Guiguinto, Bulacan, and my grandmother was from Naic, Cavite. Both of my father's parents were from Cavite province.

My father, Eduardo Gruta, joined the U.S. Navy in 1957 from Sangley Point Naval Station in Cavite City. Cavite City is across the bay from Manila City. Although we lived in Cavite City, I was born in Manila, in the University of Santo Tomas Hospital, because my mother did not trust the local hospital on the U.S. Naval Base. She said the Americans there don't give you the TLC [tender loving care] treatment; they make you walk and deliver the child. My father was not home the day I was born. He was aboard the U.S.S. *Hancock,* an aircraft carrier.

Although my father started out as a steward, after two years in the United States, he converted to the AK rating, or aviation storekeeper. My dad was the studious one in our family. He worked very hard and got good grades. I really admire my dad for that. He wanted to be a jet mechanic, but in those days, since the jet technology was so new, you had to have a security clearance. My father was not a U.S. citizen, so he could not get a security clearance. He did not become a citizen until 1969. For his entire career, he worked in the aviation community of the U.S. Navy.

My father's brother, Fernando, also joined the U.S. Navy. He stayed in the steward rating and was promoted to the rank of master chief, an E-9. He was the most senior enlisted man at the Chief of Naval Education Training Command back in the early eighties. In fact, he made Filipino history by being the first Filipino to write the mess specialist exam.

On my mother's side of the family, two of her brothers were U.S. Navy men. Uncle Adolfo started out as a steward and then converted to aviation storekeeper. Like my dad, he retired as a chief petty officer, an E-7. My mother's youngest brother, Florencio, was a ship storekeeper, and he retired as an E-8, a senior chief. He was the first one in our family to intermarry. He married a Japanese Italian. His wife sometimes feels like an outsider when we speak Tagalog to each other and English to her during social gatherings.

Both of my uncles from my mother's side had college backgrounds. But they joined the U.S. Navy for economic opportunities, even though they had to start out as stewards. They had a practical view of life. In the Philippines, they might earn a four-year degree but still not get a good paying job. The U.S. Navy was one way for them to get to the United States. After he joined the Navy, one of my uncles was able to finance his sister's medical school tuition.

In 1963, my father received orders to report to the Naval Air Station Whiting Field in Milton, Florida, for duty. That is about an hour east of Pensacola, Florida. We were supposed to join him. But it turned out that instead of being able to travel with us, his orders told him to travel with his ship from the Philippines to Honolulu, Hawaii. Because he was unable to accompany us, my mom decided to stay in the Philippines. My mom would not have been able to lift me and the luggage by herself. She is less than five feet tall, and I was a pretty heavy kid; so was the luggage. Who is going to help some E-4's wife carry luggage and a pudgy little kid around anyway?

So we stayed in the Philippines until I was ten years old. We had our own drug store, and my mother was the pharmacist. I grew up with a large extended family. Every Christmas, our house was packed with people exchanging gifts. After I came to America, Christmas was never the same again.

While in the Philippines, I learned how to speak English by going to Catholic school. I also attended an American school for one year. I spent nursery, kindergarten, and first grade at a Catholic school named Saint Joseph. Then, in 1969, my dad got stationed in Cubi Point. That's part of Subic Bay Naval Reservation. Because I was a dependent of a U.S. serviceman, I was able to go to any Department of Defense school in the Philippines. I attended John Paul School at Sangley Point Naval Station. I spent second grade there. Other students from the diplomatic community in Manila were bused there. That was my first exposure to Americans.

A year later, Sangley closed down. I reentered the Philippine school system. I spent all of third grade and a part of fourth grade at another Catholic school, Saint Francis de la Salle, in General Trias, Cavite.

Daniel Gruta reuniting with his wife Carmencita and oldest daughter, Katherine, after having served in Operation Desert Storm, San Diego, 1991

"I Came to America Just at the Right Age"

In 1972, when I was ten years old, we moved from Cavite City to Mira Mesa, San Diego. Until then, I did not see my dad full-time. Even when he was in the Philippines from 1969 to 1972, we lived in Cavite City and he lived in Subic. My mom did not want to go to Subic because it was a dumpy place—a place of prostitution and recreation for lonely sailors.

In 1972, my dad was in his sixteenth year of service in the U.S. Navy, and San Diego was his last assignment. So he said it was time for us to join him in the United States. By then, all of my mother's brothers and sisters had already established residence in the United States. We went through a lot of hassles before we left, because Marcos had just declared martial law. We had to pay all kinds of taxes and get all kinds of clearance.

I was glad to be in America because for one thing: there was unlimited television. For a ten-year-old, that was important. Before martial law was declared in the Philippines, we had "Hawaii Five-O" and "Star Trek," "Popeye," and "Mister Magoo." Many American shows were exported to the Philippines. After martial law, we only had the government station.

I did not have any problems adjusting to life in the United States. I spoke English well. I spoke like an American because I went to an American school in the Philippines. I also practiced English by watching U.S. shows on television.

I think I came to America just at the right age since I am able to shift back and forth between English and Tagalog. My brother, the next oldest, had a harder time adjusting because he did not know how to speak English. He was five years old when we arrived, and he had to start school right away. But my sister and my two younger brothers did not have the adjustment problems, because they were able to develop English in the subsequent years before they started school. All of us were born in the Philippines, except the youngest one, Michael, who was born in San Diego in 1975.

We lived in Mira Mesa because my dad was stationed at the nearby Miramar Naval Air Station. My parents bought their house for $22,000. Getting that loan was a shocker for my dad, because he had never been in debt before. They still live in that house today.

"Manila Mesa" and Catholic Schools

Even back in 1972, there were many Filipinos living in Mira Mesa. We called it "Manila Mesa." It was predominantly a Navy town. The biggest store in town was not Alpha Beta but the Navy Commissary store and the Navy Exchange at the Naval Air Station. Navy families develop lifelong ties. We see each other at the Navy Exchange and the Commissary store, and also at Good Shepherd [Catholic] Church. In the late 1970s, they formed the Fil-Am North County Association here in Mira Mesa.

The Filipino enlisted men tend to socialize among themselves. They go on liberty together. The wives also socialize with each other. Socially, there is no great distinction made between an E-4 and an E-7 [a third class petty officer and a chief]. The people who do make that distinction become very "famous" in the Filipino community.

But the officers have to watch how they are seen socializing with enlisted personnel, because it can be viewed as fraternization. As an officer, I have to maintain a professional relationship with the enlisted guys. For example, as a rule, subordinates may not call me by my first name, and I don't call them by their first names. I can't be their best buddy, because I'd be jeopardizing our relationship. I do not want to do that, because it would give Filipino American officers a bad name in the United States Navy. There is a distinct separation between officer and enlisted. But among the enlisted men, there is less of a distinction.

My parents first enrolled me in Mason Elementary, a public school. After a year, they felt that the public school was not giving us a good education, so in 1974, they sent me to a Catholic school. My grades rose because of encouragements from the Irish nuns and a Scottish teacher. Many Filipinos were sent to that school, and by and large we were the group that excelled.

High school was when many of the Filipino kids in the Catholic schools started to go off in different directions. Some went to public schools, and some to private schools. I went to Saint Augustine High School [Saints]. There were not too many Filipinos in this school.

By this time, my parents could not afford to pay the tuition any longer. They had four other children to support. My father had just retired from the Navy, and my mother had just started working as a pharmacy technician. She is a technician instead of a pharmacist because she needed another year of pharmacy school in the U.S. to get a license. There were four of us kids in a new country, so she made us her first priority. We would finish school before she would even think of going back.

To help pay for my tuition, I started working after school cleaning classrooms and painting buildings at Saints. That was how I paid for 75 percent of my tuition. The rest came from my parents and grants from the Diocese of San Diego.

Throughout high school, I saw myself as a Filipino American. I am a Filipino who has assimilated to the American culture, but I still speak Tagalog and I understand the Filipino culture. I do the *mano*—raising an elder's hand to my forehead. I respect my parents and elders, and maintain an appreciation for the extended family. I also value education. But then, when I was in school, I assimilated into the American culture. I ran track. I ran for government. I wrote for the school newspaper, and I competed for school honors.

I did face discrimination at school. Some of the students made racial remarks, but the funny thing was these remarks were meant for other ethnic groups. They called me Kwai Chang, this Kung Fu guy that was famous back then. They called me Tojo because of World War II. And they called me a V.C. because of the Vietnam War. I just ignored them. I did not let it bother me. I had better things to worry about, like grades.

I got even by outdoing them in school. Back then, if you did well, you did not have to take the final exams. During my first year at Saint Augustine High School, I was exempted from all the final exams. I think the other kids were just jealous of my achievements. But I always had the upper hand, because I did well in school and the authorities backed me up.

I did not have a close circle of Filipino friends. Much to my dismay, I was the outsider to the Filipino crowd. I did not fit in, because I did not dress the way they did and my hair was always short. I spoke Tagalog and they did not. I went to Catholic school, and they went to the public high school here in Mira Mesa.

They were the "ABs"—the "American Borns"—and they thought I was one of those "FOBs"—the "Fresh Off the Boats." In the late seventies and early eighties, there was a culture clash between these two groups. But I belonged to neither one.

So my problem was not assimilating with the Americans. My problem was assimilating with the Filipinos who were born and raised here, because I was not in their circle of friends. They were very tight, and I was an outsider. It bothered me, but I also saw education as my ticket out. My goal was to get a scholarship, go to college, and take myself out of this setting.

My circle of friends were and are still diverse. I had Mexican, white, Arab, Eastern European, and Polish friends. My closest friends now are still these guys that I hung out with in high school. That's the core of my friends. I tend to have few but close friends, but then I have many people I network with.

Dating in High School

In high school, I had the opportunity to go out with many women because our school had a lot of dances. Our sister school was OLP—Our Lady of Peace Academy. After school, all these girls would come by our school, or a lot of us guys would go over to their school. That's where I got my dates from usually. I was so preoccupied with my studying and a job that I planned my dates in advance. Most of the women I invited to the dances were white.

I did not take a Filipina to a dance until I was a junior in high school. The reason I rarely invited Filipinas out was because once you go out with one of them, you get paired for life. My father and mother were well known in the community, so the adults watched my social activities closely. The barrio mentality!

I had a motto in high school: date widely and lively. Never ask a girl to a dance twice. But in the Filipino community, they call you a "butterfly" if you date different Filipinas. As far as me dating out of the race, it was no problem with my parents. They knew I "played the field" and was academically responsible. All they told me was, "Look, son, if you go out with one of these Filipinas, you have to treat them differently." I respected their position.

My youngest brother, almost all of the girls that he dated have been Oriental—but not all Filipina. First, there was a Vietnamese, then a Filipina, and now a Japanese. And my sister had an Arab boyfriend. Another brother dates a Vietnamese. So they had a better mix than I did.

The U.S. Naval Academy

When I was in high school, I knew that I wanted to be a naval officer. In the summer of 1979, I took a trip back East to visit my aunt and uncle. They took me to see the U.S. Naval Academy in Annapolis, Maryland. I was impressed. I saw it as a way for me to move up, because it would open more doors for me than a regular college.

I graduated from Saint Augustine High in 1981 with honors. I was not admitted into the academy right away, however. I had good grades, but my SAT scores were not up to par. But I did get a spot in the Naval Academy preparatory school. I received my appointment to the Naval Academy in 1982. While at Annapolis, I majored in political science and served as a political science intern at the office of the Chief of Naval Operations for Political-Military Relations.

In my class, there were 25 Filipinos out of 1,300. I was probably one of two people who spoke Tagalog, and I was the only one who spoke it fluently. The others were raised in the States and never learned how to speak Tagalog.

I was closer to the Filipinos from the Philippine Military Academy than I was to Filipinos who were born here. Every year, the top 10 percent in the Philippine Military Academy compete for a spot in the U.S. service academies. These Filipinos liked me because I spoke Tagalog, I knew what went on back in the old country, and I knew something about the Philippine Navy, where I had served as a good will ambassador. I also had friends of other races; most were part of the Catholic choir. That was my support group.

In 1986, after I graduated, the Filipinos in the academy formed the Fil Am Association of the U.S. Naval Academy. The person who organized it, Max Mejia, is now a lieutenant junior grade in the Philippine Navy. As of last year [1992], there were 125 Filipinos in the academy—from all the different classes, freshmen to senior.

After receiving a Bachelor of Science degree in political science in 1986, I was commissioned as an ensign in the United States Navy. I went to flight training. I wanted to fly airplanes but I got sick and fell behind in the training, so they told me try something else.

From there, I was assigned to ships. I served aboard the U.S.S. *Fanning* as boilers and antisubmarine warfare officer. As boilers officer, I qualified as engineering officer of the watch.

During Operations Desert Shield and Desert Storm, I served as auxiliaries/electrical and fire control officer aboard the U.S.S. *Marvin Shields*. My claim to fame on the *Marvin Shields* was that since I spoke Tagalog, I was able to interview merchant ships in the Persian Gulf, because by and large they had Filipino crewmen on board. These men would tell me the information my commander required.

After that, I returned to the U.S.S. *Fanning*. We went to Central America for a counternarcotic operation. All that time, I led people in the engineering and weapons departments.

In March of 1992, I left the U.S.S. *Fanning*. The next month, I reported to the Naval Amphibious School in Coronado as a program manager for foreign military sales training. As part of this program, we teach junior officers from other countries naval shipboard operations. I train mostly officers from the Middle East. I am in charge of the computers in the international training department, and I also develop curriculum.

Marriage and Family

I got married in 1988. My wife, Carmencita, was born, raised, and educated in the Philippines. She is a nurse. She came to the United States in 1982 on a worker's visa. She was recruited by Mount Sinai Hospital in New York City. The East Coast, mainly the New York–New Jersey area, is a major entry point for Filipina nurses.

I met her in 1986 on my birthday. I was about to graduate from the Naval Academy. She was introduced to me by another Filipino from West Point. Until I reported to Pensacola, Florida later that year, I used to go up to New York City every other weekend just to see her when I had the chance.

We got married two years later in a civil ceremony here in San Diego. Then we went back to the Philippines in January of 1989 to get married in the church there.

My wife grew up in Manila, but her parents are from Tarlac province. Her father is from Victoria, and her mother is from Gerona. Her brothers and sisters were born at different locations in the Philippines because her father was with the Bureau of Internal Revenue. So they moved around often.

By the time my wife was born, they had settled in the Manila area. So she was born and raised in Manila. She went to Catholic schools all of her life. My wife has many relatives who have immigrated to the United States as professionals, mainly as accountants and lawyers.

My wife comes from a family of lawyers. But when she graduated from high school, martial law was declared in the Philippines. As a result, the courts and the legislature were suspended. So she realized that there was no profit in going on to law and decided to study nursing instead. She went to the University of Santo Tomas. She worked for Lourdes Hospital in Manila before she came to America.

Originally I had not intended to marry a Filipina because I had dated more anglos here. But in 1985, I was selected to serve as a good will ambassador to the Philippine Navy. I was back in the old country for two months. It was a personnel exchange cruise, and I got picked because I knew the culture and I knew the language.

It was on this cruise when I decided that there was something special about the Filipina for me. I hate to sound chauvinistic about marriages, but Filipinas have a way of making you feel like you are a king. They also have that tenderness, that elegance. Expressed in Tagalog, it sounds wonderful. Things get lost in the translation. And we share the same values about family, education, religion, and raising children.

So when I came back to the States, I started to look for the kind of women that I'd met in the Philippines. That was when I met my wife. To me, she looked like one of those Filipina movie stars, Vilma Santos. She had the same values that I had, plus she can stand on her own two feet. She knew New York like the back of her hand. She knew how to take charge of her life. I knew then that she was the one for me.

Religion is an important part of our marriage. We believe that no matter what hardship there is, we have God and our family. After God, the family is number one to us. We stick together. You may have to make sacrifices, but you do it for the good of the family.

My Tagalog had gotten better because of my wife. Hanging around her and her friends, I picked up the vocabulary of college-educated Filipinos. My wife's friends are all Filipinas: all the nurses, classmates from the old country, and people she worked with in New York. I still only read and write Tagalog at the third-grade level, because I came to the United States when I was in the fourth grade. So in a sense, my marriage to my wife has made me more Filipino. But my primary language of expression, my technical language, is still English. But for the social stuff, it is Tagalog.

After we got married, we moved to Mira Mesa because my parents lived here and could help my wife out, especially when I was out at sea. She also has cousins here in Mira Mesa. My mother helped care for our children. Initially my wife worked only on days that my mother was off, so we did not have to worry about child care.

I have two daughters: Katherine is three years old, and Victoria is two. I want my children to understand their Filipino heritage. I want them to know that we have strong family values—that families support each other. I want them to understand the importance of religion and the value of education. These values are not exclusively Filipino values, but they are much more accentuated among Orientals.

I want my children to know that there is a proud culture over in the Philippines—a culture of multitalented people. We also want to teach them the language. We speak in both English and Tagalog with the children. We want to show but not force the culture on them. We just want to give them the tools—the best of the Filipino culture.

But I also want them to believe that America is a land of unlimited potential. I want them to know that they will face discrimination but that they can do as well as anybody out there if they work hard enough and deal with it accordingly to reach their goals.

I want my daughters to grow up to be self-sufficient. I think I will be a protective dad, but I hope that I will be more understanding than other

Filipino parents since I grew up here. Of course, I'll always be the inquisitive dad, "Hey, what did you guys do on your date last night?" Other than that, I have always known that a lot of the women can do what the men do. I would not be where I am right now if it weren't for some women I knew back in the Naval Academy. They were the ones who helped me through math and engineering.

"What Country Are You from?"

I have met many people in the United States who do not trust people who do not speak English or do not show that they have assimilated. One of my biggest beefs about the United States is that when people speak to me on the phone, they think I was born in America. But when they meet me in person, they say, "What country are you from?" I guess we have a come a long way, but we still have a long way to go.

Once, I had a superior officer who told me that he was impressed by my performance in the engineering plant, where I gave commands over the intercom. He said, "I saw the aggressive side of you, Dan, and I liked that. I wanted to see if the men could understand you over the speaker because of the language thing." What language thing? I speak perfect English. He had heard me speak before. So despite the fact he had known me for almost a year, he still saw me for the color of my skin first.

I had another superior officer who sees minorities as causing moral decay in America. At that point, I wanted to say, "Excuse me! Do you know that Oriental Americans have the lowest rejection rate of all groups in the United States?"

I sometimes felt that I had to work much harder than the other guys to get credit for my work. Because you are Filipino, people, especially the ones in the Navy, assume that you do not have that "go-getter" attitude. I did not want to believe that at first, but those are just the facts of life, and I have to deal with it accordingly to succeed.

Balancing Community, Work, and Family

I see many subtle differences between my dad's generation and my generation. Something I notice about my dad's generation is that they are more conscious about being the only Filipinos in a setting than I am. For me, this is not so.

Another thing, the Filipino organizations in San Diego love to hold dances and talk about the old days. How do we get beyond that? How do we get ahead in this society? By and large, the older Filipinos continue to look back to the old country. But I am more concerned about my life in this country and about the future of my kids.

I do not have much time to get involved in the community now because of school and family. That's why I am stepping down from my post as a public relations officer for the Filipino American Military Officers Association [FAMOS].

FAMOS was established back in 1990. We have 120 members. They are from all the military branches but mainly the Navy. Most of the members were enlisted men prior to commissioning. I am one of the few who was commissioned through the academy. Our goal is community service. We encourage our members to make the rank. We recently established a college scholarship for deserving high school students.

I think the Filipino community in San Diego still has a strong Navy connection. Most of the Filipinos I meet here are from Navy families. But people in my age group are branching out into other occupations. Most of us are too busy working to get involved in the community. That is just my impression.

I would like to be more involved if I had more time. I am more interested in helping the young people, getting them out of gangs and letting them know that the future is promising. That's why I believe so strongly in having positive role models for our young people.

But for now, my focus is on my wife and my kids. As much as I enjoy having an extended family, I am trying to preserve my nuclear family. I decide matters with my wife and try to spend quality time with our kids. I suppose that is one of my American traits.

And although I value being able to get things done because of my family connection, if someone asked me to do him a favor that violates my sense of ethics or family well-being, I would say, "No way." That's where I draw the line.

Another difference between us and a lot of other Filipinos is that we seldom send money to relatives. I basically say to my wife that we can send money as long as it does not affect our bills and the children. So, the kids come first, then us, then everybody else.

When I was in the academy, someone asked me if I gave money to my parents. I replied, "No. Why should I? They can work. I am not going to give money to be a good son." I feel that you pay back affection by giving time and service to your parents, not money. So I am trying to balance all these things. And I have so far. My wife is pretty practical; she is my reality check.

Filipinos are a growing population in San Diego. We need to team up, because we need to be represented in this country. We can no longer be considered as excess baggage. We are part of this country.

But I feel that the Filipino community continues to be occupied with the same old stuff: the dances, the beauty pageants, the picnics. As for me, I am interested in issues like employment, representation, discrimination, training our children to be leaders, etc. I want to get the young people involved, because they are the future of the community.

There is a perception among the young people that all Filipino community leaders ever do is argue. They have these long meetings, but they never get anything done. I think that is what turns the young people off.

Before, I was more interested in international relations because I am a naval officer, and the Navy inherently depends on foreign politics. But now, I am a little bit older, I am a house owner, and I am a parent. So I have taken more of an interest in what happens in local politics.

There are three things that limit my participation in politics. One, my income. Two, I do not have that much time: I have school, and I have a family. And three, I am in the military, and professional ethics laws do not allow us to be involved in politics. Those are the reasons why I am not as active as I should be.

In the fall of 1994, I will be leaving the Navy to start a master's program in business. Afterward, I plan to pursue a career in the international arena.

Chapter 11

"I Offended Many Filipinos Because I Was an FOB"

Dario Villa

The U.S. Navy

I was born in Manila in 1958. My father, Dante, is an Ilocano from Sarrat, Ilocos Norte. His father was a well-known teacher, and his mother was a homemaker. My mother, Estelita, is a Tagalog from Putlod, Jaen Nueva Ecija. Her parents were members of the small middle class in the Philippines. Her father was a school superintendent, and her mother was a farmer.

My parents met in college in Manila. I heard stories that when my father was courting my mother, there was bias against him because he is from the Ilocos—a "different nation."

My father joined the U.S. Navy in 1960. He was studying to be an engineer when he married my mother. Life was very difficult economically. When I came along, my father decided to take his chances and joined the Navy, knowing that the only place he would go, regardless of his education, was into stewardship or as kitchen help. His older brother, who joined the Navy before him, worked in the kitchen and the mess hall, and eventually became a commissary specialist. Very few Filipinos were allowed into other rates. Those days, only U.S.–raised Filipinos were given a little bit more flexibility. That situation did not change until the late sixties, when my father, who is fairly bright, was given the opportunity to become a hospital corpsman.

My father was recruited out of Sangley Point Naval Base near Manila. The U.S. Navy advertised in the Philippine newspapers for male high school graduates between the ages of eighteen to twenty-four. College-educated men were not desirable, because the military didn't want bright Filipinos. So those who were in college or who had a college degree lied about their level of education.

My father left for the United States on December 5, 1960, the same day that my sister was born. I was two years old then. I have this old picture of my father right before he took off for America. While my father was away, I was being raised by my maternal grandparents and my mother. I did not miss having a father because I had an extended family of uncles, great-uncles, and older male cousins. My mother went to school and became a teacher—a status she would lose because the U.S. system did not recognize her Philippine education.

My father's decision to join the U.S. Navy was purely economic. When he started out, he made sixty dollars a month and sent half of this to my mother. It was a sacrifice, but I suppose when you get the feeling that you are supporting your family and that life is better for them, the distance mattered little.

Because of my father's ROTC experience in college, while in training his drill instructor trusted him to do the drills. As a result, he received some special privileges, such as using the drill sergeant's bathroom. I also heard stories about his experience with racism in West Virginia. While traveling there, he realized that there were separate trains and facilities for whites and blacks. He related that whenever he used either bathroom, he got the same stares from both groups. So he decided to use whichever bathroom became available first. I am not fully sure how his experience with racism affected him. My father is a man of few words.

Leaving the Philippines

We left the Philippines for California on March 31, 1976. I was seventeen years old and in my third year of high school. My sister Emma was fifteen, and my brother Dindo was only three.

My father decided that it would be best for us to leave at that time for two reasons: one, because he wanted our family to stay together; and two, because the Philippines was in turmoil politically and economically. The country's general deterioration contributed to our need to leave. But we also were being pulled toward what we perceived to be better opportunities in the United States. At that time, I thought that the streets of the U.S. were paved with gold, devoid of garbage and flies, and that everyone was beautiful.

Leaving the Philippines was a frightening experience for me. One of the saddest moments in my life was the day we were to leave for the U.S. Even at my young age of seventeen, I understood that I would never return and that even if I did, it would be different, because I would be a different

*Dario Villa taking Filipino students to a weekend retreat in
Laguna Mountain, where the group discussed Filipino American
history and family relations, 1992*

person. I knew that I would never again live in my village, that I was stretching my umbilical cords so far that even if they stayed connected, they would never snap back so that I could end up the same place that I started.

I remember crying and trying to hide, not wanting to go, while knowing all the time that I must. My emotions were mixed. I was excited by what I knew of America from books, magazines, movies, and former classmates who had lived in America, but at the same time I was feeling insecure.

I also had a fiancée at the age of seventeen. We have known each other since we were in the sixth grade. Having a fiancée added to my agonies, but the lifelong promises we made to each other gave me strength. Before I left the Philippines, I told her parents that I would come back for her when I had become successful. But distance took a toll on our relationship. Even though I dated other women while I was in San Diego, deep in my heart, I knew that when I was ready to get married, I would go home. Unfortunately, she did not feel the same way. Promises were broken, and she got married in 1979.

When I saw her again in 1982, I discovered that the love I was feeling was no longer for her but for the memories. It was love of the events that took place in my life when I was growing up with her. I learned, however, that I cannot forget her, because that would mean forgetting some of the best years of my youth. Eventually, I was able to put things in proper perspectives, but she definitely broke my heart and ruined some magnificent dreams that I had.

"Fresh Off the Boat!"

We came directly to San Diego because my father was stationed here. I would say that the great majority of Filipinos in San Diego are Navy-related. Many were able to immigrate here due to their military connection, even if they themselves were not in the Navy. For example, my family is in the process of sponsoring two uncles to immigrate here. These uncles are not in the Navy, but because my father joined the Navy many years ago, they are now able to come.

When we arrived in San Diego in 1976, I attended Montgomery High School in South San Diego. I was happy to be there because I saw many Filipino faces that reminded me of home. Assuming that their hearts and thoughts were like mine, I was very friendly toward them.

To my surprise, I offended many Filipinos because I was an "FOB"— "Fresh Off the Boat." That made my immigration experience more painful. I was ridiculed because my accent reminded them of their parents. It was their shame coming out at my expense. A number of times in my classes, there were Filipinas who giggled and displayed bodily discomfort when I spoke. I was a reminder of the image they hate, part of themselves. One time I'd had it, so I turned around and said to them, "I know why you are laughing at me. I dress like your parents. I speak like them. I remind you of them and that bothers the heck out of you, because you are embarrassed by them."

The overt racism from the Filipino Americans broke my heart. At first I didn't know all the negative connotations that came with the term "FOB." I thought it meant that I was new. So when somebody said, "FOB," I laughed, because I thought, "Hey, here is a Filipino who is inviting me into his world by calling me a newcomer." I didn't know that they were making fun of me behind my back. Then somebody explained to me that being called a FOB is like being a "nigger, somebody who is dumb and stupid." Learning that being labeled FOB is the same as being called dumb, stupid, and unworthy hurt me terribly.

I longed for my old friends in the Philippines, the types who would catch a bullet for me if necessary. I thought Americans were not capable of such deep friendships and were not as warm as my village mates. I considered the locally raised Filipinos "American." To keep my sanity, I rationalized why I should not like "those" Filipinos. It was a double-edged sword. They thought I was not good enough, and I thought the same of them: "They aren't really Filipinos. How could they be? They don't speak their parents' language. They don't even know anything about their ancestral land."

So I had very few Filipino friends in high school, not because I didn't want to be friends with them, but because they didn't want to be friends with somebody who was their own but not really theirs. In their opinion, because I spoke English with an accent, I was dumb. With a damaged psyche, I found comfort in the company of Mexicans, other FOBs, open-minded Filipinos, and others who accepted me unconditionally.

College Years: "I Became More Open and Accepting"

In 1977, while attending Southwestern Community College, I joined Pag-kakaisa, a Filipino student organization. I thought I was *the* only Tagalog speaker in the group, until I realized that there were others who also spoke the language but hid it. The stigma of being called an FOB was so powerful that it was easier for them to hide their Filipino-ness than to face it.

In that organization, I realized that I had an obligation to myself and to others to capitalize on our similarities. The change was gradual and mutual. When my feelings began to be more positive, so did their attitudes toward me. We all became more accepting of each other. I became more open, and so did they. So I did make some very good connections in college, Filipinos who had become friends for life. When I discussed our initial reactions to each other with a couple of those friends, one of them admitted that when she first met me in college, she did not want to be around me because I was carrying my books in a basket rather than in a backpack and I wore a straw hat and slippers. To her, I was too much of a Filipino. This basket book bag, which made others see me as a primitive, became a symbol of my pride. I carried that native basket with pride all the way to graduate school.

During that transition, I also became more comfortable with the English language. I knew that if I wanted to succeed in this country, I had to find a way to improve the way I speak English. So I read out loud, I recorded my readings, then listening to myself and repeating words I had difficulties with. As a result, I became more confident. Also, because I read so much, I felt that I had more knowledge than the next person. It may be inconsequential knowledge, but recognizing that I may know some things that other people don't gave me confidence.

It was also at this time that I became acutely more aware of other ethnic groups. When I attended school in Subic in the Philippines, I was exposed to many military brats—whites, blacks, Latinos. My perception of them was that they were rude and that they had no respect for Filipinos and the Philippines. Their maids were Filipinas; their gardeners were Filipinos; therefore, they treated Filipinos as inferior. I also remember young American sailors in Olongapo City behaving like wild animals, mistreating and abusing Filipinos, especially the women. That experience prejudiced my mind. I carried that baggage of disgust and mistrust with me for a long time. In fact, whenever I would meet someone who said that he or his father was stationed in the Philippines, my immediate thought was, "You were one of those assholes."

As my comfort zone expanded, I realized my own narrow-mindedness. I realized that there were people in the United States who cared about other people, perhaps as much or much more than I did. With that realization, my world just opened up. I became more open and accepting. Learning about other people became my passion.

One incident that sticks in my mind took place in the beginning of my junior year at San Diego State University. I made a cultural presentation to my predominantly white classmates. They fully appreciated and accepted me. They made me feel so good that after the presentation, I told them, "For the first time in my life, I feel so comfortable and so accepted by white people."

That incident was a cathartic experience which became the starting point of my full participation in campus life. I attended as many cultural and social gatherings, as many sorority and fraternity parties, that I could to gain exposure. I had decided to put aside my prejudice. I knew that if I were to understand America, the university was probably one of the best opportunities I had. I went camping and met white Americans who were down-to-earth, who would rather be barefoot than wear shoes, who were wearing slippers like I was. That just amazed me, because I thought the values that I carried with me—simplicity, love of nature, all these other stuffs—were exclusive to Filipinos and other Asians. Getting to know Mexicans, African Americans, European Americans, and many different Asian Americans whose values were like mine made my college life unforgettable.

I also dated women from different racial groups, Mexican, Vietnamese, black. I think it was part of an experiment—not in a sexist sense. It was not planned; it just turned out that way. I felt fortunate that I was able to experience different people. But not all of my experiences were positive. I remember going out with a Jewish classmate whose grandmother disapproved of me. One time when I picked her up, the old lady proceeded to tell me that I was not right for her granddaughter. I exploded and said, "Ma'am, you are only concerned about your side of the issue. You have no idea what my parents would say if they knew that I was going out with your granddaughter. So please don't give me this crap." Then I left. I am still friends with that Jewish girl. Later on, she married a Filipino who converted to Judaism.

I was one of the very few Filipinos who lived on campus. Most of the Filipinos I knew then lived at home with their parents. Although my parents' house was only half an hour away, I chose to live on campus to experience "college life." I felt that living at home would stifle my growth. Unfortunately, through the eyes of some Filipinos, especially the Filipinas, living on campus made me look too progressive, too "American." Just when I thought that the discrimination issue with other Filipinos was resolving itself, I found out I was wrong. Whenever I invited a Filipina to have dinner at my apartment, I was immediately rejected. They were afraid that I'd become so Americanized that the real reason why I was inviting them for a meal of rice and *adobo* [a stew-like dish] was to get into their pants. It was ironic, because on the other hand, I was still walking around with my slippers and shorts and my basket from the Philippines, and that made me "too Filipino" in their eyes. I thought I was becoming more acceptable to Filipino Americans, but to my dismay, I was wrong again.

Working in Santa Maria, California

After completing my master's degree in counseling in 1983, I applied everywhere for a job. I found a teaching and counseling job at Saint Joseph High School in Santa Maria, a small agricultural town on the California central coast. The only thing I knew about Santa Maria was based on Carlos Bulosan's autobiography, *America Is in the Heart*.★ I stayed at this parochial, all-white school for three years, teaching sociology and psychology. I believe I was the first ethnic teacher there.

It was my years in Santa Maria which restored my faith in Filipinos. As soon as I got into town, I went to the Filipino store owned by a one-armed man from Cavite. We both spoke Tagalog, so he decided to help me. With his assistance, I met Jun and Lu Garcia, both originally from Pangasinan. I told them that we used to travel through their town because my father was from the north. My knowledge about Pangasinan became our common bond, and they agreed to take me on as a boarder. Eventually I moved into a small house behind a bigger house owned by a sweet and kind Filipina named Virginia.

In Santa Maria, I was amidst Filipinos who treated me like family. Their kindness and acceptance reminded me so much of home. This would never have happened in San Diego, because city people are less trusting and are not as down-to-earth as people who work on the farms. That was another common thing that I had with the people I lived with: I also grew up on the farms. In fact, some weekends when I was off, I went to the farm with them for a few hours, picking sugar peas and strawberries.

★*America Is in the Heart* is an account of what it was like to be a Filipino in California and its sister states during the 1930s. First published in 1946, *America Is in the Heart* is a required text for all students of the Filipino experience in the United States.

Culture and Identity

When I arrived in America at the age of seventeen, I knew only of my Filipino-ness. I knew only one way of living, and that was dictated by the values that I had learned in the Philippines. But along the way, I have incorporated American values into my life to a point that it is hard to separate the two.

I am able to walk smoothly in both worlds—the Filipino and the American worlds. Deep in my heart, I don't think I can say that I am only American or that I am only Filipino. Even for Filipinos in the Philippines, what is a true Filipino value these days? The Philippines is so Westernized that unless you are one of the indigenous people, you cannot really say that you are a true Filipino. It would be hypocritical of me to say that I am 100 percent Filipino, because there is no such thing.

Because of my strong connection with my roots, when I speak there is no denying that I am as Filipino as one can get. I speak the language as fluently as the next Filipino, and I know our history probably better than most. On the other hand, because I have done what it takes to become comfortable in the American world, I also can be considered a full-blown American.

Many Filipinos have become Americanized by discarding their Filipino values. In my case, what I have is an amalgamation of values. I have been able to find a comfort zone between both cultures, taking advantage of the values that I learned as a kid and adopting the American values that I think will make me a much wholler, more knowledgeable individual. For example, I use both the Filipino value of family interdependence *and* the American value of independence to the best interests of myself and my family. I also have incorporated those American values that enrich my life, such as being less chauvinistic than my contemporaries in the Philippines, and being open-minded to people and new experiences.

I have been careful not to lose myself in the process of becoming a well-adjusted individual in my adopted country. I want to make sure that what is important to me stays with me. But in the process of Americanization, you invariably feel like you have given up or that you have lost some values. I may have, but I refuse to look at it this way. I believe that I have gained more than I have lost. For example, my sense of family is still very Filipino. That has not changed. I still like having a big, extended family. I don't believe in the nuclear family. In fact, I purchased a home in South San Diego that is only twelve houses away from my parents' house so that I could be close to them.

I am proud of where I came from, and I am proud of my ability to understand the soul of my culture. It's hard to say what non-Filipinos think of me, but I hope that they see me as a Filipino American. Whenever somebody says to me, "I just see you as a man," I tell them, "You have to see me as a *brown* man, because that's what I am. If you see me just as a man, you are taking my background away from me. You are not seeing me as a whole person. You are seeing only the American part of me and not the strong ethnic pride that I have."

I am sure that non-Filipinos see me as an Asian. When I was at San Diego State, I was a member of the Asian American Student Alliance. Obviously, I have a lot in common with people who are from that part of the world, because we share many of the same values. I enjoyed the company of the Chinese, the Japanese, the Vietnamese, and other Southeast Asians that I met in college, and I still am very close to some of them. But when it comes to describing myself, then I am not Asian, I am Filipino.

I think we Filipinos are for the most part culturally different from other Asians, definitely different from the Japanese and Chinese because of our misfortune of being colonized by Spain and then the United States. That definitely changed the way we lived our lives. The Western values that were implanted in the Philippines made us Westerners in Asia. That's how I see the modern-day Filipinos, which includes me.

Marriage to a Non-Filipina

In 1991, I married Rebecca Starr, a European American with a dash of Native American blood. I met Becky while I was teaching in Santa Maria. It was her humble ways and her strong family values that first attracted me to her. I had not intended to marry an anglo person or even a Filipina who was raised in the States because of the cultural differences. But as I became more open to different ethnic groups, I realized that the values I held dearly were not exclusive to the Filipinos. What mattered was that we understood and loved each other. Becky and I knew from the start that we were better off with each other than without.

When I told my parents about my intention to marry Becky, they were very concerned. They said, "Couples from the same ethnic group don't always see eye to eye. How is it going to be with you?" I knew a long-term engagement was required. We met in 1983 but did not marry until 1991. Before we got married, I asked Becky's parents to allow her to live with my family so she could understand our dynamics. It was important to me that she liked my family and that my family liked her. Fortunately that was the way things turned out.

I know other Filipinos in San Diego, especially some of the elders, always have something to say about my marriage to Becky. It makes me sad, because I value their opinion. I try to tell them that the values they think are important are the values that my wife has. For example, one time I took Becky to an all-Filipino party. She was accepted immediately when she was offered some goat meat and rice, and she went at it. The Filipinos at the party were impressed. They saw her as stretching herself to become like us, but she really was just being herself. She is an open-minded person, willing to try anything.

Initially, Becky's parents had reservations about our relationship, because they have not known many Filipinos. I knew that it would take time. But they were very, very nice people. They welcomed me into their home as if I were family and definitely contributed to the good relationship that I have with my wife, because they also value family the way I value family.

Getting married is a process of discovery. First I realized that my expectations were very traditional. I grew up in a home where women did certain things and men did certain things—strict division of labor. I thought I'd gotten over those expectations, but I discovered that when we first got married, I wanted Becky to do all the cooking and other "womanly" housework. I have since recovered—but talk about collision of values! My old value tells me she is supposed to do these chores; my new value tells me whoever has the time should do them.

Now we have a daughter, Rio Jacinta. Raising this child is going to be challenging, and my wife and I are going to question each other from time to time. Before my wife gave birth, one of my female colleagues pointed out to me that since my wife became pregnant, I had been acting differently—somewhat more chauvinistic. I thought about it and said, "I grew up for seventeen years in a society that embedded in me the idea that a man becomes a real man when he impregnates someone." For her, I was being chauvinistic; but for me, it was the way that I, a father-to-be, was supposed to act. So I said to this colleague, "If the first seventeen years of your life have affected you, then mine have affected me too."

Becky and I would like for our daughter to be bicultural. We know we must provide the example. But we cannot choose for her, we can only guide her. With her own mind and her own heart, if she chooses to travel a path that is different from mine or from my wife's, and if that is going to make her happy, we'll accept that. But as parents, we'll be happiest if she accepts the path that we think would be best for her.

We would like Rio Jacinta to be able to feel comfortable in either culture. We'll do our best to give her the best of both cultures, but she is the only one who can decide that when the time comes. I would like for her to have all the values that I admire, that I love, and that I keep in my pocket all the time—little things such as liking Filipino food, talking stories at night, sitting in the backyard doing nothing, having respect for the elders, calling me *Tatay* rather than "Dad," and calling my parents *Lolo* and *Lola* rather than "Grandpa" and "Grandma." It is important to me that the cultural ties remain intact—stretched but intact.

My wife is learning Tagalog to better understand my culture and to teach our daughter. I speak to my wife in Tagalog about 30 percent of the time. Her embracing my culture has made things a lot easier. She has learned to prepare Filipino dishes. Her *adobo* is better than mine, and I cook a better hamburger dish than she does. I think we have come to that point where a mixture of our two cultures has enhanced our existence.

I also think that being exposed to my culture has made Becky more interested in her Native American heritage. It has been a hidden heritage, repressed or suppressed by her grandparents because of the history of prejudice against Native Americans in this country. But now my wife is more open to it. She's gone through her own evolution in terms of who she is. I told her, "Maybe it is your Native American heritage that makes you so simple and so down-to-earth."

Experiences with Racism

Today I work as a guidance counselor at Eastlake High School in Chula Vista. Am I aware of racism? YES! I have had white colleagues make comments such as, "If I were competing for a job with you, I would be afraid because I am white." I answered that one by saying, "What makes me better qualified are my *additional skills,* such as being almost trilingual in English, Tagalog, and Spanish, my multiculturalism, sensitivity, and understanding of other cultures. Yes, you should be afraid, not because you are white, but because you are not as good."

I have seen that kind of racism occurring quite a bit in the last couple of years—people who think that we are still not good enough. On the issues of affirmative action and quotas, I have my opinion. Yes, there is affirmative action in this country, but not for me. White people have the best affirmative action in this country. We need just to look at history. Who's been running this country? Which group has benefited more? Quotas? Just look at the top corporations and companies in the United States. You'll be lucky to find a handful of nonwhites at the top. Yes, there are quotas, but they have been reserved for whites.

I know many Filipinos would deny that they have been discriminated against. Too many are so thankful to be here that they shut their eyes to avoid seeing the injustices, political and economic injustices. Then there are those who simply don't care. This type of attitude stifles our community.

Many of us have limited our definition of success to mean middle-class materialism. But I think as we grow older, we redefine our notion of "making it." Just because you own a nice house in East Lake, in La Jolla, or in Mira Mesa, it does not necessarily mean that you have made it. Maybe financially you have, but can you really feel comfortable participating in mainstream America? Most Filipinos don't. For me, I feel comfortable but not to the same degree that a white person would. I am not sure how to explain it.

I think it's a combination of two things: race and economics. I may do certain things because I can afford it financially and because I don't think being Filipino has anything to do with it. On the other hand, if I didn't feel comfortable, even if I had the money, I wouldn't do it. Most Filipinos, like me, still sometimes hesitate when we deal with mainstream America. I don't know if that is an inferiority complex or just feeling different.

The people from the European background, once they have mastered the English language, you can't tell them from the others. But you and me, we may speak better than the most educated white folks, but we still are not going to be accepted as equal because of our racial differences. I refuse to take on that battle every day. I have better things to do. I know that it is there. I feel it, but it doesn't change me a bit. I feel sorry for people who are that narrow-minded.

Ties to the Philippines

We plan regular visits to the Philippines. Two years ago I took Becky to my village, and she loved it. When my grandmother first met Becky, she was concerned because my wife was not a Filipina. But when she got to know Becky, she realized that they shared many of the same values. I knew that my relatives liked and accepted Becky when they said, "She is like a Filipina." Next year we plan to take our daughter to the Philippines.

Honestly I do not know if I would go back to the Philippines to live permanently. I have changed so much, and I am not particularly interested in returning to farm work. I have transplanted my life to the United States and have gotten used to the convenience of living here. It is not that I can no longer live in the village. I probably could adjust to living anywhere in the world, but I prefer to live in a more comfortable environment. People in my village, they live on a farm, they wake up early, farm all day, go home in the evening, chat with their family, have dinner, and go to sleep. I don't think I can do that any more. And my wife liked to visit there, but I don't know if she would like to live there.

But I will always visit the Philippines to reestablish connections, to share stories and laughter with old friends and relatives. I will visit often, because part of me will always live there. I am proud of who I am and where I came from.

Chapter 12

"I Could
Not Cope
with Life"

Joey Laguda

Early Years in Cicero, Illinois

I was born in Chicago, Illinois, in June of 1969. Both of my parents were from the Visayas, Philippines. My mother had immigrated to Chicago in 1965 to complete her studies to be a laboratory technologist. She was here on an exchange-visitor's program, and sponsored my father and two older brothers as her dependents. They came to the U.S. a few years later than she did. My father had graduated in the Philippines with a bachelor's degree in criminology but couldn't get a job as a police officer here because he was not a U.S. citizen. So he only worked blue-collar jobs.

My younger brother and I were the only ones born in the States, and we consider ourselves to be Americans. My family lived in Cicero, a suburban area on the outskirts of Chicago. The area we lived in consisted mostly of Italians. About five blocks away, there were blacks and other ethnic groups, but they were outside of Cicero. Except for my family, there were no colors other than white in Cicero. That was it. No other ethnic group really stuck out in my mind.

When I attended elementary school there, I didn't understand the racial differences that would prove later to be a great challenge in my life. My friends at school were white Italians, and I had assimilated pretty well into that group. At first, they thought I was Chinese. When I told them that I was Filipino, they asked me what was a Filipino. I didn't really know the answer to that. The most I understood was that we were from the Philippines, because that was what my parents taught me at home. But I didn't know where the Philippines was. I would not have been able to point it out on a map.

From what I understand, my two older brothers, who were born in the Philippines, didn't fit in as well because they had Filipino accents, and the kids made fun of them. They eventually made their own friends, but there was a call to lose their ethnic identity, to fit in.

My parents worked very hard to provide for our family. Sometimes, they worked multiple jobs to make ends meet. I remember that they were not home much of the time, so my two older brothers took turns at raising me and my younger brother. My mother believed that if we could have a taste of the better things in life, we would never settle for second best. Our taste in food, clothing, cars, and other material things was first-rate. Maybe we couldn't afford such luxuries, but we always had the best. Because of this, I always wanted to have or be the best. Whenever someone told me that I wasn't good enough, I went out of my way to prove them wrong.

Moving to San Diego

We lived in Cicero until I was about seven years old. I had assimilated into the white society there and felt a part of that community. Then in 1976 my family moved to San Diego because my mother has a sister here.

In San Diego, things were much different, because I didn't quite fit in so readily. We moved to Rancho Penasquitos, a suburb in north San Diego. Back then, in the mid-1970s, Penasquitos was predominantly white. We were among the first group of Filipinos to move there. The majority white population was not tolerant of any minorities. This I got to experience from watching racial fights my brothers were involved in and seeing the words "Flips go home" spraypainted on the house of one of my best friends. Some of the fights would even take place right in front of our house. My parents were working most of the time so they did not witness these fights, and we never really talked about them. At that time, they were working so much that we didn't want to burden them with our problems.

I could not understand what was going on, because I felt that I was being rejected from a group that I had always belonged to. So I went out to prove them wrong. I felt I had to prove that I could get along with them or that I was better than what they said I was. That led to much confusion in my life.

Racial Problems and Gang Activities

In Cicero and during my first couple of years in Rancho Penasquitos, I didn't have any Filipino friends. But after what my brothers had gone through, they told me that Filipinos needed to stick together and watch out for one another. There would always be strength in numbers. It was sort of a defense that we could all fall back on.

That was when I started hanging around Filipinos. My generation of

Joey Laguda (center) drinking a soda at a social function after having attended the Twelve-Step program, San Diego, 1993

friends consisted of Filipinos who had been born in the States, like myself. They spoke with no accents and had assimilated into society as well as possible. As far as we were concerned, we were Americans. I felt more at ease with these Filipino friends, because whites would tend to ask me things like, "Why do you have Chinky eyes? Why do you have this and that?" I didn't know. I was born that way.

Filipinos made up most of my friends, but they were not my only friends. I still was able to incorporate other ethnic groups. My generation seemed to get along pretty well with the white majority, and things were peaceful at that level. We were pretty much the few Filipinos who hung around and understood white people.

I saw both sides very clearly. I could see that it was hard for Filipinos like my older brothers, who were born in the Philippines, to fit in. I knew what it was like to be alienated for no reason other than your accent or your physical characteristics. On the other hand, I could see that it was a big misunderstanding, because whites and Filipinos did not really talk to each other.

In order for me to understand what was going on, I had to see the other side. I wanted to know exactly what it was that Filipinos were doing that made whites angry or uncomfortable. I noticed that when I went into stores, the store people would eye me suspiciously. Maybe they've had bad experiences with a few Filipinos. That did not make it right, but I could understand their position.

Basically, I was trying to switch back and forth so much that sometimes I lost myself. What the hell were these Filipinos doing? What the hell were these white people doing? I saw Filipinos fighting white people for no other reason than because this guy or that guy looked at them funny. Then on the other hand, I saw the white guys that I played football with fighting Filipinos. I was mad at both groups. I bounced back and forth, and in trying to understand both sides, I got caught up in a lot of things. I got really lost, and I started to get involved in alcohol, drug abuse, and gangs. I was trying to understand what didn't really make much sense. I was trying to figure out why I was so unique, why I didn't quite fit either mold—the Filipino or the white mold.

There also were problems at home with my parents. Even in San Diego, my parents still had to work a lot, and I saw very little of them. I understand now that they worked hard so that they could provide the best for us. But back then, I felt that they wanted to get away from me and that they were abandoning me. I didn't feel a part of the family. I felt hurt, lonely, and abandoned.

I wanted to prove to my parents that I was worthy of their attention. So when I got involved in extracurricular activities, I strove to be the best. For example, when I played Pop Warner football, I started at every position I had. I received high marks throughout junior high and the early years of high school. This seemed to capture my parents' attention for a little while, but it was temporary. I seemed to understand that if I received a B grade, I needed to get an A to win their approval. If I didn't get the most tackles on the team, then I wasn't a good enough football player—even though I started both offense and defense and all special teams.

After a while, I found I could not achieve the best status always and that I could not possibly please my parents. So I began to lose interest in some of my positive goals. They didn't seem to be important to me any more. My grades dropped, and I quit playing football. The only time I felt that I got my parents' attention was when I got into trouble, which increased when I went from junior high to high school. When I separated myself from my parents, I turned to my friends. That was where the troubles of my life started.

I concentrated more on getting my friends' approval. When I was with my friends, I felt that I was a part of something. I looked up to them, and they looked up to me. We shared a bond that is hard to describe, except that I felt that I belonged to something that went beyond having friends who were fun to be around. I had friends that I could confide in, friends that would encourage me in whatever I did, friends that would be there for me till the very end, regardless of whether I was right or wrong. What I found myself to be was wrong more times than right.

When I partied with the people of my generation, I set out to prove that I could party harder than any of them. I wanted to be the one who could drink the most, who was the funniest, the craziest, the wildest. My generation got along with everyone, so I turned out to be the biggest people-pleaser in town.

It was when I was around older generations of Filipinos, like my brothers and their friends, that I started noticing the differences between white and brown. These older Filipinos had been affected more by racial tensions than I had. When I was around them, I saw a real hatred for white people. They would say things like, "Screw the white guys. Forget the white guys. I don't want to deal with them." They mistrusted everyone and felt that the world was out to get them. They had such a chip on their shoulder. Through them, I began to feel that no one could be trusted and that we could make it on our own.

The thing was that I seemed to make sense of it all, and it was all justified. Filipinos were being slurred and slandered, and therefore it was right for us to retaliate. I was involved in many fights because of this. When I got angry about anyone thinking that I was less than human, I made sure they knew I was someone to be reckoned with. I felt there was no reason why they shouldn't accept me. So I forced them to look at my side. I would get into fights to prove that I was not a weak, timid, little Filipino. At 5'9" and 195 pounds, I am a fairly large Filipino. I don't fit the stereotypical norms. I had always been a little bigger than the rest of the guys when I was growing up. So whenever there was a conflict to be resolved, I was sure to be one of the guys to get involved.

I remember that I would not take anything from anybody. If you said something bad about me or my friends, I was sure to get into a fight over it. If you said you didn't want me at your party, or kicked me or my friends out, I'd be in a fight. If you looked at me strangely or stared me down, I'd give serious thought to getting into a fight. I felt that I constantly had to prove myself and that I had to get everyone's attention.

When the problems of race subsided, all that hate and fear transferred into gang activities. What you had was a group of Filipinos with a lot of rage who always wanted to prove themselves. I remember partying with these guys and having to prove that I could do the most drugs, drink the most beer, and get into the most fights.

So I became pretty good at drinking and drugging and fighting. It was kind of weird, because the more experienced in these things I became, the more I did. It wasn't like I didn't have any morals. In fact, the more bad things I did, the more I drank. I had to at the time. It was a way for me to cope with what I was doing. I couldn't go home to Mom and say that I was involved in a big brawl because some guys looked at me funny, or that I had finished a case of beer all by myself the other night, much less tell her that I was involved in drugs.

Having to hide such things, dealing with the guilt of getting involved with them in the first place, having to deal with beating up somebody just because he was at the wrong place at the wrong time, led me to increase my drug and alcohol abuse. It was the only way I knew how to cope. I did not have anyone to turn to. If I went to my friends, they would probably offer me a drink. If I went to my parents, I'd probably get punished. I didn't like either option, and I felt really alone. I was surrounded by people, and I felt alone. Being alone when I was confused was a difficult position for me to be in. I had ruined every relationship that I had been involved in, because I had so many things to hide. I tried to please everyone, and I felt I was failing miserably. Things just seemed to get crazier and crazier.

During my senior year in high school, things got better for a little while. I was getting along with a lot of people. The older Filipinos did not have that much effect on me any more because they had already graduated. So I was sticking around more with my generation of Filipinos.

There was another group of Filipinos at my school that wasn't a part of the group I was around. They were Filipinos who were new to the States. You could tell who they were because they were a lot smaller than the ones who were born here. I felt odd about how different we were from each other by the way we spoke and the way we looked at things. I got along with them, but we still had separate groups. I didn't see too much of them because they were usually gone after school.

I remember one day, a few of these Filipinos got into a fight with one white boy. I told them exactly what I felt at that time: "Listen, you guys had better cut it out. You're going to make all of us look bad. It is all going to come back to us that Filipinos are like this and like that." I didn't want to be associated with any negative generalization such as, "All Filipinos hate white people." That was strange coming from me, but I felt good that I told these Filipinos how I felt.

It turned out that the fight had started because one of the Filipinos claimed that the white boy had been staring him down. That sounded quite familiar to me, but I was trying to start a new life where I could be at peace. I wanted to leave my past behind. I didn't want to see the fightings continue, and I had Filipinos disliking me because of this. So it turned around on me again. No matter what I tried to do, it was never quite right.

I was getting along with the people around me, and I was content. But this peace only lasted for a little while because I soon graduated. After graduation, I started hanging around the older generation again, and I found myself to be bitter and lonely again.

Getting Help

There came a point when my drinking and drugging weren't working any more. My parents were always on my case on how I wasn't getting things done around the house and how I wasn't attending school. In fact, I really hadn't graduated from high school because I had done so poorly at school. That affected me a lot, because I wanted so bad to graduate with my friends that I had grown up with. I remember at the graduation ceremony, the mother of a long-time friend of mine walked up and hugged me, congratulating me. I felt so low at that point.

From that point on, my life seemed to get lower and lower. I held many odd jobs here and there, but I really wasn't going anywhere with my life. My relationship with my parents was disintegrating. They always wondered what was going on when I stayed away from home for days at a time. When they confronted me at home, I was really moody and reacted severely to their questioning.

I used to get so frustrated that I would bang my head against the wall and created a hole. It was a great way to get away from dealing with the issues at hand. The reality of it all was that I could not cope with life. With the things I was doing, I could not go to my parents for help. My friends also were slowly slipping away because I was getting out of hand. It just seemed that everyone was slipping away from me, and the drinking and drugging weren't helping me through these hard times any more.

I remember being asked to go to a Twelve-Step meeting, sponsored by Alcoholics Anonymous, at which I could get help. I felt insulted when I was confronted with the information that I even had a problem, but soon after, I had no choice but to concede to that fact. I no longer could talk to my family. I couldn't hold on to a job. I had no education worth mentioning. My friends were those I either used dope with or drank with or sold dope to. Even greater than that, the ultimate turning point in my life was that I was miserable. I could not look at myself in the mirror. I couldn't look anyone in the eye because I felt so ashamed. I realized that I didn't fit in anywhere and that I needed help. So I decided to go to the Twelve-Step meeting soon after it was offered to me. Having to accept that help just seemed another blow to my ego.

But it was just the blow that I needed. I eventually was able to put aside the alcohol and drugs and be able to reevaluate my life. I saw the incredible strain that I put on myself and what destruction it led to. It was me who pushed everyone out of my life. I was responsible for all the fights that I was involved in. Nobody was forcing me into those fights, nor was I obligated to fight everyone else's cause. I was able to take a long and hard look at what I had done in my life and not be ashamed of it any more. That was the key for me. I learned that I needed to forgive myself. I learned how to rebuild the relationship between myself and my family, and that has meant a lot to me.

Reflections on Culture and Identity

At home, I don't remember any attempt by my parents to teach me the Filipino language other than being at the dinner table and saying certain foods in Tagalog. I can understand when they say "rice" or "set the table" but that is about it. At one point, I was interested in taking classes to learn the Filipino language but since the classes weren't available, I didn't go out looking all over the place for someone to teach me.

I learned about the Philippines mostly through the history books. The school gave me a very shallow view of Philippine history, but I took it a step further by reading more about it on my own. I learned that many things that are Filipino have been influenced by the Spanish culture. I also read about Filipino American history. I found it interesting that not all Filipinos came over on a boat. There were people who worked on the railroad. There were servants. And there were Filipinos all over the world, not just in the United States. That's why I can see that not all Filipinos are the same, because not everybody came the same way and not everybody went into the same environments.

I still don't know much about Filipino culture. I like Filipino food, and I know how to cook it. There are certain things that I like about the Filipino culture, like the social events and the traditional dances. I feel proud of these traditions because they are beautiful and they have been handed down from generation to generation. I feel that I am a part of that tradition, and I take that seriously. For example, when I try to teach some friends how to cook Filipino food and they want to cook it their way, I tell them that there is a reason why you cook it a certain way. Some people can't see the difference, but I can see the difference. I can take pride in that.

I feel now that I can pick and choose what I want and what I don't want from the Filipino culture. When I go to a Filipino social function and people expect me to behave a certain way, I tell them that I do not have to. I am comfortable telling them that without feeling like I am rejecting my race. Before, certain parts of the Filipino culture were forced onto me, and that made me uncomfortable. I didn't know why I was expected to behave a certain way other than because I am brown. Now I can pick and choose what is right for me. I have taken a step past learning about the culture to asking if it is really important. If something is not appropriate for me, why just not throw it out?

Through the Twelve-Step program, I learned who I am and what I want to do. I see myself now as a Filipino American—a Filipino who was born and raised in the United States. I have never thought of just being Filipino.

That is a given. I don't have to *be* a Filipino; I *am* Filipino because of my genetic make-up. The bottom line is my values are unique to me. They are not Filipino values, and they are not American values; they are *my* values. I also can easily say that I am American, because there is no so-called American model. Pretty much everybody makes up the model.

I also learned what is valid and what is invalid. If someone calls me a Flip, is his opinion valid, and why should I let it bother me? I could let someone push me over, or I could stop them from doing so. It is entirely up to me to decide if the payoff is worth it. I look at things now as payoffs. What am I going to get out of this? Am I going to wind up hurt? Am I compromising myself and my values? Before I was always compromising my values, so I ended up losing myself. Now I don't compromise my values, except that now my values are a little bit more broad-based. I am more accepting of people—regardless of their ethnic background.

I know there are people out there who discriminate against me just because of my physical characteristics. But I am not going to let anybody put me down for what I am. If somebody says something negative about the Filipino culture, I correct them, and let them know what is accurate and what is inaccurate. Now I take pride in being different. It does not necessarily mean that I am proud because I have a flat nose or dark hair, but more because I think differently. I don't have to dress like the norm. I don't have to act like the norm. I can be a little bit different.

When I have children, I would like them to know basically where the Philippines is and where my family comes from. I would show them the family tree so they would know why I am different. Other than that, I wouldn't put much into it, because my way of thinking is not very similar to that of the other Filipinos. So I would let my children learn about the Filipino philosophy on their own. But most of all, I want them to know that the United States is multicultural and that they do not have to fit into any preset mold. I want them to focus on what feels right and appropriate for them.

I am not sure if I want to marry a Filipina. I go back and forth with that question. It would be nice to carry the culture through and to make more of a connection. But if I find the perfect woman who meets my wants and needs, and if I meet her wants and needs, I think that will be the more immediate calling. As far as gender roles, since I come from a family of four boys, we cook and clean and do everything else. I say the more you learn and the more you can break down these gender barriers, the better. If a man can learn everything that a stereotypical woman can do, and if a woman can do everything that a stereotypical man can do, all the better. I don't think it is appropriate when the Filipinos say men shouldn't cry, because I have seen a lot of healing through crying.

Religion is taking a big part in my life now, not so much religion but spirituality. Again, the most important thing is, how does it make me feel? And if my belief does not feel right for my children, I am not going to push it on them. To force a certain religion on them would be to push them further away from it. So I would just let them come into it. And if they can see something in the Catholic Church that makes them want to join, then it is all the better.

"I Am Working for a Better Future"

To have my family back and to be loved were the most important things for me to go on in life. This feeling has transferred into how I treat my life now. I went back to school and was able to obtain my high school diploma, and I am now currently enrolled at a local community college. I am taking courses so that I may be able to become a counselor someday.

I am trying to take some action to help the Filipino community understand the youth. I feel I must take a part in my community so that I may give back what was given to me. I do volunteer work and guest speak at various Filipino and Asian community group meetings that address drugs and gangs. I talk directly with the young Filipinos, because there is nobody out there that they can connect to. I am not saying that they can only connect with a Filipino person, but if I can make a difference, all the better. Sometimes when I tell the high school students my story, they don't quite relate to my particular situation. But when I say, "This is what I felt at the time: lonely, alienated . . . ," then they say, "Gee, I felt that way too." And that is how we make the connection.

The gang problems, the drugs, the alcohol, these have always been there in the Filipino community. But they are more recognized now because they are next-door to you instead of over there in southeast San Diego. These problems have always been bad, but we didn't use to get caught all the time. Back then, we were more careful because we didn't want to get in trouble; we didn't want to be put in jail. It seems like kids nowadays don't really care if they are caught. They don't value their lives or their relationship with their parents very much.

I feel that Filipino parents put so much emphasis on making money. They work all the time and have no time for their children. I believe there should be an appropriate portion of time spent with the children so that they feel a part of something. Many of the kids are getting more and more away from their homes. In my case, I was still tied to my home. Even though I went against my parents' wishes, I still thought their wishes were valid. But now, because there is so little time spent with the children, what the parents have to say do not seem as valid as before.

I want to make a little sense of the world around us, for what I had lost was my sanity. I was confused with what I wanted and where I was going.

Having some direction has given me back my sanity, and this is what I hope to spread to others when I speak at these community meetings.

I want to be the best example that I can be, not for other people's benefit but for my own. I wouldn't be able to help others if I could not back it up with my own life. I have been there and done that. I am neither above nor below anyone, because I know what it is like to be out there, and I know what it is like to get better. I have no regrets on my past life, and I am moving on. Things get hard sometimes, but that is life. I am happy where I am today, and I am working for a better future.

Chapter 13

"Everybody
Seemed to Be
Either White
or Black,
a Full Race"

Lisa Graham

"My Mom Is Filipino, and My Dad Is American"

I was born in San Clemente, California, in 1976. My dad is in the Marine Corps. He is a master sergeant. I think he went straight into the military at the age of seventeen. He was in Vietnam when he was eighteen years old.

My mom is Filipino, and my dad is American. My dad met my mom in a restaurant in Manila when he was stationed in the Philippines. She was a waitress there. They dated for a while, and when he came back to the States, they decided to get married. My mom was twenty-three years old, and my dad was eighteen years old when they got married. My mom already had a son at that time, but they didn't have enough money to bring my brother over. So my mom left my brother with some relatives when she came to the United States.

I don't think my mom's family objected at all to her marrying my dad. But I do remember my mom telling me that when she was younger, her parents always wanted to give her an arranged marriage. My mom ended up running away and working as a maid because she did not want to marry this man that her parents wanted her to marry. But then the person that she was working for made her feel really uncomfortable. So she stopped working there and started waitressing. And that was how she met my dad.

My mom told me that she used to be afraid that if she married an American, the in-laws wouldn't like her. So she would pray, wish, and hope that when she did get married, it would be with someone that she didn't have to deal with in-laws. Well, my dad's parents died when he was really young. So everything worked out as my mom wanted.

I don't really know my mom's family. They write letters, and they always tell my mom to say "hi" to us, but I have not met them personally. I never met my grandparents. My grandma died when my mom was very young. Then her father remarried, and I guess my mom and her stepmother never really got along. Her father also died a couple of years ago. My mom has one brother and one sister, but I only know the sister. Actually, my mom set her sister, who was still in the Philippines, up with one of her friends here. He was already thirty-something and had never been married. They ended up getting married, even though they only knew each other by letters. That was how my aunt was able to come to the United States. So she is really the only one that I know, besides a couple of my mom's relatives who are living in Los Angeles.

I have not been to the Philippines. My mom wants to go back to visit, but her priority is to pay off our bills. All of our money goes to paying the mortgage. My dad is starting his own construction business to make more money on the side. I don't think my mom would want to live in the Philippines permanently. I think she has become more Americanized. She hasn't forgotten her Filipino heritage and her culture, but with marrying an American man and then having two daughters here, I think she prefers to stay here.

I want to go to the Philippines for a visit. I think that would be fun. My mom and my aunt always talk about the Philippines when they get together, and it sounds so interesting. So I want to go there and see it for myself.

Settling in San Diego

After I was born, we stayed in San Clemente only for a couple of months. Then we moved to Kentucky because my dad was transferred there, and that's where my sister was born. When I was almost four years old, we moved back to the San Diego area. We lived near the Del Mar area for a while because we were waiting for base housing. When base housing became available, we moved back to San Onofre Base, near San Clemente.

We lived in San Clemente until I was maybe eleven or twelve years old, and then we bought this house here in Oceanside. Because we'd always lived on base, my mom wanted a house. That was all she ever talked about. Before we got this house, my dad bought a nice, nice boat, but my mom said, "Gosh, we could have put that money down toward the house." We bought this house before it was even built. We got it for $128,000, and now it's worth over $200,000. This was five years ago. All my friends think that

Lisa Graham after the Fil Am Cultural Association's beauty pageant, where she was selected first princess, Oceanside, 1992

I am rich because I live in this neighborhood, but we are not rich. My parents have to work really hard to keep up with the mortgage.

As soon as we came back to San Diego, one of my mom's Filipino friends told her about a job at this place that made water sprinklers. She worked there for a long time, for twelve years or so, as an assembler. But then the company moved to Texas, and my mom was unemployed for a year before she found a new job assembling electronics parts. At first, she didn't really like her new job. She was always really tired when she got home. But I think it is better now because she knows more people at work. I know that there are a lot of Filipinos at my mom's work, because they would have parties where they would bring all these Filipino foods.

Most of my mom's friends are Filipinos. But in our neighborhood, most of the people are whites. Well, my mom usually is not home that much because she is always working overtime for extra money. My dad pays the house bill, but my mom pays for everything else. My mom gets along well with the people in our neighborhood, but sometimes I think that she would rather have some Filipino friends around here. I don't think it really matters, but whenever we have things like block parties, my mom is the only Filipino out there, and all the other people are white.

When my mom's son, my brother, was about thirteen years old, my parents had saved enough money to bring him here from the Philippines. I remember exactly when my brother first came over. He was thirteen years old, and I was five, and my sister was three. We went to the airport to pick him up. I remember that he was crying because he'd left all of his aunts and uncles who had raised him behind in the Philippines.

On the way home, it was weird for me and my sister because all of a sudden, we had a brother. I guess my parents must have explained the whole situation to us beforehand. In the car, we were laughing, and I told my sister, "Touch him. Touch him." And he was laughing at us. He spoke English. He had a heavy accent at first, but now, not really. No, I didn't make fun of his accent because my mom has an accent too.

My brother adapted easily to living here with us. He lived with us until he was about twenty-one. Because my dad was always away—sometimes he would be overseas for a year and then he was gone for a long time during the Gulf War—he asked my brother to stick around for a while to watch over us. My brother did, and as soon as my dad came back from Desert Storm, he stayed for probably another two weeks, and then he moved out. He is now living with some of his Filipino friends. He is a very good guitarist. He and his friends have a heavy metal band. They are just waiting for their break.

Culture, Race, and Dating

My mom doesn't really tell me that much about the Filipino culture, but she always says to me, "Well, in the Philippines, I didn't do that, I didn't do this when I was your age." Well, her growing up in the Philippines is different from my growing up here.

It's hard sometimes for my mom to get her points across. I understand what she is saying, but often because my dad is American, they both see things differently. When I was in elementary school and we had parent conferences, I usually asked my dad to go with me, because I sometimes felt that my mom wouldn't understand.

My mom and dad differ mostly on the teenage years, over dating and things like that. My dad gives me a little bit more freedom, but my mom feels more comfortable if I am home all the time. I think it was like that for my mom in the Philippines because she would always say things like, "I didn't have to go out like that. I didn't have to spend the night at my friend's house." But then my dad would say, "Go ahead and go."

In our family, my dad is the dominant one. What he says usually goes. But when I have my own family, I intend to be the dominant one. When I told my mom that I am going to be making all the rules in my family, she said, "Watch! When you get married, it is not going to be like that." In a way, it wouldn't really matter if my husband was dominant over me as long as it doesn't get to the point where he makes all the decisions and I have no say.

Once, when I was going out with my boyfriend, he wanted me to wear this skirt that I didn't want to wear. So I decided to wear something else. When I told my mom about it, she said, "Well, why didn't you wear it? You're supposed to." She said that! And I was not even married to him! I think that is how it is with her and my dad. She does what my dad wants, and she believes that when I get married, I am supposed to do what my husband wants. That's how my mom sees things, but that's not how I see things. I don't want to feel like I have to make all the decisions by myself, but I also don't want to feel like I have no say.

Even though my parents told me that I couldn't date until I was sixteen, when I was in eighth grade, I dated this one guy named Gabriel, and my mom loved him. He is half-Mexican and half-white. We stayed together for almost two years. My parents really liked us together. When my dad was overseas, Gabriel would always be around the house too. My mom felt comfortable having him here when my brother was out with his band. But we ended up breaking up at the beginning of my tenth grade.

Now I have another boyfriend, but I don't feel that he is welcome here. My dad is nice, and he tries not to be mean. But my mom, her whole attitude has changed toward boyfriends. She tells me not to have a boyfriend now and to concentrate on school. When my new boyfriend comes around, she is really quiet. She won't say "hi" or really talk to him. It makes him feel uncomfortable. I also feel uncomfortable when he comes over, so I really don't invite him to come over here that much. Then he feels like I am ashamed of him, but I am not.

My boyfriend now, Ray, is full Mexican. I think that's why my mom doesn't really like him. She wants me to be with white Americans. I don't even think she would approve of me dating Filipinos. If Ray were full Filipino, I still don't think it would make any difference. If he were white American, I think she would be a little bit more okay with it. Gabriel was half-American, so my mom didn't have a problem with him.

When we talk about marriage, my mom always tells me, "Marry an American. If he is half-Mexican, half-American, it's good too." I never ask her why because she'll just say, "Because." She never gives me a straight answer. And the person has to be tall. She wants me to marry a tall American because she wants beautiful grandchildren. Gabriel is about six feet tall, and my mom likes that. My boyfriend now is 5'8". To me, he is tall, because I am short. But to my mom, he still is not tall enough.

When I have children, I want them to consider themselves Filipino. But if I married someone who is half-something and half-something-else, then my children will have four different parts. That would be crazy because then they would want to know about every little part. I want them to focus more on the Filipino part, because I never got to.

I don't know what I can teach my children about Filipino culture because I really don't know all that much. I wish I knew more. But I never really got the chance, because in our family Filipino culture just doesn't come up; everything is American, American here. The only thing Filipino in this house is the food. Also, my mom is the best cleaner in the world, and I know I can clean. So maybe those are Filipino traits: cleaning and cooking. Me and my sister don't know Tagalog. When I asked my mom how come she never taught us Tagalog, she said she never really thought about it. I guess it was probably because of my dad. He probably told my mom that only English will be spoken in our home. Once in a while, I would ask my mom how to say this and that in Tagalog. I always hear her talking Tagalog on the phone. I wish there were a Tagalog class at school so I could learn.

Before, when my sister and I were younger, we used to go to church with our parents every Sunday. That was when we lived on base. But as soon as we moved down here to Oceanside, everything changed. We stopped going to church. When my dad left for overseas or when he was in Desert Storm, then we would go to church and pray for him. But I haven't really sat through a church session in a long time. Before it was like top priority for us to go to church, but now we only go when my mom gets the chance. Sunday is the only day that she has time to do anything else besides work. But sometimes my mom's Filipino friends come over, and we'll do the rosary together.

I want to learn more about Filipino culture, but I don't know how to go about it. I wish they would teach that kind of stuff in school because it would make things a lot easier. But if you want to learn about the Filipino culture, you have to go do your own research on your own time.

In school, they don't really teach us about the Philippines. Once in a while in world history, the teacher will mention the Philippines. That class usually puts me to sleep, but when the teacher says anything about the Philippines, I wake up. I am interested. I want to know more about the Philippines, because it has something to do with me. Because we are here in America, that's all we learn about. Everything in school is about America. That gets boring after a while. It's not anything against my dad and this country, it's just that I hear more about America, and I already know about that. But I don't know that much about Filipino culture or heritage, so that's why that interests me more when it comes up in school. Sometimes when they say anything about the Philippine culture or history, I feel funny because I wonder if anybody in the class knows that I am half-Filipino. I always think like that because I feel good when people know that I am Filipino.

I can ask my mom about the Filipino culture, but I know she'll try to put things in my head like in the Philippines, girls never have boyfriends, and they never do this and that.

The Fil Am Cultural Association Beauty Pageant

When I was fifteen years old, this Filipino lady from the Fil Am Cultural Association of North San Diego County called the house and asked my mom if she was interested in putting me in the beauty pageant that they were sponsoring. My mom has never been a member of the Fil Am organization. But whenever we go to the Filipino store in Oceanside, a lot of people would tell my mom, "Your daughter is so pretty." I think maybe that's where they knew us from. My mom told the lady who called that I was only fifteen years old but that she would consider putting me in the pageant the following year. So when the next year came [1992], my mom asked me if I wanted to do it, and I told her yes.

I went to the first pageant meeting to see how it was. Cora Lego, the lady who coordinated the event, told me, "Just come to the first meeting. You can decide from there whether you want to be in it or not." At first, I felt really uncomfortable about joining the pageant because I thought that all the girls would be full Filipinos. I figured since it is a Filipino cultural event, everyone would want a full Filipino to win. I felt like I really wasn't going to fit in because I was only half-Filipino. But when I went to the first meeting, my friend Maria Cotter was there, and she also is half-Filipino and half-white. That made me feel a little bit better. Maria ended up dropping out, but I decided to stick with it.

At the second meeting, I met all of the girls, and we got along perfectly. So I relaxed and felt like this was going to be fun. These girls were really Americanized so I didn't feel any different, because I am Americanized too. In fact, when we all talked together, we started realizing how many of the Filipinos living in America today are so Americanized. It seems like they forget sometimes that they are really Filipino.

When it came toward the end of the pageant and the judging, I felt insecure again. I kept thinking, "Well, the person who is going to win has to compete at the San Diego Miss Philippines pageant, so they are really going to want somebody who looks real Filipino." That thought kept running through my head. But I was happy with the results; I got first princess. It was better than I thought. Overall, I was happy with the whole pageant because I felt like I did fit in. It was the first time that I felt comfortable in an all-Filipino setting. I enjoyed the experience of just being around other Filipinos. It's funny because all the Filipinos call me Lisa Marie, and they all spell my name "Liza" instead of "Lisa."

All the girls had to sell tickets to the pageant, and I think I sold the most tickets. I know I sold about 175 tickets. I just called all of my friends, plus the people from my neighborhood. And all of my mom's Filipino friends bought tickets, and my dad got some people from his work to buy. I was surprised that a lot of my friends wanted to go, because I thought they would feel uncomfortable, out of place. But they came, and they were all cheering for me. They were really loud. I could hear them from the stage.

Actually I joined the Fil Am beauty pageant because of my mom. My mom is really into the beauty stuff like beauty contests and modeling and all that. My mom and I would sit down and watch beauty pageants together. My sister was taking these modeling classes, and she was in the Harbor's Day [an Oceanside event] pageant, but I never got to do anything like that. Mostly when things like that came up, my mom would talk to my sister first, telling her that she should be in a pageant. My mom probably thinks my sister is prettier because she is lighter than I am. It was always like that. So in a way, I wanted to join the pageant because I wanted to prove to my mom that I can also do something like that. She was so proud that I got first princess. But I also joined because I was interested in the Fil Am Association; I was excited about becoming part of the association.

Racial Discrimination

Sometimes, I wish I were one full race. I wish that when people ask me about my nationality, I could just say, "I am Filipino," or "I am white."

But if I could be just one race, I wouldn't know which one to choose. There are advantages to both sides, so it is good sometimes to be in the middle. I think it is easier if you are a white American because Americans have more advantages than Filipinos, especially here in the United States in terms of jobs and things like that. I know that's how society works. Me myself, I don't feel discriminated against at all about being Filipino, but that is probably because I am half-American. If I were full Filipino, it might be different, because Filipinos do get discriminated against.

For people who don't have to face discrimination, they don't realize that it is everywhere. Even though I don't face it, I can see it around me—like my aunt's situation with her in-laws. Her mother-in-law is really rude to her because she is a Filipina. I really feel sorry for my aunt because she should not be treated that way. If I married a full American and his parents wanted him to marry a full American, maybe my being half-Filipino would bother them. Some people are like that. They want one full race, not a bunch of different mixtures. Now I understand why my mom was always hoping to marry a man without parents so she wouldn't have to face what my aunt is going through. I think my mom had always planned to marry an American.

Even though Filipinos are discriminated against, I still wouldn't want to be full Filipino either. I want both. I wouldn't want my life to be completely based on what my mom believes, and I wouldn't want it to be completely based on what my dad believes.

At school, I really feel discriminated against by blacks. A lot of the black girls, the ones who are seniors, have something against me. I don't know what it is. It can't be my race because they don't do that to full Filipinos, but they are really rude to me. I have no idea why. It may be jealousy. Like this one girl, during her freshman year, she did really well in speech and got all the recognition for her performances. But then she quit. Now that I am getting recognition for dramatic interpretation and acting, she is jealous about it and is using that against me. Then this other girl, when it came to homecoming court and snowball court, I was chosen princess, and she was not. So she also had something against me.

I am also class council president, and there are all these girls, most of them black, who don't want me to be president. But I had more votes, so I won the election. The girl who was running against me for president was black. So everybody made it into a racial thing. All the blacks were cheering for her, and all the white Americans, Filipinos, and the rest were cheering for me. She had signs up saying, "Who is African American and wants to be your president?" My sign was "Vote for Lisa Graham" and things like that. When she went up on stage to give her speech, she did an African dance. She tried to win on popularity. If she would have won, it would have definitely been because of popularity. But I won.

I know that blacks face discrimination, but what makes me really mad is that they feel they are the only ones who get discriminated against. Even those who are not really being discriminated against, they think that because they are black, there is discrimination against them. I think that's why they feel they always have to be on top. Because they weren't superior before, now that they have more freedom, more advantages, more things going their way, I think they are looking down on the other people.

Being Half-Filipino and Half-White

A lot of people don't know what my nationality is because I don't look full Filipino or full white. They try to guess what I am. Everyone thinks that I am Mexican. Usually, when people try to figure out someone's nationality, they only think of one race. I feel sort of unique when it comes to that, because I have two races. For some reason, it bothers me when people tell me that they couldn't tell that I was part Filipino. It makes me happy when people come up to me and say, "You have to be half-Filipino." It makes me happy that they can tell.

Our high school, Oceanside High, is mostly Mexicans. There is one group of about six Filipinos who only hang around with each other. But there are other Filipinos and people who are half-Filipino and half-white who hang around whites. I don't think I could tell at first who were half-Filipino and half-white. I thought they were Mexican too. But we would talk, and I would say I am half-Filipino and half-white, and they would say they were too.

From sixth grade till the end of tenth grade, my best friend was half-Indian Cherokee and half-American. My other friend was full Mexican; I think she was mostly Spanish or something because she had light skin. Another friend was full Indian from India. And then me. So we had a variety right there in our group. I have never had a close friend who is full Filipino.

For some reason, I feel weird around people who are full Filipino. I think I feel insecure around them because I am only half-Filipino and because I don't speak Tagalog. Sometimes, I am afraid that they might be saying to themselves, "She is not really Filipino." That makes me really uncomfortable. But I really don't meet many people who are full Filipino. Where I have been living, especially on the bases, people are mostly half-and-half.

But now that I think about it, I also feel a little uncomfortable when I am with a group of full Americans, because it is all of them and then just me. For example, if all our parents were to get together and they were all white, I would feel uncomfortable, and I think my mom would feel uncomfortable too. That's why most of my friends are a variety of nationalities. None of my friends are full white.

When I was younger, I used to say, "I am American, I am American. I am white." It was just because everybody seemed to be either black or white, a full race. In school, when we had to fill out those cards for nationality, I was always confused because I never knew what to put. The teachers would say, "Mark down what you most look like." Well, that was even worse. I didn't know what to put. I hated that. I remember one time when I was in elementary school, I asked my dad what I should mark down. He told me to mark down "American." I think my mom said "American" too. I also thought "American," because I was born and raised in America; I wasn't born in the Philippines.

Starting in junior high, it became important for me to say that I was Filipino because of my mom. I just can't ignore the fact that I have Filipino blood in me and say that I am only American. I am proud to be Filipino. Even though you are not supposed to, sometimes I just mark both "Filipino" and "white" down on those nationality cards. Other times, I just marked off "Filipino." I never just marked off "white" though. I either put "Filipino" or both. I wish they would have something like "half-and-half," because if you are not one full race, you don't know what to put down. They have Asian American, Native American, and all these different Americans, but they don't have "half-and-half."

I realize that the first thing I usually say now is, "I am Filipino," because there are so many whites around. But whenever I have said that, people usually respond with, "You are not full Filipino." So then I had to say, "Yah, I am half-white." But then I don't look full white either. When I think of "white," I see light, light brown hair or blonde hair, and I don't look like that. Also, when people at my school make fun of the white boys and the white girls, saying things like, "Get out of here, white girl," I would say, "I am not white. I am Filipino."

But now my whole attitude is changing. Now I say that I am half-Filipino and half-white.

Bibliography

Agbayani, Amefil R. "Community Impacts of Migration: Recent Ilokano Migration to Hawai'i." *Social Process in Hawaii* 33 (1991): 73–90.

Agbayani-Siewert, Pauline. "Filipino American Immigrants: Social Role Strain, Self-Esteem, Locus of Control, Social Networks, Coping, Stress, and Mental Health Outcome." Ph.D. dissertation, University of California, Los Angeles, 1993.

Alcantara, Ruben R. "The Filipino Community in Wailua." Ph.D. dissertation, University of Hawaii at Honolulu, 1973.

———. "The Filipino Wedding in Wailua, Hawaii. Ritual Retention and Ethnic Subculture in a New Setting." *Amerasia Journal* 1 (February 1972): 1–12.

———. *Sakada: Filipino Adaptation in Hawaii.* Washington, D.C.: University Press of America, 1981.

Alegado, Dean T. "The Filipino Community in Hawaii: Development and Change." *Social Process in Hawaii* 33 (1991): 12–38.

Almirol, Edwin B. *Ethnic Identity and Social Negotiation: A Study of a Filipino Community in California.* New York: AMS Press, 1985.

———. "Exclusion and Acceptance of Filipinos in America." *Asian Profile* 13 (1985): 395–408.

———. "Filipino Voluntary Associations: Balancing Social Pressures and Ethnic Images." *Ethnic Groups* 2 (1978): 65–92.

———. "Rights and Obligations in Filipino American Families." *Journal of Comparative Family Studies* 8:3 (1982): 291–305.

Alsaybar, Bangele. "Santana's: Ethnography of a Filipino American Brotherhood." M.A. thesis, University of California, Los Angeles, 1993.

Ancheta, Shirley, Jaime Jacinto, and Jeff Tagami, eds. *Without Names: A Collection of Poems by Bay Area Pilipino American Writers.* San Francisco: Kearny Street Workshop Press, 1985.

Anderson, Robert N. *Filipinos in Rural Hawaii.* Honolulu: University of Hawaii Press, 1984.

Anderson, Warwick. "Where Every Prospect Pleases and Only Man Is Vile: Laboratory Medicine as Colonial Discourse." *Critical Inquiry* 18 (1992): 506–29.

Angeles, Rodolfo Boye. "Selected Los Angeles County Filipino Immigrants' Perception of Acculturation." Ed.D. dissertation, University of San Francisco, 1991.

Aquino, Valentin R. "The Filipino Community in Los Angeles." M.A. thesis, University of Southern California, 1952.

Arnold, Fred. "Birds of Passage No More: Migration Decision Making Among Filipino Immigrants in Hawaii." *International Migration Review* 25:1 (1987): 41–61.

Arnold, Fred, Benjamin V. Cariño, James T. Fawcett, and Insook Han Park. "Estimating the Immigration Multiplier: An Analysis of Recent Korean and Filipino Immigration to the United States." *International Migration Review* 23 (1989): 813–38.

Asis, Maruja Mila Gros Billones. "Immigrant Women and Occupational Changes: A Comparison of Filipino and Korean Women in Transition." Ph.D. dissertation, Bowling Green State University, 1989.

――――. *To the U.S. and into the Labor Force: Occupational Expectations of Filipina and Korean Immigrant Women.* Honolulu: East-West Center, 1991.

Ave, Mario Paguia. "Characteristics of Filipino Social Organizations in Los Angeles." Ph.D. dissertation, University of Southern California, 1956.

Azores-Gunter, Tania Fortunata M. "Educational Attainment and Upward Mobility: Prospects for Filipino Americans." *Amerasia Journal* 13:1 (1986–87): 39–52.

――――. "Filipino Education Study: A Study of Factors Affecting the Educational Aspirations of Filipino Twelfth-Grade Students." M.A. thesis, University of California, Los Angeles, 1982.

――――. "Status Achievement Patterns of Filipinos in the United States." Ph.D. dissertation, University of California, Los Angeles, 1987.

Bacho, Peter. *Cebu.* Seattle: University of Washington Press, 1991.

Baluarte, Librado L. "A Ministry to Filipino-Americans." D.Min. dissertation, United Theological Seminary, 1989.

Bello, Madge, and Vince Reyes. "Filipino Americans and the Marcos Overthrow: The Transformation of Political Consciousness." *Amerasia Journal* 13:1 (1986–87): 73–83.

Berry, William E., Jr. *U.S. Bases in the Philippines: The Evolution of a Special Relationship.* Boulder, Colo.: Westview Press, 1989.

Bogardus, Emory S. "Filipino Americans." In *One America,* 3rd ed., edited by Francis J. Brown and Joseph S. Roucek, pp. 361–72. New York: Prentice-Hall, 1952.

――――. "Filipino Immigrant Attitudes." *Sociology and Social Research* 14 (1930): 469–79.

Bottomley, Allen William Thompson. *A Statement Concerning the Sugar Industry in Hawaii; Labor Conditions on Hawaiian Sugar Plantations; Filipino Laborers Thereon; and the Alleged Filipino "Strike" of 1924.* Honolulu: Advertiser Press, 1924.

Boyd, Monica. "Oriental Immigration: The Experience of the Chinese, Japanese, and Filipino Populations in the United States." *International Migration Review* 5 (1971): 48–61.

Boylan, Dan. "Crosscurrents: Filipinos in Hawai'i Politics." *Social Process in Hawaii* 33 (1991): 39–55.

Brainard, Cecilia Manguerra. *Philippine Women in America: Essays by Cecilia Manguerra Brainard.* Quezon City: New Day Publishers, 1991.

――――. *Song of Yvonne.* Quezon City: New Day Publishers, 1991.

Bresnahan, Roger J. *Conversations with Filipino Writers.* Quezon City: New Day Publishers, 1990.

Buaken, Manuel. *I Have Lived with the American People.* Caldwell, Idaho: Caxton Printers, 1948.

Bulosan, Carlos. *America Is in the Heart: A Personal History.* 1943. Reprint. Seattle: University of Washington Press, 1973.

————. *If You Want to Know What We Are.* Minneapolis: West End Press, 1983.

————. *The Power of the People.* Manila: National Book Store, 1986.

Buttny, Richard. "Legitimation Techniques for Intermarriage: Accounts of Motives for Intermarriage from U.S. Servicemen and Philippine Women." *Communication Quarterly* 35 (Spring 1987): 125–43.

Cabezas, Amado, and Gary Kawaguchi. "Race, Gender, and Class for Filipino Americans." In *A Look Beyond the Model Minority Image,* edited by Grace Yun, pp. 88–106. New York: Minority Rights Group Inc., 1989.

Cabezas, Amado, Larry H. Shinagawa, and Gary Kawaguchi. "New Inquiries into the Socioeconomic Status of Pilipino Americans in California." *Amerasia Journal* 13:1 (1986–87): 1–21.

Caces, Fe. "Immigrant Recruitment into the Labor Force: Social Networks among Filipinos in Hawaii." *Amerasia Journal* 13:1 (1986–87): 23–38.

————. "Personal Networks and the Material Adaptation of Recent Immigrants: A Case Study of Filipinos in Hawaii." Ph.D. dissertation, University of Hawaii, 1985.

Campomanes, Oscar V. "Filipinos in the United States and Their Literature of Exile." In *Reading the Literatures of Asia America,* edited by Shirley Geok-Lin Lim and Amy Ling, pp. 49–78. Philadelphia: Temple University Press, 1992.

Card, Josefina Jayme. "The Aftermath of Migration to the U.S. Versus Return Home: Data from the 1970 Cohort of Filipino Grad Students in the U.S." *Philippine Sociological Review* 30 (1982): 63–77.

————. "Assimilation and Adaptation: Filipino Migrants in San Francisco." *Philippine Sociological Review* 32 (1984): 55–67.

————. "The Correspondence Between Migration Intentions and Migration Behavior: Data from the 1970 Cohort of Filipino Graduate Students in the United States." *Population and Environment* 5 (1982): 3–25.

Cariaga, Roman R. *The Filipinos in Hawaii: A Survey of Their Economic and Social Conditions.* San Francisco: R & E Research Associates, 1974.

Cariño, Benjamin V. "The Philippines and Southeast Asia: Historical Roots and Contemporary Linkages." In *Pacific Bridges: The New Immigration from Asia and the Pacific Islands,* edited by James T. Fawcett and Benjamin V. Cariño. Staten Island, N.Y.: Center for Migration Studies, 1987: 302–25.

Cariño, Benjamin V., James T. Fawcett, Robert W. Gardner, and Fred Arnold. *The New Filipino Immigrants to the United States: Increasing Diversity and Change.* Honolulu: East-West Center, 1990.

Carlson, Alvar W. "Filipino and Indian Immigrants in Detroit and Suburbs, 1961–1974." *Philippine Geographical Journal* 19 (1975): 199–209.

Castillo-Tsuchida, Adelaida. *Filipino Migrants in San Diego, 1900–1946*. San Diego: San Diego Society, Title Insurance and Trust Collection, 1979.

Castro, Patricia A. "Filipino Writers in America." M.A. thesis, Columbia University, 1951).

Catapusan, Benicio T. "The Social Adjustments of Filipinos in the United States." M.A. thesis, University of Southern California, 1940.

Clark, Erlinda T. "Filipino Labor Experiences in the U.S." Ph.D. dissertation, Texas Technical University, 1971.

Coloma, Casiano Pagilao. *A Study of the Filipino Repatriation Movement*. San Francisco: R & E Research Associates, 1974.

Cordova, Fred. *Filipinos: Forgotten Asian Americans, A Pictorial Essay, 1763–1963*. Dubuque, Iowa: Kendall/Hunt Publishing Co., 1983.

Corpus, Severino F. *An Analysis of the Racial Adjustment Activities and Problems of the Filipino-American Christian Fellowship in Los Angeles*. San Francisco: R & E Research Associates, 1975.

Cortes, Josefina. "Factors Associated with the Outflow of High-Level Philippine Manpower." *Philippine Sociological Review* 18 (1970): 159–68.

Crouchett, Loraine Jacobs. *Filipinos in California: From the Days of the Galleons to the Present*. El Cerrito, Calif.: Downey Place Publishing House, 1982.

Cruz, Jon D. "Filipino-American Community Organizations in Washington, 1900s–1930s." In *People of Color in the American West,* edited by Sucheng Chan, Douglas Henry Daniels, Mario T. Garcia, and Terry P. Wilson, pp. 235–45. Lexington, Mass.: D. C. Heath and Company, 1994.

Cullinane, Michael. "The Filipino Federation of America: The Prewar Years, 1925–1940—An Overview." *Crossroads* 1 (1983): 74–85.

De Castro, Steven. "Identity in Action: A Filipino American's Perspective." In *The State of Asian America,* edited by Karin Aguilar-San Juan, pp. 295–320. Boston: South End Press, 1994.

De la Llana Decenteceo, Lenore A. "Language Switching in Story Retelling Tasks Among Filipino Bilingual Children." *Philippine Journal of Psychology* 24:2 (December 1991): 1–19.

Demonstration Project for Asian Americans. *Health Assessment of Elderly Filipinos in the International District, Seattle, Washington*. Seattle: DPAA, 1972.

De Vera, Arleen Garcia. "An Unfinished Agenda: Filipino Immigrant Workers in the Era of McCarthyism; A Case Study of the Cannery Workers and Farm Laborers Union, 1948–55." M.A. thesis, University of California, Los Angeles, 1990.

De Witt, Howard A. *Anti-Filipino Movements in California: A History, Bibliography, and Study Guide*. San Francisco: R & E Research Associates, 1976.

———. "The Filipino Labor Union: The Salinas Lettuce Strike of 1934." *Amerasia Journal* 5:2 (1978): 1–22.

————. *Violence in the Fields: California Filipino Farm Labor Unionization During the Great Depression.* Saratoga, Calif.: Century Twenty-One Publishers, 1980.

Domingo, Benjamin B. *The Philippines and Hawaii.* Manila: Foreign Service Institute, 1983.

Dorita, Mary. *Filipino Immigration to Hawaii.* San Francisco: R & E Research Associates, 1975.

Epinosa-Schneider, Mila. "Examining the Ethnic Identity of the Filipino Americans Relative to Their Perceptions of Employment Discrimination." Ph.D. dissertation, United States International University, 1983.

Espina, Marina E. *Filipinos in Louisiana.* New Orleans: A. F. Laborde & Sons, 1988.

Espiritu, Augusto Fauni. "The Rise and Fall of the Filipino Town Campaign in Los Angeles: A Study of Filipino American Leadership." M.A. thesis, University of California, Los Angeles, 1992.

Ethnic Studies Oral History Project. *The 1924 Filipino Strike in Kauai.* Honolulu: University of Hawaii at Manoa, Ethnic Studies Program, 1979.

Evangelista, Susan. *Carlos Bulosan and His Poetry: A Biography and Anthology.* Seattle: University of Washington Press, 1985.

Feleo-Gonzalez, Marina. *A Song for Manong.* Daly City, Calif.: Likha Promotions, 1988.

Felipe, Virgilio Menor. "Hawaii: A Pilipino Dream." M.A. thesis, University of Hawaii, 1972.

Feria, Dolores S., ed. *Sound of Falling Light; Letters in Exile.* Quezon City: University of the Philippines, 1960.

Fermin, Patricia Natividad. "A Descriptive Analysis of the Cognitive Style(s) of Selected Filipino Immigrant Children at the Filipino Education Center." Ed.D. dissertation, University of San Francisco, 1990.

"The Filipino in America: Filipino American Literature." *Philippine American Journal* 1:4 (Summer–Fall 1990): special issue.

Filipino Oral History Project. *Voices: A Filipino American Oral History.* Stockton, Calif.: Filipino Oral History Project, 1984.

Flaskerud, Jacquelyn H. "Diagnostic and Treatment Differences Among Five Ethnic Groups." *Psychological Reports* 58:1 (February 1986): 219–35.

Forman, Sheila M. "Filipino Participation in Civil Rights Policies and Practices in Hawai'i." *Social Process in Hawaii* 33 (1991): 1–11.

Foronda, Marvelino, Jr. "America Is in the Heart: Ilokano Immigration to the United States, 1906–1930." *Bulletin of the American Historical Collection* 4 (1976): 46–73.

Foster, Nellie. "Legal Status of Filipino Intermarriage in California." *Sociology and Social Research* 16 (1932): 441–54.

Francisco, Luzviminda. "The First Vietnam—The Philippine-American War 1899–1902." In *Letters in Exile: An Introductory Reader on the History of Pilipinos in America,* edited by Jesse Quinsaat et al., pp. 1–22. Los Angeles: UCLA Asian American Studies Center, 1976.

Fujii, Edwin T., and James Mak. "On the Relative Economic Progress of U.S.-Born Filipino Men." *Economic Development and Cultural Change* 33:3 (1985): 557–73.

Galedo, Lillian, et al. *Roadblocks to Community Building: A Case Study of the Stockton Filipino Community Center Project.* Davis: University of California, Asian American Research Center, 1970.

Gan, Leticia V. "The Quality of Life of the Filipino Elderly: An Exploratory Study in Los Angeles County." M.S.W. thesis, California State University, Long Beach, 1989.

Gomez, Consuelo Tukay. "Cultural Identity and Academic Achievement: The Development of a Cultural Identity Index for Filipino-American Students." Ed.D. dissertation, University of San Francisco, 1981.

Graff, Henry F., ed. *American Imperialism and the Philippine Insurrection.* Boston: Little, Brown, 1969.

Griffiths, Stephen L. "Emigrant and Returned Migrant Investment in a Philippine Village." *Amerasia Journal* 5 (1978): 45–67.

Gupta, M. L. "Outflow of High-Level Manpower from the Philippines: With Special Reference to the Period 1965–1971." *International Labor Review* (February 1973): 167–91.

Gutelius, Rebecca S. M. "A Study of the Relationship Between the Value Orientation and Academic Achievement of Filipino-American Students." Ed.D. dissertation, University of San Francisco School of Education, 1981.

Haas, Michael. "Filipinos in Hawaii and Institutional Racism." *Philippine Sociological Review* 32 (1984): 41–52.

Hagedorn, Jessica. *Dogeaters.* New York: Pantheon, 1990.

Heras, Patricia. "Acculturation, Generational Status, and Family Environment of Pilipino Americans: A Study of Cultural Adaptation." Ph.D. dissertation, California School of Professional Psychology, 1985.

Herminger, Carol. "Little Manila: The Filipinos in Stockton Prior to W. W. II." *The Pacific Historian* 24 (1980): 21–34.

Ignacio, Lemuel F. *Asian Americans and Pacific Islanders: (Is There Such an Ethnic Group?)* San Jose, Calif.: Pilipino Development Associates, 1976.

Ignacio, Melissa Macagba. *The Philippines, Roots of My Heritage: A Journey of Discovery by a Pilipina American Teenager.* San Jose, Calif.: Pilipino Development Associates, 1976.

Jiobu, Robert M. *Ethnicity and Assimilation: Blacks, Chinese, Filipinos, Japanese, Koreans, Mexicans, Vietnamese, and Whites.* Albany: State University of New York Press, 1988.

Joyce, Richard E., and Chester L. Hunt. "Philippine Nurses and the Brain Drain." *Social Science and Medicine* 16:12 (1982): 1223–33.

Junasa, Bienvenido. "Filipino Experience in Hawai'i." *Social Process in Hawaii* 29 (1982): 95–104.

———. "Study of Some Social Factors Related to the Plans and Aspirations of the Filipino Youth in Waipahu." M.A. thesis, University of Hawaii, Honolulu, 1961.

Keely, Charles B. "Philippine Migration: Internal Movements and Emigration to the United States." *International Migration Review* 7 (1973): 177–87.

Kim, Hyung-Chan, and Cynthia Mejia, eds. *The Filipinos in America, 1898–1974: A Chronology and Fact Book.* New York: Oceana Publications, 1976.

Kitano, Harry H. L. "Asian Americans: The Chinese, Japanese, Pilipinos, and Southeast Asians." *Annals of the American Academy of Political and Social Science* 454: (March 1981): 125–38.

Lasker, Bruno. *Filipino Immigration to Continental United States and to Hawaii.* 1931. Reprint. New York: Arno Press and the New York Times, 1969.

Lauby, J., and O. Stark. "Individual Migration as a Family Strategy: Young Women in the Philippines." *Population Studies* 42:3 (November 1988): 473–86.

Lawcock, Larry Arden. "Filipino Students in the United States and the Philippine Independence Movement: 1900–1935." Ph.D. dissertation, University of California, Berkeley, 1975.

Lee, Hye-Kyung. "Socioeconomic Attainment of Recent Korean and Filipino Immigrant Men and Women in the Los Angeles Metropolitan Area, 1980." Ph.D. dissertation, University of California, Los Angeles, 1988.

Lee, Joann Fuang Jean. *Asian American Experiences in the United States: Oral Histories of First to Fourth Generation Americans from China, the Philippines, Japan, India, the Pacific Islands, Vietnam, and Cambodia.* Jefferson, N.C.: McFarland & Company, 1991.

Lee, Sun-Hee. *Why People Intend to Move: Individual and Community-Level Factors of Out-Migration in the Philippines.* Boulder, Colo.: Westview Press, 1975.

Le Vasseur, Patricia. "Identity Patterns Among Pilipino American Youth." M.A. thesis, University of California, Berkeley, 1973.

Liljeblad, Sue Ellen. *Filipino Alaska: A Heritage.* Anchorage: Alaska Historical Commission, 1981.

———. *The Filipinos and the Alaska Salmon Industry.* Anchorage: Alaska Historical Commission, 1978.

Liu, John M., Paul M. Ong, and Carolyn Rosenstein. "Dual Chain Migration: Post-1965 Filipino Immigration to the United States." *International Migration Review* 25:3 (Fall 1991): 487–517.

Lopez, Naty. "The Acculturation of Selected Filipino Nurses to Nursing Practice in the U.S." Ph.D. dissertation, University of Pennsylvania, 1990.

Madison, Leonard David. "Planning with an Ethnic Enclave: Filipinos in Seattle's International District." M.A. thesis, University of Washington, 1973.

Manlapit, Pablo. *Filipinos Fight for Justice: Case of the Filipino Laborers in the Big Strike of 1924.* Honolulu: Kamalae Publishing Company, 1933.

Mariano, Honorante. *The Filipino Immigrants in the United States.* San Francisco: R & E Research Associates, 1972.

Mason, Sarah R. "The Filipinos." In *They Chose Minnesota*, edited by June D. Holmquist, pp. 546–59. St. Paul: Minnesota Historical Society, 1981.

Masson, Jack K., and Donald L. Guimary. "Pilipinos and Unionization of the Alaskan Canned Salmon Industry." *Amerasia Journal* 8:2 (1981): 1–30.

Matsuoka, J. K., and D. H. Ryujin. "Asian American Immigrants: A Comparison of the Chinese, Japanese, and Filipinos." *Journal of Sociology and Social Welfare* 18:3 (1991): 123–33.

May, Glenn. "The State of Philippine American Studies." In *A Past Recovered: Essays on Philippine History and Historiography*, edited by Glen May pp. 174–89. Quezon City: New Day Publishers, 1987.

McCallus, Joseph. "The Rhetoric of Journalism: The Filipino-American Press and Its Washington, D.C., Audience." Ph.D. dissertation, The Catholic University of America, 1987.

McKenzie, L. "A Descriptive Study of the Traditional Folk Medical Beliefs and Practices Among Selected Filipinos in Seattle." M.A. thesis, University of Washington, 1974.

McWilliams, Carey. *Brothers Under the Skin*. Boston: Little, Brown, 1964.

————. *Factories in the Field: The Study of Migratory Farm Labor in California*. 1935. Reprint. Hamden, Conn.: Archon Books, 1969.

Medina, Belen T. G., and Josefina Natividad. "Filipino Chain Migration to the United States." *Philippine Population Journal* 1:4 (1985): 67–94.

Melendy, H. Brett. *Asians in America: Filipinos, Koreans, and East Indians*. Boston: Twayne Publishers, 1977.

————. "California's Discrimination Against Filipinos, 1927–1935." In *Racism in California*, edited by R. Daniels and S. C. Olin, Jr., pp. 141–51. New York: Macmillan, 1972.

————. "Filipinos in the United States." *Pacific Historical Review* 43 (1974): 520–47.

Menez, Herminia Quimpo. *Folklore Communication Among Filipinos in California*. New York: Arno Press, 1980.

Miller, Stuart Creighton. *Benevolent Assimilation: The American Conquest of the Philippines, 1899–1903*. New Haven: Yale University Press, 1982.

Min, Pyong Gap. "Filipino and Korean Immigrants in Small Business: A Comparative Analysis." *Amerasia Journal* 13:1 (1986–87): 53–71.

Montepio, Susan N. "Folk Medicine in the Filipino American Experience." *Amerasia Journal* 13:1 (1986–87): 135–49.

Morales, Royal F. *Makibaka: The Filipino American Struggle*. Los Angeles: Mountainview Publishers, 1974.

Morante, P. C. *Remembering Carlos Bulosan*. Quezon City: New Day Publishers, 1984.

Munoz, Alfredo N. *The Filipinos in America*. Los Angeles: Mountainview Publishers, 1971.

Navarro, Jovina, ed. *Diwang Pilipino: Philippine Consciousness*. Davis, Calif.: University of California, Asian American Studies, 1974.

————, ed. *Lahing Pilipino*. Davis, Calif.: University of California, Asian American Studies, 1976.

Nee, Victor, and Jimy M. Sanders. "The Road to Parity: Determinants of the Socioeconomic Achievements of Asian Americans." *Ethnic and Racial Studies* 8:1 (1985): 75–93.

Nomura, Gail M. "Within the Law: The Establishment of Filipino Leasing Rights on the Yakima Indian Reservation." *Amerasia Journal* 13:1 (1986–87): 99–117.

Okamura, Jonathan. "Beyond Adaptationism: Immigrant Filipino Ethnicity in Hawai'i." *Social Process in Hawaii* 33 (1991): 56–72.

————. "Filipino Hometown Associations in Hawaii." *Ethnology* 22:4 (1983): 341–53.

————. "Filipino Voluntary Associations and the Filipino Community in Hawaii." *Ethnic Groups* 5 (1984): 279–305.

————. "Immigrant Filipino Ethnicity in Honolulu, Hawaii." Ph.D. dissertation, University of London, 1983.

Osumi, Megumi Dick. "Asians and California's Anti-Miscegenation Laws." In *Asian and Pacific American Experiences: Women's Perspectives*, edited by Nobuya Tsuchida, pp. 1–37. Minneapolis: University of Minnesota, Asian/Pacific American Learning Resources Center, 1982.

Penaranda, Oscar, Serafin Syquia, and Sam Tagatac. "An Introduction to Filipino American Literature," in *Aiiieeeee! An Anthology of Asian American Writers*, edited by Frank Chin et al., pp. 37–54. Washington, D.C.: Howard University Press, 1974.

Pernia, Ernesto M. "The Question of the Brain Drain from the Philippines." *International Migration Review* 10 (1976): 63–72.

Philippine Commission. *Report of the Superintendent of Filipino Students in the United States Covering the Filipino Student Movement from Its Inception to June 30, 1904*, pt. 3, pp. 919-30. Washington, D.C.: U.S. War Department, Bureau of Insular Affairs, Philippine Commission, 1905.

Pido, Antonio J. A. *The Pilipinos in America: Macro/Micro Dimensions of Immigration and Integration*. Staten Island, N.Y.: Center for Migration Studies, 1986.

Pimental, L. "The Perception of Illness Among the Immigrant Filipinos in Sacramento Valley." M.A. thesis, Sacramento State College, 1968.

Pomeroy, William J. "The Philippines: A Case History of Neocolonialism." In *Remaking Asia: Essays on the American Uses of Power*, edited by Mark Selden, pp. 157–99. New York: Pantheon Books, 1974.

Posadas, Barbara M. "At a Crossroad: Filipino American History and the Old Timers' Generation." *Amerasia Journal* 13:1 (1986–87): 85–97.

————. "Crossed Boundaries in Interracial Chicago: Pilipino American Families Since 1925." *Amerasia Journal* 8:2 (1981): 31–52.

————. "The Hierarchy of Color." *Labor History* 23:3 (1982): 349–73.

Posadas, Barbara M., and Ronald L. Guyotte. "Unintentional Immigrants: Chicago's Filipino Foreign Students Become Settlers, 1900–1941." *Journal of American Ethnic History* 9 (Spring 1990): 26–48.

Provido, Generoso Pacificar. *Oriental Immigration from an American Dependency.* San Francisco: R & E Research Associates, 1974.

Quinsaat, Jesse, ed. *Letters in Exile: An Introductory Reader on the History of Pilipinos in America.* Los Angeles: UCLA Asian American Studies Center, 1976.

Rebamontan, Anthony Umengan. "Filipino High School Students and Higher Education: A Look at the Family Support System." M.S.W. thesis, California State University, Long Beach, 1989.

Renato, Constantino. *A History of the Philippines: From the Spanish Colonization to the Second World War.* New York: Monthly Review Press, 1975.

————. *Neocolonial Identity and Counter-Consciousness: Essays on Cultural Decolonization.* London: Merlin Press, 1978.

Reyes, José. "Filipino Students in the U.S.: A Survey of Conditions in the States of Oregon, California, Washington, Idaho, Montana, and Wyoming." M.A. thesis, Reed College, 1930.

Rojo, Trinidad. "Across the Pacific: A Three-Act Play." M.A. thesis, University of Washington, 1937.

Salazar, Leticia G. *Filipino Migration to Alaska.* Anchorage: Alaska Historical Commission, 1979.

San Buenaventura, Steffi. "The Master and the Federation: A Filipino-American Social Movement in California and Hawaii." *Social Process in Hawaii* 33 (1991): 169–93.

————. "Nativism and Ethnicity in a Filipino-American Experience." Ph.D. dissertation, University of Hawaii at Manoa, 1990.

Saniel, J. M., ed. *The Filipino Exclusion Movement, 1927–1935.* Quezon City: University of the Philippines, Institute of Asian Studies, 1967.

San Juan, Epifanio, Jr. *Carlos Bulosan and the Imagination of the Class Struggle.* Quezon City: University of the Philippines Press, 1972.

————. "Filipino Writing in the United States: Reclaiming Whose America." *Philippine Studies* 41 (1993): 141–66.

————. "Mapping the Boundaries: The Filipino American Writer in the U.S.A." *Journal of Ethnic Studies* 19:1 (1991): 117–31.

————. "The Predicament of Filipinos in the United States." In *The State of Asian America,* edited by Karin Aguilar-San Juan, pp. 205–18. Boston: South End Press, 1994.

Santos, Bienvenido N. *Scent of Apples.* Seattle: University of Washington Press, 1979.

Scharlin,, Craig, and Lilia V. Villanueva. *Philip Vera Cruz: A Personal History of Filipino Immigrants and the Farmworkers Movement.* Los Angeles: UCLA Labor Center, Institute of Labor Relations, and UCLA Asian American Studies Center, 1992.

Schoen, Robert, and Barbara Thomas. "Intergroup Marriage in Hawaii, 1969–71 and 1971–81." *Sociological Perspectives* 32:3 (Fall 1989): 365–82.

Sharma, Miriam. "Labor Migration and Class Formation Among the Filipinos in Hawaii, 1906–1946." In *Labor Immigration Under Capitalism: Asian Workers in the United States Before World War II,* edited by Lucie Cheng and Edna Bonacich, pp. 579–611. Berkeley and Los Angeles: University of California Press, 1984.

————. "The Philippines: A Case of Migration to Hawaii, 1906–1946." In *Labor Immigration Under Capitalism: Asian Workers in the United States Before World War II,* edited by Lucie Cheng and Edna Bonacich, pp. 337–58. Berkeley and Los Angeles: University of California Press, 1984.

————. "Pinoy in Paradise: Environment and Adaptation of Pilipinos in Hawaii, 1906–1946." *Amerasia Journal* 7:2 (1980): 91–117.

Sibayan, Bonifacio P. "The Intellectualization of Filipino." *International Journal of the Sociology of Language* 88 (1991): 261–77.

Silva-Netto, Benoni Reyes. "Culture, Personality, and Mental Health: An Ethnographic Study of Filipino Immigrant Families." Ph.D. dissertation, Northwestern University, 1978.

Smith, Peter C. "The Social Demography of Filipino Migrations Abroad." *International Migration Review* 10 (1976): 307–53.

Solland, Sonja. "A Study of Conflict in a Multi-Ethnic Community." Ph.D. dissertation, University of Washington, 1974.

Soriano, Fred. "Filipino Hawaiian Migration and Adaptation: New Paradigms for Analysis." *Social Process in Hawaii* 29 (1982): 163–79.

Stegner, Wallace Earl. "Legally Undesirable Heroes: The Filipino in America." In *One Nation,* edited by Wallace Stegner and the editors of *Look,* pp. 19–43. Boston: Houghton Mifflin, 1945.

Stern, Jennifer. *The Filipino Americans.* New York: Chelsea House, 1989.

Stier, Haya. "Immigrant Women Go to Work: Analysis of Immigrant Wives Labor Supply for Six Asian Groups." *Social Science Quarterly* 72:1 (1991): 67–82.

Sycip, Lynna-Marie. "Values, Work, and Entrepreneurship: A Comparative Study of Filipino and Korean Immigrants to the United States." Ph.D. dissertation, University of Hawaii at Manoa, 1990.

Sycip, Lynna-Marie, and James T. Fawcett. "Expectations, Family Networks, and Emigration: A Study of Filipino Decision-Making." *Philippine Journal of Psychology* 21 (1988): 56–71.

Teodoro, Luis V., Jr., ed. *Out of This Struggle: The Filipinos in Hawaii.* Honolulu: University Press of Hawaii, 1981.

Thompson, David. "The Filipino Federation of America, Incorporated: A Study in the Natural History of a Social Institution." *Social Process* 7 (1941): 24–35.

Torres, Mary Eileen. "Elder Abuse in the Filipino Community: Does It Exist?" M.S.W. thesis, California State University, Long Beach, 1992.

Ty-Casper, Linda. *Wings of Stone.* London: Readers International 1987.

United Cannery, Agricultural, Packing, and Allied Workers of America, Local 7. *Excerpts on Alaska Congressional Fisheries Hearing.* Seattle: UCAPAWA, Local 7, 1939.

U.S. Congress, House of Representatives. *Hearings on Exclusion of Immigration from the Philippine Islands.* 71st Cong., 2d sess., 1930, H. Rept. 8708, vol. 1.

———. *Naturalization of Filipinos: Hearings, November 22, 1944, on H.R. 2012, 2776, 3633, 4003, 4229, and 4826.* 78th Cong., 2d sess., 1944.

University of Hawaii at Manoa, Ethnic Studies Oral History Project. *The 1924 Filipino Strike on Kauai.* Honolulu: University of Hawaii at Manoa, Ethnic Studies Program, 1979.

Vallangca, Caridad Concepcion. *The Second Wave: Pinoy and Pinay, 1945–1965.* San Francisco: Strawberry Hill Press, 1987.

Vallangca, Roberto V. *Pinoy: The First Wave, 1898–1941.* San Francisco: Strawberry Hill Press, 1977.

Velez, Gonzalo Alunan. "A Study of the Historical Development of the Congress of Filipino American Citizens." Ed.D. dissertation, Rutgers University, 1983.

Venzke, Linda Jean. "The Advancement Patterns of Filipino-American Nurses into Nursing Management." M.S.N thesis, University of Texas, 1990.

Wallovitts, Sonia Emily. *The Filipinos in California.* San Francisco: R & E Associates, 1972.

Wentworth, Edna Louise. *Filipino Plantation Workers in Hawaii: A Study of Incomes, Expenditures, and Living Standards of Filipino Families on an Hawaiian Sugar Plantation.* Shanghai: Kelly & Walsh, 1941.

———. *Living Standards of Filipino Families on an Hawaiian Sugar Plantation.* Honolulu: Institute of Pacific Relations, 1936.

Williams, L., and L. J. Domingo. "The Social Status of Elderly Women and Men Within the Filipino Family." *The Journal of Marriage and the Family* 55:2 (1993): 415–26.

Wong, Morrison G. "The Cost of Being Chinese, Japanese, and Filipino in the United States: 1960, 1970, 1976." *Pacific Sociological Review* 25:1 (1982): 59–78.

———. "The Education of White, Chinese, Filipino, and Japanese Students: A Look at High School and Beyond." *Sociological Perspectives* 33:3 (Fall 1990): 355–74.

Wu, John T. "The Relationship Between Ethnic Identity and Achievement Motivation in Chinese-Americans and Filipino-Americans." Ph.D. dissertation, Harvard University, 1992.

Yu, Elena S. H. "Filipino Migration and Community Organizations in the United States." *California Sociologist* 3:2 (1980): 76–102.

Also in the *Asian American History and Culture* series: